I drove my car out of our parking garage and stopped to let a delivery boy pass by, pushing a dolly. A woman in a knee-length coat and headscarf lagged behind a terrier on a leash.

As I waited, I noticed a white Peugeot parked across the street in the shade of a sycamore tree. The driver, a clean-shaven man, was staring at me. As soon as I noticed him, he seemed to spot me. He quickly leaned forward to start his car and said to the man sitting next to him so clearly that I could read his lips, "It's her."

I hesitated for a few seconds, then pulled past the electronic gates, and turned right onto the street. The white Peugeot was struggling to get out of its tight parking spot, but through the rearview mirror I saw a gray sedan veer out onto the street and pull up close behind me. It was a brand-new Renault L-90, factory stickers still on its windshield.

I glanced into the side mirror. The Renault was obviously tailing me. I made another right onto busy Africa Street, the main thoroughfare of our neighborhood, and from the sound of honking cars I could tell that the Renault had cut into the lane to stay with me.

With sweaty palms, I changed gears and moved into a different lane before stopping at a traffic light. The street was packed with cars and motorcycles. Drivers were turning left and right, cutting each other off as they did on any other day in the bustling Iranian capital.

I'd left the Peugeot behind—there was no way it could keep up with me—but before any relief could register, the Renault pulled up alongside my car. I pretended to adjust my side mirrors. A drop of sweat slid down my upper lip.

Only government forces would tail you so brazenly. They'd already arrested thousands of protestors and hundreds of former government officials, activists, and independent reporters, including my sources. I speculated they were after me because I had defied a ban: the government had ordered me, along with every other reporter working for the foreign media, not to cover the protests. My colleagues with the *New York Times* who had flown into Iran to cover the elections had left. An Iranian friend with *Newsweek* had been arrested the week before.

As I was adjusting the side mirrors, two motorcycles—each bearing two riders—pulled up on either side of my car. Red mud flaps arched over the front wheels of the trail bikes. Government forces had appeared on those motorcycles only two weeks ago to club the demonstrators.

SURVEILLANCE

I slipped into my long coat, which I used as an Islamic dress, and pulled a scarf over my hair. It was the morning of June 27, 2009, and I was rushing out the door to meet a political analyst, something I'd done countless times in my ten years as the only *New York Times* correspondent in the country. The routine of getting dressed to go out in public should have felt familiar, but this time the smell of smoke and tear gas on my coat evoked a sense of uncertainty about the future.

Massive protests had erupted three weeks earlier, after a presidential election that many Iranians believed to have been stolen by the incumbent, Mahmoud Ahmadinejad. At first some three million demonstrators had marched in silence, demanding only new elections. But then government forces had attacked them, shooting at people and jailing scores of protestors. Outraged by the brutality, demonstrators continued to pour into the streets and now clashed with government forces. The demonstrations were the largest in three decades. I needed to make sense of these events. What did the confrontation mean for the future of Iran?

The tree-lined street where I lived with my husband and two children was quiet under a scorching sun on this Saturday afternoon. Tall new apartment buildings, with their granite façades, towered over older, two-story brick houses. Over the past decade the neighborhood's lush gardens had given way to garages and cement yards. The modern apartment buildings, one of which we lived in, had robbed the neighborhood of its charm.

tapes, notes, videos, newspaper clips, and other published sources. On occasion I have reconstructed dialogue from memory or changed the names of certain individuals (or simply refrained from using their full names in order to protect their identities), but I have only taken liberties like these when doing so had no impact on the veracity and substance of the story.

History has many narrators. In this account, the story is mine: that of a girl who grew up after the revolution, became a journalist, and witnessed the metamorphosis of the society around her. I hope that other Iranians will add their voices to mine, just as I have contributed my tale to the river of stories flowing from Iran. Mine is the story of the hope and perseverance of a nation that has never surrendered to tyranny.

continuing to work from within to reform their political system—an effort that is sure to yield the transformation they have been seeking but that could easily be undone by a war or an external threat. A trauma like Iraq's invasion of Iran in 1980 would radicalize the nation and rally even the opponents of the regime to defend the country—a fact that other foreign powers would do well to keep in mind as they continue to engage with, and seek to influence, Iran.

This book tells the story of a country and its people struggling to find their way, but it is also my story. I was nine years old when the revolution swept into Iran and set the country on its current course. As I grew up, I watched my homeland continue to change around me. So while the evolution described in this book is Iran's, it is also mine: the story of how a girl grew into a woman, discovered a world beyond the one she had imagined, and eventually was forced to choose between the two.

The choice wasn't easy. When, roughly a decade after the revolution, I decided to pursue a career as a professional journalist, I knew that I would be putting myself at risk. What I couldn't know—indeed, what none of my countrymen could have known at the time—was that Iran would be transformed so profoundly over the next two decades that many of its people and their children would rise against the very government they had ushered in with the revolution. This uprising was the biggest story of my career, but in covering it I earned myself the enmity of the regime. Once they had merely treated me with suspicion, but now they were determined to incarcerate me. So in July 2009, at the height of the crisis, my family and I slipped out of Iran. To this day we have not returned.

It has not been easy to write this story, for reasons both personal and practical. I have relied on my memory in reconstructing some of the events that took place during the first decade after the 1979 revolution, but when possible I have also used YouTube videos and newspaper articles to compose scenes and verify facts. For the second and the third parts of the book, which describe what took place after the death of Ayatollah Khomeini in 1989, I have used thousands of documents I gathered over a period of two decades. These include my interviews,

that is wobbly. Except for the Revolutionary Courts and the Revolutionary Guards—two law enforcement apparatuses set up in the early weeks
after the shah's ouster in 1979—and the leader of the revolution (as the
supreme religious leader is known), the fundamentalist ideals that the
Islamic regime spawned have completely lost their appeal. The leader,
the Revolutionary Courts, and the Guards remain ideological, while
elected governments headed by presidents have become more pragmatic
in the face of changing public opinion and international pressure.

The Iranian people, meanwhile, have taken on the role of trans-
forming their society. By imposing draconian and inflexible restrictions
on Iranians' personal freedoms, the regime gave them no choice but to
challenge its policies, turning many law-abiding citizens into defiant
rebels. Iranians' longing for freedom was on full display in 2009, when
many believed the regime had stolen the presidential election on behalf
of the incumbent at the time, Mahmoud Ahmadinejad. The resulting
protests, which have come to be known in the West as the Green Uprising, after the political movement that gave them their impetus, were violently put down but testify to an enduring truth about Iranians: like the
citizens of many other nations, Iranians vie for honesty in their politics.

Many of the revolutionaries who created the inner workings of
the system have turned into anti-revolutionaries today. Many of them
evolved into pro-democracy activists and are now living in exile or in
prison. In a letter from prison in the summer of 2010, a deputy interior
minister, Mostafa Tajzadeh, pleaded for forgiveness—not from the regime, but from the people. He apologized for building what he termed
a regime "that is a far cry from the democratic pledges of its leader, who
had once promised to embrace freedom and human rights." Some activists are more vociferous in their opposition. Another revolutionary who
fled the country in 2009, Mojtaba Vahedi, called for overthrowing the
regime altogether.

But the idea of overthrowing the Islamic government is no longer
as palatable to many Iranians as it once was. The majority of people
fear instability and institutional breakdown. The bloodshed after Iran's
revolution and eight years of war—and even more recently the erup-
tion of what many called a civil war in neighboring Iraq after the fall
of Saddam—are evidence fueling those fears. Therefore Iranians are

population was born after the revolution; these young men and women studied, traveled abroad, and—from the early 1990s on—were exposed to new ideas and opinions through technologies such as satellite television and the Internet. Today, more than 70 percent of Iran's population lives in cities, compared to less than 50 percent before the revolution. More than 60 percent of Iranian university students are women, and Iranians under the age of twenty-four have a literacy rate of over 99 percent. By 2009, 43 percent of the population was identified as middle-class—30 percent of which is rural—and another 40 percent as lower-middle-class, together more than two-thirds of Iran's population.

This newly expanded middle class longs for a regime that can deal with critical matters of running the country rather than busying itself with what its citizens do in their private lives. Satellite television and the Internet have exposed the population to a global culture that defines the job of the government as providing comfort and opportunities for its citizens. As a result the desire for economic prosperity and political and social freedoms has spread among the majority of people.

Whereas technology has propelled positive change in Iran, the country's vast material wealth has often impeded it. The revenue from the country's thriving oil industry enabled the regimes both before and after the revolution to splurge on their political goals without needing a genuine base of support. Nationalized in 1952, the oil industry has been a source of inequality as well as progress. The Islamic regime relied on oil revenue to wage eight years of war with Iraq and to solidify its rule by rallying the Iranian people against an outside enemy. Yet the regime also rewarded its supporters with jobs in the civil sector, provided free public education from kindergarten to university to all Iranians, and thereby expanded the very middle class that would someday come to oppose many of its most hard-line policies.

Iran's economic progress since the revolution has left much to be desired, but after a sharp decline in the 1980s, the economy has been growing steadily. Since the mid-1990s, it has expanded at a rate of about 3.5 percent per year. In 2008, after oil prices rose sharply, per capita income caught up with its prerevolution peak.

Nearly thirty-six years after the revolution, there is nothing left of Iran's revolutionary regime other than its ideological skeleton—and even

The revolution changed every aspect of our lives. By the age of eleven, I could no longer choose what clothes to wear. The new regime dictated the styles and colors that were acceptable for girls and women. We could only wear dead colors: black, grey, dark blue, or brown. One of the requisite articles of clothing was a headscarf, knotted under the chin and on the throat—a reminder with every breath that the regime was in control of your life. If you appeared in public without one, you could be whipped with an electric cord on your back: seventy-four lashes that would leave deep, bloody welts.

The revolution took away Iranians' personal liberties, but it also gave many people a taste of power and opportunity that had long been denied to them. Those who continued supporting the Islamic regime despite its repression came from impoverished and traditional families that had never embraced the former regime's modernizing policies. Whereas the shah had robbed them of their religious identity by introducing secular schools and secular courts to Iran, the new regime's leader, Ayatollah Ruhollah Khomeini, reorganized Iranian society in a way that prioritized religious values. The regime drove the old governing classes out of power and replaced them with its own supporters. It mustered all levels of conservative Iranian society, encouraging traditional women to take responsibility outside the house. After the regime enforced gender segregation, families that had balked at the prospect of coed public spaces finally felt comfortable sending their daughters to school, to university, and into the workforce. Far from chafing at the new regime's restrictions, these women felt empowered.

The regime drew a huge number of Iranians from the margins of society into its center—and not just women. To satisfy its rural supporters, the government improved the quality of life in villages. It provided rural areas with electricity and clean water, and built roads that connected them to modern city life. The country's new leaders offered rural Iranians upward mobility on a fast track, in the process providing the rural poor with a new identity: they became the enforcers of the new laws.

Over the years, a large section of this once-impoverished population became part of Iran's middle class, in a socioeconomic revolution driven by major demographic changes. Two-thirds of the country's

PREFACE

When I was ten years old and entering the third grade, my mother stopped my younger sister and me at the front door of our Tehran apartment on the first day of school. "If anyone asks you whether your parents support the revolution," she told us, "you must say, 'Yes, they do.'"

I nodded solemnly. She didn't have to explain; these were the rules of the new Iran, and although I was only a child, I understood them all too well.

Less than a year had passed since the 1979 revolution that replaced the Iranian monarch, Shah Mohammad Reza Pahlavi, with a conservative Islamic government, but we had already learned that if our parents were identified as anti-revolutionaries, they could face the firing squad. My friend's father had been executed, my father's friend was killed, and we knew many ordinary young people who had disappeared into the country's prisons, all for the crime of opposing the new regime. The first lesson the revolution taught me, then, was to lie to protect my family and myself.

I was born a few days before the end of 1970, but as it is for every Iranian of my generation, my story truly begins with the revolution. The events of 1979 transformed our world in ways that we are still struggling to understand. For me, the change was profoundly traumatic. It was as if there had been a calm music to life until then, as if even the leaves danced to the breath of the wind and the singing of the birds. But that music ended in the winter of 1979, and a new sound began: the drumbeats of the new regime, which drew its inspiration from Islam and which intended to wipe out secular people to create a theocracy.

CONTENTS

For my parents, my children, and my husband,
whose love gave me strength.
And for the people of Iran,
whose perseverance gave me hope.

Published by Basic Books,
A Member of the Perseus Books Group

Books published by Basic Books are available at special discounts for
bulk purchases in the United States by corporations, institutions, and other
organizations. For more information, please contact the Special Markets
Department at the Perseus Books Group, 2300 Chestnut Street, Suite 200,
Philadelphia, PA 19103, or call (800) 810-4145, ext. 5000, or e-mail
special.markets@perseusbooks.com.

Designed by Jack Lenzo

Library of Congress Cataloging-in-Publication Data
Fathi, Nazila, 1970-
    The lonely war : one woman's account of the struggle for modern Iran /
Nazila Fathi.
        pages cm
    Includes bibliographical references and index.
    ISBN 978-0-465-06999-6 (hardback : alkaline paper) —
ISBN 978-0-465-04092-6 (ebook)
    1. Iran—History—Revolution, 1979—Influence.   2. Iran—Politics and
government—1979–1997.   3. Iran—Politics and government—1997–
4. Fathi, Nazila, 1970–   5. Fathi, Nazila, 1970—Childhood and youth.
6. Women—Iran—Biography.   7. Women journalists—Iran—Biography.
8. Social change—Iran.   9. Middle class—Iran.   10. Iran—Social conditions.
I. Title.
    DS318.81.F38 2014
    955.05'4092—dc23
    [B]
                                                                2014035829

10 9 8 7 6 5 4 3 2 1

THE
LONELY WAR

ONE WOMAN'S ACCOUNT *of the*
STRUGGLE *for* MODERN IRAN

NAZILA FATHI

BASIC BOOKS
A MEMBER OF THE PERSEUS BOOKS GROUP
NEW YORK

THE LONELY WAR

More Advance Praise for *The Lonely War*

"Nazila Fathi's *The Lonely War* is both a touching personal story that illuminates the struggles of life in Iran and a broader reflection on the sociopolitical effects of the Islamic revolution on the Iranian people. With so much misinformation about Iran in the national discourse, Fathi's book is a valuable resource for anyone looking to read beyond the headlines."

—Hooman Majd,
author of *The Ayatollah Begs to Differ:*
The Paradox of Modern Iran

"A poignant portrait of Iran's tortured contemporary history through the eyes of one of the country's most thoughtful and courageous journalists."

—Karim Sadjadpour,
Carnegie Endowment for International Peace

"As fearless as it is honest, *The Lonely War* tells the inside story of how Iranians have grappled with—and also been inspired by—their Islamic Republic. Journalist Nazila Fathi gives us a powerful personal account of coming of age in revolutionary Iran, exploring Iran's turbulent modern history through a remarkable cast of real characters, and deftly navigating Iran's cultural and political divide to provide us a superb picture of what makes Iran today."

—Scott Peterson,
author of *Let the Swords Encircle Me:*
Iran—A Journey Behind the Headlines

"Drawing on more than a decade of reporting for the *New York Times* in Iran, Nazila Fathi has written a lucid and highly engaging portrait of Iranian politics from the 1979 revolution to today. One of the book's most illuminating features is her vivid portrait of the impoverished recruits for the paramilitary Basij and Revolutionary Guard Corps—including their subsequent disillusionment and adoption of a more middle class, secular life style. Highly recommended for college courses."

—Janet Afary,
author of *Sexual Politics in Modern Iran*

Now one of the riders, with dark stubble, was staring at me. The one behind him craned his neck to look inside my car.

I rolled up my windows and locked the doors. I knew that I couldn't go to the analyst's home with my escort, or I would put him in danger too. He was one of the few remaining free analysts who were critical of the government and had also agreed to speak to me. A visit from me would certainly land him in prison.

At the green light, I drove around the block, headed back to my street, and sped into our garage. Shutting the electronic gate behind me, I hurried into the elevator to take refuge in my fifth-floor apartment.

They'd come for me.

I was still sweating when I entered the apartment. My son, Chayan, age five, and my daughter, Tina, three and a half, ran to me and yelled, "Mommy, you're back." I held them and smelled their tousled hair. Their soft arms gripped my neck. Tina pulled my headscarf off and wrapped it around herself. I felt a pang of guilt as the smell of smoke and tear gas wafted into the air.

I knew what I needed to do next: get a lawyer. Legal representation couldn't keep you out of prison—the authorities jailed its citizens with impunity, and without any kind of formal procedure. But a good lawyer could sometimes find a way to secure someone's release, even if it took months. And having a lawyer was a crucial safeguard against abuse; without anyone to represent you and to speak on your behalf, you could easily vanish into prison and never be heard from again.

In my case, the government was likely to force me to confess on national television that I was a spy. They had already done this with many high-profile activists and journalists; it was all part of the regime's strategy of blaming foreign scapegoats in an attempt to cover up the fact that its own people had risen against it. The charge was so common that after my friend at *Newsweek* was arrested, I wrote a formal letter to my editor in New York explaining that the paper should consider any statements I made while under arrest to be lies extracted under duress.

I pulled myself from Chayan and Tina's embraces, and they rushed back to play with my mother, whom I had asked to take care of them while I met with the analyst. At my computer I punched in the name of a prominent lawyer I knew. I dialed the number of his cell phone and waited. My desk was covered with piles of notebooks, newspaper clips, and memory drives of videos I had captured during the past weeks. As I listened to the phone ring, it occurred to me that I needed to get all of this potentially incriminating material out of the house.

After five rings, a voice responded: *"Alo."* It was the lawyer. He immediately recognized my voice; I'd interviewed him just the day before to ask about several of his clients.

I told him about the surveillance team. He was silent. Then he explained that I needed to sign certain documents granting him authority to legally represent me. He said that he could not represent some of his clients because they hadn't had preexisting agreements and prison authorities were not letting them sign the papers in jail.

I needed to provide the lawyer with original signed copies of the documents, but I was reluctant to leave our apartment to go to his office. The convoluted bureaucracy of repression in Iran sometimes allows security forces to seize you on the street, but they often cannot enter your home without a proper arrest warrant.

I called Reza, the young driver who'd taken me around town over the past month. He showed up half an hour later, and I buzzed him in. I told him about the men outside in a hushed tone. I'd always suspected that my apartment was bugged. Reza looked at me sadly but agreed to retrieve the documents from the attorney's office so I could sign them.

Reza was true to his word and returned an hour later with the documents. I signed them, and he delivered them. I had a lawyer.

I called my editor in New York and told her about the agents who had tailed me. I presumed that my phone was tapped and the agents were also listening in. I wanted them to hear that I was informing my newspaper, which would publicize my case if anything happened to me. As the paper's only correspondent in Iran for over a decade, I'd become the longest serving Iranian reporter for an American publication. I knew the analyst was probably wondering where I was, but I decided not to call him so as to avoid drawing any attention to him.

I went on the roof of my building to adjust a BGAN, a satellite device that the *New York Times* had given me to connect to the Internet. The local provider had disconnected my Internet some weeks ago on the pretext that the cables leading to our building were damaged beyond repair. It was clear now that the government was behind the move. I put the BGAN in a corner, and as I waited for it to pick up a signal, I looked over the low wall around the roof to spy on the agents on the street below.

From my vantage point I could see five of the agents standing in a cluster, gesturing passionately as though they were arguing. Their shirts hung over their pants, just like the way members of the government-linked militia force dressed. Two others shuffled around in rubber sandals. Farther down, two more leaned against a wall near a trail bike. One man was speaking on a walkie-talkie near a car I hadn't noticed before.

Sixteen men were staking out my building. Why so many? And what were they waiting for?

I was back in the apartment when my husband, Babak Pasha, returned home from work. His worried face told me that he'd noticed the agents, too. He looked tired and aged; the grey hair at his temples appeared more pronounced than usual. "Have you seen them?" he asked me. "They have sent a whole gang for you."

Babak walked into the kitchen, poured himself a glass of water, and said, "We need to find out when they leave, and then you should go to the airport." He looked at me, the urgency clear in his eyes. "Get on any flight that leaves the country," he said. "We'll join you later." Sensing my doubts, he added, "Think of the kids."

My heart sank at his words. I couldn't let my children watch the agents barge into our home at dawn and drag me out of bed in front of my family, as they had done to so many others. I had heard the stories about how their terrified kids continued to tremble at every knock at the door. I didn't want my children to experience that horror.

I felt depleted. The hope that had driven me for weeks was gone.

That surge of optimism had begun on the night of June 12. That day, Iran had held nationwide elections to determine whether the incumbent president, Mahmoud Ahmadinejad, would stay in power or would be replaced by one of several reform-minded candidates. Within hours of the polls' closing, a surprisingly early count put Ahmadinejad in the lead. Riot police showed up on the streets early the next morning in black gear, holding batons and shields, as though the regime expected demonstrations. People began calling the election a coup d'état and felt enraged that the regime had deprived them of even the most basic right of choosing their own president—a right that had been enshrined in Iran's revolutionary constitution but that the government now seemed to be flagrantly violating.

Sure enough, not long after Ahmadinejad was announced the victor, demonstrators began appearing on the streets—the equivalent to a full-fledged revolt in the eyes of the regime, which tolerated little in the way of open dissent. When the troops began shooting, gassing, and jailing these protestors, their numbers only seemed to grow.

The news of the uprising and the violence that followed made international headlines. Embarrassed by the coverage, the government expelled visiting reporters and banned resident journalists from leaving their offices to cover the clashes. I continued to go out and write stories every day.

It wasn't long before the violence found me, too. Ten days later a government source called and warned, "Nazila, they have given your photo to snipers." As if I didn't understand the implications of this news, he continued: "Stop going out. They have orders to shoot you."

Normally, my source's warning would have scared me. But somehow my fear had evaporated, as it had for many other Iranians. From my living room window I watched my neighbors march down our normally quiet boulevard in their running shoes, heading to join the sea of people flowing down the main Valiasr Avenue, which had become the scene of many protests. They didn't look intimidated by the shooting or the arrests.

You have to have lived in Iran to understand how being harassed daily, over the course of decades, for purely personal matters—what you wear, eat, drink, listen to, or where you go and with whom—can make you less afraid, not more. You do all those things in your home, try to enjoy it in your seclusion, but the intimidation never stops. Every day the regime comes up with a new excuse to repress you. One day they nab you because they dislike your sunglasses; another day it's the color of your coat or even your white socks.

Iranians had endured all of this for years, seething at the indignities until one issue, the stealing of the election, caused that simmering anger to erupt. Iranians had thought that the other candidate would give them more breathing room if he were elected, and their disappointment surely contributed to the force of the explosion. Across the country, people seemed to be saying, "Enough is enough."

I had shared their fearless frustration—and so, at the time, I didn't tell anyone about the phone call. Instead I went out into the streets to join the rising tide.

Iran was my country, after all. My neighbors were making history, and I wanted to witness it. I had no idea that the act of bearing witness would change my life forever.

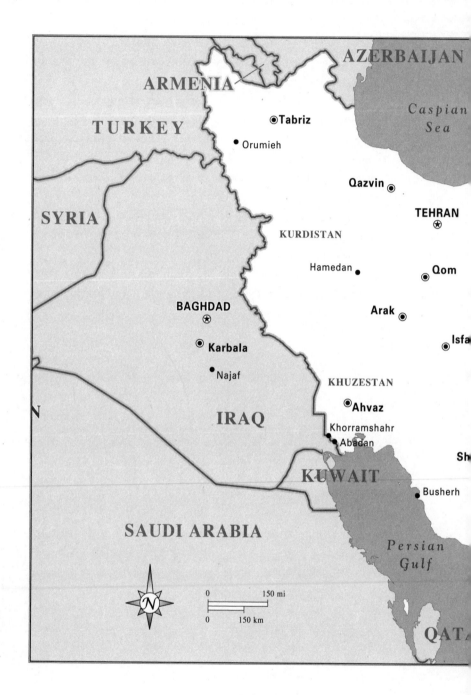

PART ONE

THE FORMATIVE YEARS

1979–1989

CHAPTER ONE

———•◆•◆•———

THE REVOLUTION

In the winter of 1979, when I was nine and my sister was six and a half, the incessant drumming of a bouncing ball triggered utter boredom in me. Schools had been closed on and off for weeks because of anti-regime demonstrations, and my sister, Golnaz, whom I called Goli, had grown fond of a small rubber ball. While I busied myself rearranging my Barbie dolls, Goli walked around our apartment, dropping her heavy ball on the parquet floor, grabbing it when it sprang up, and letting it drop again in a monotonous, hammering beat. For me, the sound had become synonymous with the disruption of the world around us.

People were flooding the streets of our hometown, Tehran, and staging rallies against the king, Mohammad Reza Pahlavi, demanding that he step down. Our parents had told us that the demonstrations were so large that Pahlavi—whom everyone referred to by his Persian title, shah—had brought out the army, with tanks and machine guns, to confront the protestors. The soldiers had opened fire, killing scores of people. The demonstrators reappeared, dressed in white, the color of shrouds in Iran, to symbolize their readiness to die.

Because of the demonstrations, our parents took us outside only for quick and urgent trips. My parents feared that shooting could take place at anytime, anywhere. A tragic fire at a cinema had deepened the fear. In August 1978 a fire broke out in a movie theatre in the southern city of Abadan. Someone had locked the doors from the outside, and four hundred people, including many children, burned to death.

It was clearly not an accident but unclear who had been behind the massacre—the shah's men or the opposition?

Secular, middle-class opponents of the shah had united with leftist intellectuals as well as Muslim activists. Together they'd launched a campaign of civil resistance that attracted civil servants and oil indus-try workers, who went on strikes and took part in demonstrations. The opposition had initially called for more political liberalization, but then as the strikes and demonstrations paralyzed the country in the final months of 1978, they demanded that the shah abdicate.

We often felt lucky that we lived in a gated housing complex, an oasis in the middle of the capital called Behjat Abad. A cluster of four-teen twelve-story buildings, the first high-rises in the country, Behjat Abad housed some four hundred middle- and upper-class families on seven acres of land. Right in the center a lush garden surrounded a pool. The garden was our own private world where in the warmer months we played with dozens of other children. Now it was too cold to play outside, and most parents were too nervous to let their children out of their sight.

As I waited for normalcy to return, Goli bounced the ball in the background. When I complained about it, she simply looked at me. Her pleading black eyes were fringed with long curling eyelashes, and her pale face was framed by straight black hair that barely touched her shoulders. The ball was her companion, her comfort. It was the exact opposite for me. The beat of the ball hitting the floor mimicked the countdown to our unknown future and served as an awful reminder of the sound of gunfire that we'd heard echoing through the city on some evenings.

One afternoon, my mother, Azar, finally gave in and agreed to take us out for ice cream. Goli and I grabbed our coats and dashed out the door. The department store that sold ice cream was only a ten-minute walk away. I remember the date: January 16. As we stepped onto the street, we heard a racket in the distance—a kind of devilish celebratory roar. My mother, who'd been jittery at every sound, quickened her pace and pulled us by the hand on either side of her toward Pahlavi Avenue, the tree-lined street that stretched from south Tehran to north.

When we reached the avenue, the street was packed with people and cars. Men and women danced in a frenzy, clambered on top of cars and buses, pounded their feet on the roofs, and swung their arms in the air. A young woman gave us candies. Drivers stopped their cars in the middle of the street, honking their horns in a singsong tone. We walked up the street and saw that the traffic had halted. The city was in ecstasy. Many of the people we passed held up the day's newspaper or rolled it around their heads like a hat. The two-word headline in bold and stark print read: "*Shah Raft*," meaning "The Shah Left."

That night my parents and I watched on state television as the shah, teary-eyed, headed toward a plane. His wife, Farah, wrapped in a fur coat and hat, stood at his side, along with their four children. Men in dark suits bowed to them continuously; a few raised the shah's hand to their lips. The shah looked uneasy. As opposition against him had peaked, he had learned that he was suffering from lymphoma. No one knew if it was the seriousness of his illness, the effect of the pills he was taking, or the rage on the streets that had weakened his will. But he had decided to leave the country he had ruled since World War II and hand over his duties to a regency council and an opposition-based prime minister. He flew with his family and a small entourage to Egypt, for what he called a vacation, on a plane he piloted himself. Later, the pilot who flew with him would return with the plane and join the revolutionaries.

On February 1, two weeks after the shah left, a newscaster announced that the revolution had triumphed. A seventy-eight-year-old cleric, Ayatollah Ruhollah Khomeini, had just returned to Iran after fourteen years in exile—first in Baghdad and then in a town near Paris—to take the helm of the revolution and complete its overhaul of the nation's political system.

"Ayatollah," a title used for senior Islamic scholars, means "sign of God," and Khomeini's arrival in Iran had the air of a religious spectacle. The historic day was broadcast on television, as millions of Iranians marched through the streets of Tehran to get a glimpse of the man who'd been the spiritual inspiration for their resistance to the shah. "Once the monster left, the angel appeared," people chanted. Khomeini descended from an Air France plane, leaning against the arm of its pilot, showing no visible sentiment despite the crowd's outpouring of emotion. He wore a black turban, a sign in Islam of a *sayyid*, a descendant of Prophet Muhammad through his two grandsons, Hassan and Hussein.

Filming from a helicopter, the state network TV camera captured a human river flowing down the wide avenues leading from the airport to the capital. The people waved their fists in the air and smiled broadly. Men in tight-fitting suits, some sporting thick mustaches, tried to reach a Chevy Blazer surrounded by the crowd. Inside, Khomeini was on his way to the city. People tried to climb over the moving car, but the vehicle continued to move through the throngs.

Then the television showed Tehran's vast Beheshteh Zahra cemetery, crowded with people. On his first day Khomeini went to pay his respects to those who'd given up their lives for the revolution. The television showed Khomeini's men push back swarms of fervent followers to make room for the Ayatollah's helicopter to land. At some point he'd been put on a helicopter to reach the cemetery in southern Tehran. A few moments later, Khomeini was seated on a platform with a group of supporters. Scuffles broke out as Khomeini's bearded guards roughly pushed back people in the audience who wanted to get close to the cleric. Eventually the guards cleared a space between the crowd and Khomeini, and he began to speak.

Khomeini's voice sounded dry, and his words were strange to my ears. He came from a rural background, and he wasn't as eloquent as the officials in the former regime. As an eight-year-old, I was amused by his accent, the way he dragged the words out and added an extra *a* at the end of every sentence. My parents, who had never heard Khomeini before, were immediately shocked that many of their educated friends had been captivated by his passionate speeches against the shah. The camera zoomed in on the faces of his supporters as they sat crosslegged in the dirt, mesmerized by his words, their eyes unblinking.

"We are going to elevate your financial status as well as your morality," he said, in a singsong tone. "Don't think that we will only build you housing. Electricity and water will be free too. Public transportation will be free."

"Good luck," my father said with a chuckle, breaking the silence in our apartment. "He probably thinks that he can run the country like he would run a seminary. Free electricity and water for a population of thirty million?" My father was a senior manager at the Ministry of Power, responsible for expanding the electric grid.

But the crowd on television took the ayatollah at his word. As he made these outlandish promises, the people at the cemetery burst into applause. They'd struggled to overthrow the shah and his dictatorship, and a freer country finally seemed within their reach. Khomeini had led their revolution to victory, and now that he was promising to deliver more, they believed him.

People were still clapping, cheering, and whistling when a full-bearded man sitting next to Khomeini rose. "*Allah Akbar,*" he chanted from the top of his lungs—"God is great" in Arabic.

Khomeini deemed clapping perverse, too Western, and not at all Islamic. From the outset of the revolution, he had been determined to introduce the nation to a realm of sin and virtue, the parameters of which would be his to determine. This new chant was the first indication to many Iranians of these grand designs—and of just how different this new regime would be.

On television, we could see people look at one another in confusion. The bearded man raised his arms and invited the crowd to chant with him. After a brief commotion, they joined him: "*Allah-o Akbar, Allah-o Akbar.*"

CHAPTER TWO

NESSA

Nessa dropped the knife on the floor and tapped on her eyelids with her index finger. "I swear on the life of my children, I saw his face with this pair of eyes," she said, sitting cross-legged on the floor with a big pile of herbs. She picked up the knife and began mincing the herbs again on a wooden cutting board.

My mother was washing the herbs at the sink to prepare *ghormeh sabzi*, an aromatic Persian stew. She raised an eyebrow and cast Nessa a skeptical look. "On the moon?" she asked.

Nessa nodded. "With these two eyes." She dropped the knife again and tapped on her eyelids, leaving a small piece of herb above one eye. "My daughter says he is the savior of the poor and this was a sign."

"Are you sure that you didn't hear about it from your daughter?" my mother asked.

"He is a man of God," Nessa responded with a wide smile, flashing eight little teeth and a row of toothless gums.

Nessa was our maid. She came to our house once a week to clean, making the long trip from her home in the slums on the south side of the capital to our apartment complex in the city center. For my relatively well-off family, Nessa provided insight into the thoughts and opinions of the underclass that had supported the revolution. And now, a few days after Khomeini's return to Iran, it was clear that she was utterly in the thrall of the new leader.

Nessa was telling my mother that she'd become a devotee of Khomeini back in August, when a rumor had circulated that his face had appeared on the moon. My mother recognized this as a tactic of the cleric and his followers to make him appeal to less educated Iranians; it was all part of an effort to raise Khomeini's stature and to make him a mystical figure before he returned from exile. It worked; some people had gazed into the dark sky every night for weeks searching for his visage again. Yet no one, not even secular activists, dared dismiss the rumors and risk being accused of undermining the new leader. Khomeini had ignited the emotional engine of the revolution and brought the masses into the streets. Everyone was now referring to him by his religious title: Ayatollah Khomeini.

Nessa was exactly the sort of Iranian whom the regime had targeted. She had never attended school and was unable to write even her name. She was tall and thin, her face like a sculpture with high cheekbones and a snub nose. She came from a Turkish-speaking village in northwestern Iran, where her parents had married her off at the age of fourteen to a street vendor who brought her to Tehran. She gave birth to three children in three years.

One morning, Nessa's husband left her and never returned. He divorced her and so to feed her children she began working as a housemaid. Soon she remarried, but this time as a temporary wife known as *sigheh*—a practice common among the lower classes.

Sigheh is a legal contract between a man and a woman for the purpose of having a sexual relationship, and it is endorsed by Shiite clerics. This type of marriage can be informal and the ceremony performed verbally, or formal and the ceremony performed by a notary like all Iranian marriages; it can last for a few minutes, for hours, or for years. The couple can terminate it unilaterally whenever they wish. The man may agree to give money, a gift, or even property to the bride. The child produced in a *sigheh* relationship is considered legitimate, and the father is required to provide for her or his upbringing. Religious clerics argue that *sigheh* binds men to act responsibly when they engage in random sexual affairs. But more educated people look down on the practice and consider it prostitution in disguise.

Nessa had two more children from two *sigheh* marriages. Her first temporary husband turned out to be an opium addict and left her. The second one was a medical doctor, she claimed; he fathered her youngest child, a two-year-old boy. My mother suspected that it must have been a brief affair. Despite their so-called obligations, neither of the two men paid child support—a violation of the *sigheh* contract, but a transgression they could both get away with, given the vulnerability of their one-time partner.

I learned how poor Nessa was a few weeks later, when I accompanied my mother and one of her friends to Nessa's home to deliver rice. Rice is the staple food in Iran, and every six months one of Nessa's clients gave her enough of it to support her family. The bags weighed fifty pounds each, and Nessa couldn't carry them home on public transportation, so my mother had offered to deliver it to her.

We drove for a long time through the shantytowns of southern Tehran, unable to find Nessa's street. Finally, when the roads turned into narrow alleys, we parked the car, and my mother and her friend, in their coiffured hair and knee-length coats, took me in tow as they continued the search on foot.

As we walked through Nessa's neighborhood, gardens and trees vanished, and rows of clumsily laid brick walls with low metal doors appeared. On the doorsteps of these homes, dark-skinned men sat in an opium daze, staring into the distance. In one alleyway, young boys with shaved heads kicked a plastic ball with bare feet.

My mother stopped to get directions from a young man who, as it turned out, knew Nessa's family. We followed him through narrow alleys, where we saw a woman beating a mattress with a wooden stick and a skinny man sitting on the pavement on a box he'd turned upside down, selling cigarettes.

At last, our guide led us through a door and down a narrow path that led to a yard. There, half a dozen women squatted around a hose, each with their own rubber washtubs. They were chatting as they shared the hose to wash dishes, clothes, and fruit, emptying the dirty water on the ground near a drain. Around the yard were carpeted but sparsely furnished rooms with large windows. We crossed the enclosure, went into another narrow passageway, and finally arrived at another door.

The young man knocked, and one of Nessa's daughters, Iran, opened the door. I recognized her immediately; she was nine, just my age, and sometimes she came to our home with her younger sister, Parvin, to play while their mother cleaned.

Iran and Parvin's home could not have been more different from mine. As the door swung open, an odor of body sweat and meat fat rushed out. Their home was actually a single room, small and windowless. A thin carpet covered the floor and several mattresses were piled on top of one another against the wall. A pot sat on a kerosene burner, lid rattling. The only other furniture in the room was a wooden trunk; there was no sign of a television, telephone, air conditioning, refrigerator, or even a radio.

I was shocked at the size of their home. Our apartment was not nearly as big as the houses of many of our friends, but it seemed like a mansion compared to Nessa's home. We had three bedrooms, two bathrooms, central air, and a modern kitchen. Nessa had to fetch water from the yard and share a toilet with the other residents of her compound. In the past, Iran and Parvin had spoken excitedly of the public bath in their neighborhood, and now I understood why going to the public bath must have been an adventure.

This was the first real glimpse I had of the class structure that divided Iranian society. The roots of this division stretched back to Iran's traditional feudal system, under which landlords were considered *arbab* or *Khan*, "masters," and their rural inhabitants, *ra'iyat*, meaning "agricultural laborer." The shah had introduced land reform in 1963 to eliminate this source of inequality by taking land from landlords—including many clerics—and giving it to the peasants. This policy had increased the peasants' wealth but failed to give them a new identity. People still referred to them as former *ra'iyat*. Social mobility through income and education was rare at the time; the children of these peasants, like Nessa, had migrated to urban areas in search of work in the 1970s, but they couldn't shed the stigma of their *ra'iyat* backgrounds.

Nessa's two older kids were out, and Nessa was still at work, cleaning other people's homes. Parvin and Iran were watching after their two-year-old brother. Our young guide offered to get the bags of rice from the car with a cart, and so we left our cargo with him and headed back to the city center.

In February, Nessa informed my mother that she'd started going to the Friday Prayer, an event that Khomeini's regime held at Tehran University in the center of the capital. From atop a makeshift podium in the yard of the university, a senior cleric preached one sermon on religion and another on politics before leading the audience in prayer. His voice blasted from speakers attached to tree trunks around the yard. Rows of men knelt on the ground during the sermons, while women sat in the back, separated by a curtain. This complete segregation was actually liberating to thousands of traditional women like Nessa, who had been reluctant to participate in public events because it would require them to mingle with men, something that was traditionally forbidden. Now they began flooding the campus every Friday, knowing that they would not even have to see the male cleric or the men in the audience.

"It's fun," Nessa explained to my mother every week. "We have nothing to do on Fridays. A bus picks us up in the neighborhood for free. I take snacks, and we spend the whole afternoon with other women. The kids get to play around on the campus too, until the bus drops us off at home."

Nessa's eldest daughter, Roya, was eighteen years old and had become a staunch supporter of Khomeini. Unlike her mother, she was educated; in fact, she was about to graduate from high school. She was also religious, like her mother, and was a regular at the neighborhood mosque. She'd started going to the mosque the previous year to pray, but she made friends there and kept going back to socialize. There wasn't much to do in her neighborhood, and the mosque had become a hangout for young men and women like her.

In the months leading up to the revolution, the cleric at the mosque had introduced Nessa and her peers to Khomeini's ideas. Nessa had told us that Roya heard Khomeini preach on cassette tapes that had been smuggled into Iran from Najaf in Iraq, and later from Paris after the Iraqi government expelled Khomeini because of his activism.

In the tapes, Khomeini had denounced the shah as an evil traitor and accused him of plundering the country's wealth. By modernizing the country, Khomeini charged, the shah was pushing Iran toward decadence and trampling on its religious values. The shah and his father had introduced secular education to Iran and had instituted a legal system that had reduced the power of the clergy—whom the shah had angered further when he had divided their land among the country's peasants.

But Khomeini claimed that the shah had done the most harm to the Iranian people, not the clerics. Khomeini wanted the shah to leave Iran, he said, so that its people could found a democracy, a system in which they would be able to vote freely and express their views without fear of persecution. He vowed that everyone would be free. The new system would be based on religious law, not mere tyranny like that which Iran had experienced under the shah's oppressive regime. Equality, freedom, and independence from Western culture would be the values of the new Iran. Khomeini even vowed that he'd remain a spiritual leader and not seek power.

No one had ever denounced the shah with such courage. And Khomeini was not just anyone—he was the most senior cleric in Shiite Islam in Iran, a grand ayatollah, and his black turban signaled that he was a descendant of Prophet Muhammad. Khomeini's outspokenness, drawing from the Shiite principle of struggling against tyranny, struck a chord with many religious Iranians like Roya.

The majority of Muslims in the world are Sunni, while some 90 percent of Iranians are Shiite, a separate sect. The split between the two groups springs from the debate over who deserved to succeed Prophet Muhammad as the leader of the Islamic world after his death in 632 CE. Shiites believe that his legitimate successor was Ali, a cousin whom Prophet Muhammad raised from childhood and who later married Muhammad's daughter. Sunni Muslims appointed another leader after the prophet's death, and Ali found himself in the position of a dissident. He was passed over twice more during subsequent successions and spent a total of twenty-three years on the fringes of Islamic culture. He finally reached the supreme post in 656, a time of intense internal conflict, and was assassinated just five years later. Shiites passed the mantle of resistance to Ali's son Hassan and later to his youngest son, Hussein. They consider Ali the first of twelve successors of Prophet Muhammad known as Imams. The twelfth, the Shiites claim, was still a young child when he passed into an occult state, apart from the world but aware of its suffering. They refer to him as Mahdi, meaning the savior and the messiah who will one day return to earth to reward true believers and punish the wicked.

By the time the Arabs conquered Persia—an empire that would eventually become the modern state of Iran—in 637, five years after Prophet Muhammad's death, Persians already had a long experience of foreign invasions and had learned to assimilate foreign cultures to their liking. Muslim Arabs viewed Persians' Zoroastrian faith as a kind of paganism and forced Persians to convert to the nascent Islamic religion. The Persians had no choice but to accept Muhammad as God's prophet and the Koran as God's word, but over a period of centuries they fashioned traditions that were quite different from those of their Arab conquerors. To this day, Persians retain ancient Zoroastrian traditions, including celebrating the feast of fire by jumping over a bonfire on the last Tuesday night of the year. Fire is the Zoroastrian symbol of purity, and the ceremony is meant to cleanse people of disease and the evil eye. There are other differences as well; Arabs celebrate the New Year based on a lunar calendar, while Persians mark the New Year on the first day of spring in accordance with a solar calendar. They inaugurate the New Year with the Zoroastrian tradition of sitting at a table with seven items that represent health, wealth, and happiness as they read a verse from the Koran.

In adapting the Islamic faith to their own culture, the Persians went so far as to claim that Hussein married a Persian princess who gave birth to the fourth Imam. By the sixteenth century, when Persia officially became a Shiite state, they had reshaped Shiite Islam into a faith that reinforced a Persian identity. They introduced into the faith ancient Zoroastrian notions such as self-sacrifice and the eternality of the battle of good against evil in pursuit of justice, and it was within that framework that Persians embraced the martyrdom of Ali and his youngest son, Hussein.

Iran's unique brand of Islam has its own set of rituals and values that have intimately influenced the country's politics. For instance, Sunni Muslims celebrate the anniversary of Hussein's martyrdom, called Ashura, by fasting because it coincides with the same day that Moses fasted after God saved his followers from the enemy in Egypt. But Iranians immerse themselves in mourning as though the suicidal battle—in which Hussein and his seventy-two fighters faced an army of thirty thousand soldiers from a rival Islamic caliphate—took place the previous day.

The martyrdom of Hussein looms especially large in Persian memory. I heard accounts of it at school and neighborhood events, retellings not unlike Christian passion plays. A preacher would narrate the details of the battle in a singsong tone: "Hussein's allies fought even after some of them were dismembered; the enemy did not spare Hussein's six-month-old infant and carried his body on a spear; Hussein was decapitated, his body mutilated, even his finger chopped off for his ring." The account would inevitably arouse intense grief from the assembled mourners, who would beat their chests rhythmically and in unison, sobbing and fainting. Then, residents would reenact the battle in *tazieh*, a theatrical play Iranians introduced into the faith from their Persian past. To this day, handsome men compete to play the role of Hussein and his companions while rougher men are assigned to play the role of the enemy. After the ceremony, men flog themselves until they become bloody and carry heavy metal banners on their shoulders to endure the pain that Hussein suffered, all traditions that come from the Persians' Zoroastrian past and that Sunni Muslims look down on. During the ritual, the preacher reminds Shiites that the struggle for justice has not ended and that learned clerics are still leading the way for Mahdi to return.

These were the stories that young Iranians had grown up with, and as Ayatollah Khomeini and his followers laid the groundwork for the revolution in Iran, they used these powerful religious traditions to great effect. Nessa told us that Roya learned at the mosque that Khomeini was one of the clerics laying the groundwork for the messiah's return. Khomeini was offering a path to liberation, and it was Shiites' duty to follow him.

Roya, like many other young believers, played a crucial role in the revolution of 1979. That past summer, she had knelt on the carpeted floor in the mosque's back room for hours, helping duplicate Khomeini's tapes. Without these tapes, Khomeini's fiery speeches would have never reached his followers in Iran. Revolutionaries like Roya were able to disseminate these speeches in part because the shah was more scared of the communists than he was of the Islamists; Khomeini was in exile, he believed, and the Islamists were not sophisticated enough to create the kind of complex networks that the leftists had spent decades building. But the mosques in every town and village had created a vast network, turning ordinary Iranians into fervent opponents of the shah.

After Khomeini's return to Iran in February 1979, Nessa told us that Roya had changed the way she wore the chador, the black head-to-toe garment that she and her mother had worn in public all their lives. Nessa still wore the chador the way she always had: in a traditional way, keeping herself covered by holding the chador under her chin. If her hands were full, she bit the chador with her teeth. The garment sometimes slipped over her shoulders and revealed her long silky hair, but Nessa didn't seem to mind—and for most of her life, neither had Roya.

Now, to avoid showing her hair, Roya began wearing a hood, a cone-shaped head-covering with a hole for the face. She wore a knee-length coat over a pair of loose pants. The chador was worn over the hood, the coat, and the pants. An elastic band held the chador tightly on her head. We began calling women who dressed in this way "black crows." Even Nessa confessed with a sheepish laugh that she found her daughter's look intimidating. Roya's chador was no longer the garment that traditional women had worn for over a century. It was a symbol of her ideological devotion to Khomeini's regime and of her new identity as a faithful adherent to his brand of Shiite Islam.

Khomeini had successfully drawn poor and dispossessed Iranians, including women, from the margins of society into the center of the country's politics. He needed them all to serve the revolution. Khomeini even reversed the decree he himself had issued in 1963 opposing women's suffrage, and now urged both men and women to go to the polls in April to vote for an Islamic republic—not a republic alone—a referendum that would decide the fate of the regime and the future of Iran itself.

CHAPTER THREE

THE TIME OF HORROR

A few days after Khomeini's return to Iran, I opened our mailbox to pick up the daily *Kayhan*, a state-run newspaper. The bus from my private American school had just dropped me off at the gates of our complex, and I had stopped to get the mail on my way up to our apartment.

I was in second grade, and before the chaos had broken out, my Persian language teacher had encouraged us to read the paper as a way to improve our reading skills. Classes at our school were held in English in the mornings and in Persian in the afternoons, and we were instructed to do whatever we could to refine our skills in both languages.

As I unrolled the newspaper, I froze. The front-page photo showed dead bodies lying on the ground. One lay facedown in a puddle of blood with his legs awkwardly pointing outward; another was faceup, his eyes blank, with a bullet hole in his forehead. Injuries or blood had blackened half of a third body. The photo showed three bodies, but the headline announced the execution of four of the shah's generals.

Only three days after Khomeini's return, his new regime introduced the term *mofsed-e-fel-arz*, an Arabic term meaning "corrupt on earth"; whoever was identified as such would face the firing squad. A judge, I read, had decreed these four generals to be *mofsed-e-fel-arz*—just one outcome of the many trials being held in Tehran at that time.

In the wake of the shah's departure, Ayatollah Khomeini had appointed a cleric, Sadeq Khalkhali, as chief justice and charged him with setting up Revolutionary Tribunals to deal with officials linked to the shah. Khalkhali was a white-turbaned cleric, short, chubby, and with thin lips and a fleshy nose. He wore round spectacles, and a patch of black beard stretched under his chin. His comical appearance was deceiving, however. In his new role as chief justice, Khalkhali had unleashed the worst bloodshed in the country's recent history.

The execution of the generals marked the first such killing under the new chief justice, and newspapers reported how it had taken place—a story that I would later hear grown-ups recount to one another over and over again. On February 15, the day before the article was published, Khalkhali had convened his first court at a school called Refah in southern Tehran, where he tried the four high-ranking army generals: Reza Naji, the governor of the city of Isfahan; Mehdi Rahimi, the military commander and police chief in Tehran; Manouchehr Khosrodad, head of the air force; and Nematollah Nassiri, head of the shah's intelligence agency, SAVAK (Iranian Secret and Intelligence Service in Persian). Nassiri had appeared on TV the night before the trial with a bandaged head, answering questions in a weak voice. Ironically, the shah had jailed him and a few other senior officials in December to show that he was willing to reach a compromise with the revolutionaries; the men had remained incarcerated when the shah fled and had thus become the new regime's prisoners. On TV, one of the revolutionaries asked Nassiri about his role in torturing dissidents under the shah. Beating, pulling out nails, and other forms of torture had been common, but he claimed that he was unaware of any such abuses. He was just a soldier carrying out orders, he said, his voice trembling.

At the trial, which lasted for five hours, Khalkhali acted as judge, prosecutor, and jury. He concluded that the four generals were *mofsed-e-fel-arz* and declared: "The earth needs to be cleansed of evil and corrupt people." The four men had resisted the will of the Iranian people, he charged. Khomeini, who was also at the school but in a different room, approved the death sentences immediately. A few minutes before midnight, four gunmen escorted the generals up the stairs to the school's flat roof. There, the guards tried to blindfold them. General Rahimi and Khosrodad refused the blindfolds and said they would face death like honorable men. Both men performed military salutes, and Khosrodad, the most senior in the group, gave the guards their orders: "Ready, aim, shoot." The guns roared, and the generals fell onto the ground. One guard walked to each man and lodged a final bullet in his head.

The new regime publicized what it was capable of doing to its opponents. The next day, my mother tried to pick up our newspaper before I came home from school, but I beat her to it and saw the gory picture on the front page. Pictures of other dead bodies, their faces disfigured and pierced by bullets, appeared in the papers day after day from then on; names of the dead also appeared in long columns, and the authorities ominously promised to "cleanse society of more corrupt people." I usually managed to take a peek at these articles after my parents worriedly devoured the newspapers every night. Even state television flashed footage of the bodies, often dotted by bullets.

Khalkhali had begun by killing the shah's senior generals and ministers, fearing that they might pose a threat to the new regime. But he quickly went after others: entertainers, bureaucrats, Kurdish rebels, non-Muslims, and even drug addicts, the latter of whom he accused of being a burden on society. During summary trials over a period of a year, he issued death sentences with a snap of his fingers. Exactly how many he ordered killed was not clear. "Hundreds," he boasted many years later in a memoir. "And I believe I didn't kill enough."

Within weeks of Khomeini's return, it became clear that there was a line dividing his supporters from the rest of the Iranian people. He ruled from a base that was more religious and rural, and less educated than my family and friends who lived in Tehran. His followers were from the lower classes—people like Roya and Nessa. And by 1979, the lower classes were enormous.

Massive demographic changes in Iran had laid the groundwork for the revolution. By 1979, Iran's urban population had reached 47 percent from 31 percent only two decades earlier. Many migrated during the mid-1950s, looking for jobs after the oil money began flowing, and had hoped to work in modern industries. Their children grew up in the cities and went to school in the years leading up to the revolution; some even attended universities. This new generation of city dwellers was more educated than their rural parents, but they remained impoverished and deeply religious. Capitalizing on this inequality, Khomeini referred to the poor as *Mostazafin*, meaning the deprived. He said that the upper class had robbed *Mostazafin* of their share of Iran's wealth, and he vowed to improve their lot.

To manifest their devotion to Khomeini, his male supporters grew lush beards and wore untucked and wrinkled shirts to show their humble roots. His female supporters, meanwhile, adopted the kind of outfit Roya had started to wear. They labeled those who didn't support the revolution as *Taghooti*, another new term in post-revolution Iran to describe people linked to the previous regime.

Not everyone exhibited such devotion to the ayatollah, however. The more educated and secular people, who had also opposed the shah, opted for Marxist and leftist ideas—the fashionable ideology among intellectuals in those days. After the victory of the revolution, many people realized they could not identify with Khomeini's ideals. In the tapes Khomeini had sent from exile, he'd spoken of democracy, human rights, even the rights of dissidents. Khomeini had since taken charge of Iran, but none of those ideas had become a reality. The leader who'd vowed to root out dictatorship and usher in an era of justice and freedom was becoming another tyrant.

Khomeini sensed the divide among the revolutionaries. He also realized that he couldn't count on the army or the police to protect his new regime in the case of another uprising, as both forces were loyal to the people before all else; they had put down their arms and sided with them during the revolution and would be sure to do so again. Indeed, the army was more of a danger to this government than it had been to the previous one. Khomeini's regime was executing officers, fearing that the army might stage a coup.

On February 21, only twenty days after his return, Khomeini hurriedly founded the Islamic Revolution Committees and the Revolutionary Guards Corps, two militia forces made up of his supporters known as Hezbollah, meaning the Party of God. The Guards Corps was to replace the army, while the Committees (pronounced *Komiteh* in Persian, like the French term *comité*) would also act as the new police force.

We called members of both forces Pasdar, Persian for "guard." The men wore dark olive-green fatigues and had a verse from the Koran embroidered on their sleeves: "And prepare against them whatever you are able of power and of steeds of war." The rest of the verse, "by which you may terrify the enemy," was left out, but almost everyone realized that the mission of the Pasdar was exactly that—to *terrify* people. They patrolled the streets in white Nissan SUVs, usually with two men in the front and two women in the back, looking for *the enemy*. On their vehicle was written *Yassa-rollah*, meaning "the blood of God" in Arabic.

One day, the Pasdars came for one of our neighbors, a friend of my father's. Tall and bald, with his shoulders slightly slumped, the man had served as a senior official under the shah. We'd taken rides in his light blue 1960 Buick, and he'd come to our home for dinners. His family was in the United States, and he lived alone. The neighbors saw the Guards take him away and learned that they took him to the notorious Evin prison, the big prison in Tehran where most executions were being carried out. A few weeks later, we received news of his death. How he died we never learned.

No one I knew uttered the word "Pasdar" or "Komiteh" in a neutral tone. Both terms evoked horror, like the word "Gestapo" did in movies about Europe during the 1940s. Our Gestapo was different from Germany's, of course; they called themselves "the Party of God." Their politics were extreme; no matter how pious and anti-West you were, they did not regard you as equals. The revolution had given them an identity and a chance to dominate their fellow Iranians. They felt they must use force to lead the rest of our society toward the path of God, and they waged a war of terror to show us their strength.

CHAPTER FOUR

——————•◆•——————

"WORLD POWERS DID IT!"

My father, Jafar, exhaled the smoke of his cigarette, creating a thin, cloudy layer over his head. At fifty-one, he had a wisp of gray hair over each ear. He leaned forward to reach for his glass; the ice clinked in the vodka as he took a sip. Then he placed the tumbler on the small table next to the piano.

It was May 1979, and we were at the home of two friends, four flights below our apartment. Their L-shaped living room was exactly like ours, except it was furnished differently. Our neighbor was a lung surgeon whom everyone—even his wife, Mali—called Doctor, as if it were more a name than a title. Because of the events outside, the families in the building got together after supper so the grown-ups could discuss politics while the kids played. Another couple from the building, Abbas and his wife, Sedigheh, had come that night with their two children. All six of us kids sat at the dining table a few feet away from the adults, scooping ice cream into our bowls.

The grown-ups kept meeting and talking, despite the fact that their conversations occasionally turned into harsh arguments that exposed their political differences. Indeed their conversations have continued through the present day, in one form or another, echoing off the walls of every living room in Iran. These discussions, some of them real and others only conjecture, have influenced Iranians young and old, evolving from isolated after-dinner conversations into a society-wide discourse that nurtured me and my generation.

"I really don't understand what's happening," said Abbas. "Various Marxist and nationalist groups struggled against the shah for over two decades, but now Khomeini has emerged as the leader of the revolution. How is this possible?"

Abbas was tall, with a full head of silver hair. My father admired his wit and diligence: Abbas had never finished high school, but he had nevertheless become a wealthy carpet merchant. During the early years of the Cold War, he devoured communist texts smuggled secretly into the country from the northern borders with the Soviet Union. Marxism and socialism were the politics of the avant-garde, and so Abbas became a Marxist too. When his politics eventually landed him in prison for two years in the 1960s, he taught himself French and English in his cell.

"What's there not to understand?" asked Sedigheh in a matter-of-fact tone from where she sat next to him on the couch. She smoothed her skirt. "The Western powers are behind Khomeini."

My father nodded his head in agreement. "Nothing has happened in this country over the past century without the will of Western powers."

Doctor had walked to a mahogany buffet to refill his glass, carefully setting the round crystal top of a chiseled decanter on the shiny tray and pouring the liquor into his glass, then adding Coke. Now he interjected as he returned to the round ottoman next to my father's chair, shuffling slowly in his leather slippers. "Come on, Jafar," he said to my father. "The uprising against the shah was nothing like the 1921 coup that brought the Pahlavis into power. This time we had a popular revolution."

"How can anyone believe the shah, with such a powerful army behind him, could have fallen within a few months?" my father asked.

"The majority of people were against him," Doctor objected. "He and his father were both dictators."

"They were strong leaders and that's what this country needed," my father responded. "Iranians didn't have anything until they came to power. My mother gave birth to sixteen children in the 1930s and '40s, and only seven of us survived. Now, less than half a century later, we have modern hospitals and many well-educated doctors." This last comment was directed at Doctor, who had studied in the United States and returned to serve his home country. My father had also returned to Iran after he'd lived in London for eight years and completed his studies as a banker. He was a senior executive at the Ministry of Power, responsible for connecting towns and villages to the grid.

My father turned toward Abbas. "Have you forgotten that clean water was a luxury back when we were young?" Like my father, Abbas was from Tabriz, a prosperous and Turkish-speaking city in northwestern Iran.

"That's true, but—"

My father interrupted: "My father was well off, and so the *Qanat* water first surfaced in a room in the basement of our home." (*Qanat* was an ancient Iranian system for gathering and distributing water; comprising a steep underground tunnel connected to deep wells, it could efficiently tap large quantities of subterranean water and bring it to the surface.) "We didn't have electricity and so had installed cabinets to store food in that room because the cold water reduced the temperature. The water continued its path from our home to other homes, but the poor used the water that came from the public bath, grayish and filled with the filth from other people's bodies. They got sick and died. Who fixed all that?" my father asked.

"Iran was poor," Abbas agreed. "But even when the oil money began pouring into the country, the shah didn't do enough to rid the country of its *backwardness*."

Iranians were obsessed with the word "backwardness." It had embarrassing connotations of ignorance, poverty, and underdevelopment. Whole books were penned on the subject of Iran's *backwardness*, and people uttered the word with horror and resentment, as though it were a disease in need of a cure. Illiteracy, corruption, destitution—all had their roots in backwardness.

The concept of backwardness dated back to the late eighteenth century, when Iranians began travelling to Europe during the reign of the Qajar dynasty, which ruled Iran from 1785 to 1925. Back then, the king alone had the final word on all matters. The Qajar kings had extravagant courts, with hundreds of wives and children. The combination of the kings' unchecked authority and lavish lifestyles would come to push

Iran into the pocket of foreign powers that would exploit the country and its people for nearly half a century.

To sustain their expenses, the kings gave concessions to the two great world powers at the time, Russia and Britain, in return for cash. In 1872, the king at the time, Nasir al Din Shah, sold to German-born British baron Julius de Reuter of news agency fame the right to irrigate the country's farmlands, run all its industries, exploit its mineral resources, develop railroads and streetcar lines, establish a national bank, and print its currency. When the Russians made similar demands, the shah gave them the exclusive rights to his caviar fisheries. Iranian merchants, whose business suffered as a result of these concessions, were enraged. And clerics, a community of Islamic scholars who were historically rich and powerful—and thus heavily invested in the nation's economy—were also furious.

The popular anger over Nasir al Din Shah's concessions reached all the way to the king's harem. In 1890, he sold the Iranian tobacco industry to a British company for a period of fifty years, for an annual sum of £15,000. His wives joined hundreds of thousands of angry Iranian smokers who were boycotting tobacco. The concession represented a major blow to both farmers and tobacco sellers, who had developed a long-established relationship with each other, building an industry that created two hundred thousand jobs. Now they were required to seek permits from the British tobacco authorities and inform them of the amount of tobacco they produced. Under increasing pressure, the king was forced to cancel the deal, and the victory invigorated the protestors.

Iran's sense of backwardness was deeply intertwined with its history of economic subjugation by foreign powers. Educated Iranians were proud of their ancient Persian identity, grown out of an empire founded by Cyrus the Great in 600 BCE. The empire was the largest the world has seen, stretching from the Mediterranean Sea in the west to the Indus River in the east. Cyrus's success lay in the fact that he set up a central administration that worked to the advantage and profit of his subjects. In addition, Persia developed one of the world's richest cultures, creating architectural wonders such as Persepolis as well as nurturing Sufi mystic poets like Hafiz and Rumi, whose poems have transcended national and ethnic borders for hundreds of years. Educated Iranians aspired to elevate Iran to its past glory.

I had heard from my father how his mother's cousin, Ismail Momtaz-Doleh, also from the northwestern city of Tabriz and married to my grandfather's sister, had turned to activism to root out Iran's backwardness. This cousin was worldly and educated—he had studied in Istanbul and spoke French. Momtaz-Doleh's brother Samad Momtaz-Saltaneh was a diplomat in Russia and Europe from 1883 to 1951. Momtaz-Doleh often visited his brother in Europe, particularly in Paris, where Momtaz-Saltaneh served as Iran's ambassador. Momtaz-Doleh saw that in those countries monarchs did not hold absolute power, and part of each country's wealth was also injected into education and health services. He returned home inspired by his travels and determined to curb the shah's power. He called for the establishment of a parliament, a legislative body that many European countries had created to counterbalance the power of their monarchs. People began calling him—the outspoken intellectual with a dark beard—a constitutionalist, after the document that would create his hoped-for parliament.

People like Momtaz-Doleh were religious Shiite Muslims and found a common cause with merchants and clerics who were already staging protests against the king. The three groups formed an alliance aimed at reforming Iranian politics by limiting the king's power through the creation of a parliament. International political developments seemed to be on their side; in 1905, the news of the Russian Revolution, which aimed to impose a constitution upon that country's monarchy, further emboldened Iranian activists.

A year after the Russian Revolution, constitutionalists forced the ailing king, Mozafar al din Shah, to sign a declaration granting them the right to establish a parliament, a victory that came to be known as the Constitutional Revolution. The revolutionaries quickly drafted a constitution based on Belgium's, which they considered the most progressive constitution in Europe. Iran's new parliament convened for the first time in October of that year; Momtaz-Doleh was elected a member and later served as speaker. Iran became the first country in the Middle East to have a democratic parliament.

Despite Parliament's efforts, Iran was faced with a crisis by 1920 and was on the verge of dissolution. The king, Ahmad Shah, who spent most of his time in Europe, had lost control of the country outside the capital. The Red Army controlled most of Iran's northern mainland and was preparing to march on Tehran. Fearing the Soviets' expanding influence, the British backed an illiterate but bold officer, Reza Mirpanj, in his move to seize control of the capital. Before the day of the march, the British paid 20,000 rials to Reza Shah and distributed 200,000 rials among Reza's two thousand men—efforts that have fueled rumors ever since that British cash and will are behind every political change in Iran. No Iranian could raise such a substantial amount of cash. On February 21, 1921, Reza staged a coup d'état, forced the king into exile, and became prime minister and army commander himself. At this position, Reza negotiated a treaty with the Soviet troops for the removal of their forces. After he secured the country from foreign threats, Reza formally deposed the exiled king in 1925 and declared himself monarch: Reza Shah.

Reza Shah showed no sign of loyalty to his British sponsors or the Russians after he solidified his power. He accepted no loans from foreign financiers, banned the sale of property to non-Iranians, revoked concessions that gave the British-owned Imperial Bank the exclusive right to issue Iranian currency, and even forbade officials of his foreign ministry to attend receptions at foreign embassies. In 1928, he canceled Iran's nineteenth-century capitulations to Europeans. Under the agreement, Europeans who lived and worked in Iran were subject to their own consular courts rather than to the Iranian judiciary. He famously threw Iran's contract with the Anglo-Iranian Oil Company—the firm that had discovered oil in Iran at the turn of the century—into a fireplace. The British company had long angered Iranians because it had taken Iran's oil while only giving a fraction of the revenue back to Iran. As that contract burned to ashes, Reza Shah forced the British company to raise Iran's share of the revenue from 16 to 21 percent. He also issued a decree asking foreign powers to call his country Iran, meaning "the land of the Aryans," instead of Persia, a word that foreigners had been using until then. He believed that the name Iran would restore the country's glorious past.

During World War II, Reza Shah declared Iran neutral and announced that Allied forces could not use Iranian territory to ship arms to Russia for its war efforts against Germany. The decision was strategic— by that time, Germany had become Iran's biggest trading partner—but Iran could not stay out of the conflict for long. In August 1941, Russia and Britain ignored Reza Shah and occupied Iran. They needed to secure Iranian oil fields and ensure Allied supply lines for the Soviets fighting against Axis forces and also to use Iran's railroad to send Soviets supplies. A few weeks after occupying Iran, the British ordered Reza Shah in a humiliating letter to abdicate in favor of his son. "We have a high opinion of him and will ensure his position," their letter read. "But his Highness should not think there is any other solution."

Realizing the inevitability of his ouster, Reza Shah asked to go to Canada, but the British rejected his request and sent him first to Mauritius, a British territory, and then to Johannesburg, where he died three years later. Meanwhile, his son, Mohammad Reza, had ascended to the throne—a position he would occupy for nearly four decades, until he was toppled by the 1979 Revolution.

Mohammad Reza wasn't the fierce character that his father had been, but he did pursue his father's program of modernization. He introduced a secular education and legal system, built roads, imported Western technology and industry, and even invested heavily in a strong army. His opponents argued that his efforts endangered indigenous culture and traditions, but these complaints did little to slow his reforms or dampen many Iranians' enthusiasm for their steady progress away from the backwardness of the past.

My parents were the only pro-shah people in the group assembled in Doctor's apartment, and this was not the first time their support for the fallen government had put them at odds with the others. Indeed, my father sometimes seemed happy for the chance to engage in an intellectual debate about the direction the country was taking. "Come on, Abbas," my father said. "Reza Shah laid the foundation for social reforms; he built the railroad and roads, the education and health systems. His son sent tens of thousands of young people abroad on state scholarship to study. They returned home as communists, and now we are reaping the seeds these communists sowed."

"How can you say that?" Abbas asked in his cheerfully combative tone. "No one could criticize his majesty! Both the father and the son made sure that newspapers were censored, labor unions forbidden, and opposition figures jailed, exiled, or murdered. The shah brought the revolution upon himself."

My mother, who'd been silent so far, jumped in. "Had it not been for Reza Shah, armed bandits and tribal leaders would still dominate our roads," she said emotionally. "He made Iran a nation state—a safe country."

Doctor cleared his throat. "My father used to tell us a story about a visit Reza Shah took to Hamedan." Hamedan was a city in western Iran. "I am not sure if it was a legend or if it actually happened, but either way, it's telling. Reza Shah had learned that bakers in the city were hoarding wheat to drive up prices. People were going hungry because of a shortage of bread.

"As soon as he arrived in the city, Reza Shah went to a bakery and asked for bread. Not knowing that he was the king, the baker said he had no bread. Reza Shah ordered his men to throw the baker into the oven and burn him alive. Other bakers were horrified. The next morning, every bakery was filled with low-priced bread." Doctor was silent for a moment as his story sank in, then he continued. "Yes, without doubt he brought law and order—but with the price of blood."

Abbas started to say something, but Sedigheh interrupted him. She was pointing to a portrait on the wall. "Are you going to keep it there?" she asked.

It was a framed photo of Mohammad Mossadeq, the former Iranian prime minister and a nationalist whom almost everyone in the country regarded as a patriot. Mali and Doctor had raised the photo just a few weeks earlier to signal their support for the revolution. Mossadeq had nationalized oil in 1951 and expelled the British staff of the Anglo-Iranian Oil Company. As a young man, he'd served as a member of Parliament before ascending to the post of prime minister. His vocal defense of the oil industry had earned him the admiration of many ordinary Iranians, who saw in him a champion of the people. And two nationalist groups, the National Front, which he'd founded, and the Liberation Movement, were now involved in the government, which only made Mossadeq's legacy seem more vital.

Yet Mossadeq was also a tragic figure in Iranian political history, as photos of him often reflected. The portrait hanging in Mali and

Doctor's apartment was a decent picture, showing a bald man with a beaky nose in a suit and necktie, but he was often shown in a robe, lying in bed or slumped in a chair, looking frail and dispirited.

Western powers had been instrumental in bringing down Mossadeq and—inadvertently—cementing his place as a martyr in Iranian popular memory. Enraged by the losses they had suffered from the nationalization of Iran's oil industry, the British decided to seek revenge and topple him. They tried to bring their wartime ally, the United States, on board, but Harry Truman, the US president at the time, found old-style British imperialism contemptible and sympathized with the nationalist movement in Iran.

It wasn't until the election of President Dwight Eisenhower in 1952 that the Americans joined the British effort to push Mossadeq from power. In 1953, the CIA agent Kermit Roosevelt, a grandson of President Theodore Roosevelt, came to Iran as a spy to plan a coup. The Americans feared that Mossadeq might pave the way for other opposition groups, mainly communists, to expand their influence in Iran. Roosevelt snuck into the shah's compound hiding under a blanket, and once inside the palace he tried to persuade him to cooperate with the coup. Tension between the shah and Mossadeq had also heightened; the shah feared that Mossadeq might use his popularity to abolish the monarchy. Communist groups had already attracted intellectuals and instigated anti-shah sentiments. But the shah was inherently a weak and indecisive character; it took Roosevelt a few visits until the shah caved.

For months Roosevelt recruited allies in Tehran. He hired thugs to launch staged attacks and organize riots. He bribed officers and clerics to cooperate and spent tens of thousands of dollars to turn Mossadeq allies against him. He allocated a budget of $11,000 a week for suborning members of Parliament.

The British and Americans overthrew Mossadeq's government on August 19, 1953, after tens of thousands of paid mobs, officers, and former Mossadeq allies took over the streets. But over the years, the coup became the main source of Iranians' resentment toward the United States—a sense of betrayal that has lasted until this day. Many people believed the US government had interrupted the course of Iran's democratic development. Democracy had been born at the time of the Constitutional Revolution, and it survived amidst external and internal threats, even under the reign of Reza Shah. Mossadeq's government had been the country's first democratic government that stood up to the British exploitation of the country's wealth. But the United States had helped the British crush Mossadeq and had empowered the shah, and in so doing had set Iranian democracy back on its heels.

A court sentenced Mossadeq to three years in prison and then exiled him to his village. He died in 1967, perhaps more of a broken heart than old age. But even in his death, Mossadeq remained the embodiment of nationalism. His followers, known as religious-nationalists, had joined Khomeini to overthrow the shah. They were educated and looked modern; their leader, Mehdi Bazargan, became prime minister after the fall of the shah.

Sedigheh's question drew everyone's attention to the portrait on the wall. Returning from the kitchen with a stack of clean plates, Mali, our hostess, sneered, "How can you trust the religious-nationalists when you see them with Khomeini? They've become his yes-men."

Mali took an apple, an orange, and a cucumber from a bowl of fruit on the coffee table and placed them on each plate, as Persian tradition requires, and put each plate in front of a guest. Mali had a delicate face and cropped hair. As she went around putting the plates in front of each person on the large coffee table, she said, "I am really worried that Khomeini will reverse all the progress we made. Do you remember he had opposed the shah in 1963, when he gave women the right to vote?"

"Khomeini said suffrage was un-Islamic and would corrupt women," my mother said. "I'd just started university, and we were so proud to be the first generation of women to vote. Fortunately the shah ignored Khomeini."

"Like when Reza Shah ordered men to wear Western-style hats," Doctor said with a chuckle. "The clerics opposed it and said the rim prevented men's foreheads from touching the ground during prayer. But people continued wearing them." Everyone laughed at the memory.

Doctor went on, his tone serious. "I'm afraid Khomeini is still furious over the obligatory unveiling of women in 1936, when Reza Shah required women to take off their headscarves in public." The mandatory unveiling had been part of Reza Shah's effort to modernize the face of the country, but it had created a tremendous amount of opposition, especially from conservative Muslims and the Islamic clerics. "It was around the same time that he stripped clerics of almost all their clout: he took away their schools by introducing secular education, robbed them of their judicial power by setting up secular courts; and then with unveiling, he ridiculed their authority."

"My mother celebrated by having her picture taken without the veil," my mother remembered.

"My mother too," said Sedigheh, her red lips broadening into a smile. "A cleric lived next door to us. Every time he saw my mother on the street, he cursed, 'Unveiled women will burn in hell.'"

"You ladies are exaggerating now," Abbas said. "Most women didn't leave their homes until the policy was no longer enforced, including my own mother. The veil had been part of her identity for too long for her to simply shed it. She felt naked without it. Many traditional families turned against Reza Shah because of this rule."

"That might be true about older women," my mother said, warming up for one of her lengthy responses. She never identified herself as a feminist, but she'd read French feminist Simone de Beauvoir's book *The Second Sex* several times in Persian and was familiar with feminist ideas. "Reza Shah's policies such as unveiling and obligatory education for women empowered our generation in a profound way. The veil tied older women down not just physically but also psychologically."

She paused, took a deep breath, and went on. "My mother died young. My father was educated and wealthy, but no matter what, when it came down to his three daughters, he was a traditional man. He believed a woman was only good to marry, give birth, and serve her husband. He married my older sister off in an arranged marriage when she was sixteen. She cried and objected, but none of it changed his mind. Ten years later, my second sister finished high school. To escape an arranged marriage, she secretly moved from Arak to Tehran and signed up at the Teacher's Training College. She married a man of her choice. When I finished school and got admitted to Melli University in Tehran, my father simply couldn't object because the environment had changed."

Sitting nearby where the other kids and I were playing Monopoly after finishing our ice cream, I visualized my mother as she must have looked as a young university student. I'd seen many black-and-white photos of her in knee-length dresses, her hair puffed in a beehive. She and other young women posed confidently with big smiles, their eyebrows tweezed into an arched line and their eyes enlarged by thick black eyeliner.

"I am afraid Khomeini will most likely impose obligatory veiling to reverse what Reza Shah did over four decades ago," Mali said.

"Oh come on," said Abbas. "That's the last of our worries; they are rounding up people and killing them indiscriminately, and you ladies worry about covering your hair."

"Excuse me?" shouted Sedigheh, leaning forward to stub out her cigarette, her voice startling us children. Pushing back her shoulder-length hair, neatly curled up at the bottom, she said: "Do you think that I came out with you to all those anti-shah demonstrations so that my daughter and I could be treated like second-class citizens?" Their daughter, Leila, was fourteen. Sedigheh was getting her PhD in English literature. "Can't you see that it's a lot more than a matter of covering our hair?" Sedigheh continued, exasperated. "Can't we as human beings decide how to present ourselves?"

Abbas shifted in his seat without uttering a word.

Mali intervened, changing the subject. "Have you heard about Farrokhroo Parsa?" she said in a low voice, throwing a discreet glance at us to see if we were in earshot range. Parsa had been the minister of education under the shah. "In prison, they put her in a bag before they— *mmm,*" Mali said, tapping the tips of her fingers on the table next to her. "They did not want to touch her body even after—"

A sigh went around the room. Abbas stared silently at the flowers on the carpet. Doctor slowly shook his head.

My father stood up. "It's getting late," he said. "The kids need to get to bed."

CHAPTER FIVE

THE CLEANSING

My father returned home from work on a warm afternoon in April 1980, dressed in his dark blue suit and yellow-and-blue plaid tie. It was uncharacteristically early for him; he usually didn't return home until after dinner. His job at the Ministry of Power was demanding, and even though more than a year had passed since the revolution, he had still been going to work each day, just as he had before the upheaval.

He had worked for the Ministry of Power since returning from London in 1974. It was a very good job, especially considering the nature of Iran's economy. Oil revenue had been a consistent source of wealth for the country ever since the mid-1950s, when the shah went on a spree to develop the country after the fall of Mossadeq. My father, eager to be part of the process, began serving as a senior executive, connecting towns, villages, new factories, and industries to the grid—a job that often kept him working late into the evening.

My father usually greeted us cheerfully upon returning home from work, but today his face was grim with shock. He hung his jacket in his closet, unknotted the tie, and carefully placed it on a rack that held a dozen other ones. I knew my father liked this Western style of dress, but his choice of clothing was also political. When Reza Shah had required women to discard their headscarves in 1936, he had also ordered men to wear European clothes. By the late 1970s, only minority ethnic groups, like Arabs and Kurds, still wore their traditional attire. The rest of male society wore suits, and at work many wore ties. But since the revolution, the necktie had landed at the center of a widening war of symbols.

When the many exiled revolutionaries had returned to Iran along with Khomeini, people nicknamed the clerics "turbans," and the non-clerics "neckties." It was an easy way to distinguish the nationalists and Marxists from the Islamists. But within a year after the revolution, members of both factions stopped wearing ties to show their respect for Khomeini. Khomeini had labeled neckties Western, un-Islamic, and thus a garment to be avoided. But my father wore his tie like a badge of honor, a sign that he was not willing to be swayed by winds of political change.

The day my father arrived home early was his last day at work; the Islamists had dismissed him—or *cleansed*, as they called it. Not just because of the tie. My father had studied overseas and spoke a foreign language, neither of which the new regime regarded with much respect. He was part of a small population, only 2 percent of Iranians, who'd received higher degrees abroad.

My father's story was being played out in hundreds of homes, including those of many of his coworkers. During the weeks leading up to the revolution, he had watched with dismay as many of his staff at the Ministry of Power left their desks to demonstrate against the shah; now their support for the revolution seemed to mean nothing to the new regime. On this single day in April, my father would recall years later, the Islamists fired eight hundred others at his branch, including many of those who'd helped Khomeini's ascent to power. The Islamists no longer trusted them, and perhaps for good reason; Khomeini's agenda, which evolved around dividing society into sinners and his loyal supporters, was a far cry from what they had struggled for. There was no sign of the democracy or the rights of dissidents that Khomeini had promised in his taped speeches from Paris. Many were disillusioned with the way Khomeini had divided the country into those who supported him and those who did not.

The man who replaced my father had previously delivered letters at the Ministry of Power. He'd quit his studies in middle school, perhaps because he had to work to support his family. Now he received my father's paycheck, the equivalent of $60,000 a year at the time. Many Iranians wouldn't have returned from abroad had it not been for the generous salaries that the shah paid. These salaries had long driven Iran's pervasive inequality, yet now they were changing hands—and, in the process, reversing the economic trends that had caused such wide divisions in Iranian society. Even though the value of the Iranian currency, the rial, had dropped after the revolution to nearly one-tenth of its value under the shah, leading to a huge drop in Iranians' per capita income, paychecks like my father's transformed the lives of the new employees who received them.

Khomeini was determined not to repeat the shah's mistakes. The shah had continued to pay the salaries of civil servants who protested against him; it was the strike by the workers in the oil sector that had delivered the final blow to the shah. By contrast, the new regime sacked many government employees who lacked religious zeal and replaced them with loyal supporters.

Unlike the shah, Khomeini also had the masses behind him, and he was determined to reward their support. Millions of Iranians had moved from villages to cities to work in factories and manufacturing sectors between the 1950s and late 1970s, years when the country had experienced rapid economic growth. Their children had gone to school and university but retained their traditional and religious mindsets. When they became politicized, they chose Khomeini as their leader. If it took government positions to retain these followers, so be it—and if those positions had previously been occupied by people of questionable loyalty to the new regime, all the better.

One of these lucky supporters of the new regime was Roya, Nessa's daughter, who had finished high school and promptly landed a job as principal of a school. When my aunt heard the news, she was appalled. She was a teacher and had attended a teacher's training college under the shah in order to be able to practice that profession. The principal at her school had a university degree, but the new regime had demoted her. What mattered now, it was clear, was political conviction, not expertise or education. In the great reshuffling of fortunes and fates after the revolution, people like Roya and Nessa seemed to be winning.

Khomeini was determined to lay a fresh foundation for his regime, brick by brick. The government not only moved more junior loyal employees to senior positions, but it also hired many more. Within a few short years, the public sector would swell to double its size before the revolution: from 1.7 million to 3.5 million. The growth had a significant consequence: the less educated poor assumed well-paid positions that enabled them to move up in society. Meanwhile, revenue from Iran's oil industry continued to flow (although less than before), allowing the new regime to begin electrifying remote villages, building roads, and constructing water pipes and natural gas and telephone lines—projects that hadn't been prioritized with such urgency before the revolution. People from rural areas commuted to the city, bought televisions and refrigerators—modern appliances that would transform their lifestyles and mindsets. By 1984, more than 60 percent of villages would have electricity and clean water, compared to 16 percent in 1977.

One day that April, Nessa delivered more good news: Roya had secured a two-bedroom apartment for her mother in a new suburb called Vavan in southern Tehran. The apartment was part of a project to redistribute wealth after the government had seized many people's lands, properties, factories, and industries. The industries were now under the control of the government, and the properties were divided among the new elite. Several apartments in our complex were seized and sold to regime supporters for relatively low sums. On the stolen land, meanwhile, the regime built cheaper housing for the poor and called it "revolutionary housing." Nessa's new apartment was in one of these developments. Her new home had a proper kitchen and bathroom—a far cry from the hovel I had seen when I visited Nessa shortly after the revolution. As for Roya, she had married a like-minded revolutionary and moved into a house in the middle-class neighborhood of Geesha in Tehran. Neither we nor Nessa ever found out if they received the house as a reward or if they bought it with their new, steady incomes.

Luckily, we were able to stay in our home, since my father had paid off the loan on our apartment. It made sense for us to stay, moreover, since the cost of living was low; even though Khomeini had failed to deliver on his promise of providing utilities for free, his regime had maintained their low cost.

In search of an income, my father—like other friends of our family who had orchards of their own—turned to an orchard he'd inherited in the suburbs of the northwestern city of Tabriz. At the age of fifty-two, my father became a farmer. He drove three hundred miles away from home in our 1978 Fiat and stayed there for weeks. Along with one or two workers, he picked almonds, walnuts, grapes, and apricots. The income was modest, but we were glad to have it—and glad, too, that the government had not seized the orchard, as it had so many other tracts of private land.

Still, it was difficult for people who had enjoyed privileged careers under the shah, like my father, to suddenly find themselves performing manual labor. My father returned home with his skin peeling from working under the scorching sun, his hands bleeding from bee stings and picking fruit, his body aching from the physical work. An American-educated friend, an engineer, returned from his pistachio farm in Kerman, a city in the middle of the desert, where the sun is more brutal, with blisters on his face and bald head; he died a few years later of skin cancer, an illness that may or may not have been related to his exposure to the sun during this time. Other family friends had to downgrade their homes after they lost jobs and properties—all signs of the ongoing "cleansing" of Iranian society, a rebalancing still symbolized for me, all these years later, by the image of my father's necktie.

Many affluent Iranians, my family included, slipped down the social ladder in the years immediately following the revolution—yet the atmosphere of violence that had pervaded Iran made such *cleansing* feel like the lesser of our miseries. Some people, my father among them, even mentioned their dismissals with pride. Working with a regime that was spilling blood, they felt, would be embarrassing. And blood was certainly flowing freely during this time.

Khomeini had turned against his leftist and nationalist allies and had begun to eliminate them. Every family knew someone, a relative or friend or loved one, who was in prison. My family knew many people like this, most of them the young sons and daughters of friends and relatives who'd become slightly interested in Marxist ideas and had ended up behind bars for these intellectual dalliances.

Our closest jailed relative was my mother's first cousin, Mohsen. An air force pilot with Special Forces under the shah, Mohsen had been arrested on charges of plotting to overthrow the regime. Everyone in the family believed that this was a baseless accusation. As I played with Mohsen's daughter, who was two years younger than I, his sister Guity reported to my mother: "He sings and exercises in his cell. He won't let them kill his spirit." Mohsen was on death row. Every dawn, he counted the number of the doors that clanked open in his section. Then he heard the rumbling of guns in the prison yard.

Despite the violence, people didn't remain quiet. We heard about dissent at Tehran University from Sedigheh, Abbas's wife, who was completing her PhD there. Many students and academics felt the country had exchanged one tyranny for another. The regime had created Islamic Associations on college campuses to monitor the students. To confront the Islamists, the students and professors had founded Democratic Councils.

But Khomeini didn't take to being reined in by his opponents. On April 18, he called for a jihad against the students. "Jihad" was a new word to us, another Arabic word meaning "holy struggle." By calling it a jihad, he made it a religious obligation for his followers to take action against the students whom he accused of turning the campuses into "war rooms." He said that his regime feared only "the training of our youth in the interests of West or East." By West, he meant the influence that capitalism was thought to have upon the nationalists; by East, the influence of Soviet ideology on the Marxists. Minutes after his speech, his supporters, the Islamist Hezbollah, attacked the university. They were mob-like forces who'd become tasked with breaking up events that were not to the liking of the regime—a tactic not dissimilar to the rent-a-thug approach the shah had used to break up demonstrations. There were often members of the Revolutionary Guards to lead the raids. That day, Hezbollah stormed all major campuses around the country, beating the students, killing dozens, arresting hundreds, and ultimately taking control of the universities.

Two days later, on April 20, Khomeini decreed all universities to be shut down for three years. Sedigheh stopped going to school, and so did dozens of other young students in our complex. Instead, they lingered on the benches around the pool.

Now that he had taken control of the universities, Khomeini aimed to give them a makeover. He set up a council to screen professors, students, and courses, calling the effort a "Cultural Revolution," much like Mao's Red Guards had done in China. But Khomeini's cultural revolution was aimed at eliminating the influence of the communists, who had developed a vast network around the country since the early 1920s through the Communist Party of Iran as well as the Tudeh Party in the 1940s. Even though Khomeini had used the leftist parties' resources during the revolution, now he perceived them as a threat. For three years, the universities remained closed; even courses such as music were deemed un-Islamic and eliminated; hundreds of students and professors were purged.

As the new changes began to take place, we saw more traditional women dressed in black head-to-toe garb on the streets, just like Roya. They had been influenced by a book called *Mass'aleh-ye Hijab*, a broad reference to the head covering and dress code. Written by the cleric Morteza Motahari, the book branded women who showed their hair as "nude" and accused them of being responsible for men's sexual desire— "one that can never be fulfilled." Men, Motahari said, are physically and intellectually superior to women, but it is still a woman's duty to avoid provoking their sexual desires, which, like oil wells, are constantly aflame. To restrain the fire in men, he prescribed for women loose knee-length coats, pants, and headscarves that would cover their hair. The new "power women," who would soon assume government positions, the ones Khomeini relied on, wore the chador too.

The new dress, like my father's tie, was a political statement—one that was also integral to the identities of these women. You could tell just by looking at them that they belonged to Khomeini. They were everywhere: schools, the public sector, prisons. A handful were even in Parliament. There was no reason for them to work in the cottage industry of carpet making, in which less educated women commonly got jobs. The regime needed these women, and they needed it.

Khomeini had brought these traditional women out of their domestic sphere and into society, saving them from their fathers, brothers, and husbands who'd historically confined them to housework and raising children. In a referendum held in April 1979 to decide what form the new regime would take, Khomeini urged men, as well as women, to vote for an Islamic Republic, not a Republic alone. The regime announced that 99.9 percent voted for an Islamic Republic. While that number was certainly inflated, the true number was high—and many of the voters had been women.

As these women fanned across society, the Islamic regime cleansed secular and modern women from the workforce. It closed 140 fields to women at universities and purged women judges from courts, claiming that they were too emotional to rule objectively.

Ironically, even as Khomeini empowered some women, he also found ways of oppressing their entire gender. The regime replaced the shah's secular law with an Islamic law, which allowed men to marry up to four wives, to divorce them whenever the husbands wished, and to retain custody of children. The law put the value of a woman's life at half of that of a man's life, and the value of her testimony at half that of a man's testimony.

Thus women in Iran became watchdogs and scapegoats, both the foot soldiers of the new regime and its victims. Newly empowered, they were also newly oppressed. Theirs was a paradoxical plight—and at the time, no one could have foreseen how it would one day make women a force of enormous change in Iran.

CHAPTER SIX

THE WAR

On September 22, 1980, a day before schools were to open, we gathered on a bench near the pool to enjoy the last day of summer. It was a perfect day: the sun beamed into the blue depths of the water, its light a reminder of the tranquility we had maintained at the edges of the pool despite the madness around us. This was our space, with its own music—the perpetual murmur of the trees and chirping of crickets at dusk. We'd swum in the pool the entire summer and chased one another in the lush garden until sundown, when fatigue finally forced us to go home; then, bruised and muddy, we'd returned to the pool the next morning to repeat the same ritual. Now this idyllic season was coming to an end. In a few days, the building management would empty the water, the leaves would change color, and by the end of November, we would get our first snow. Our only consolation was that, once the snow fell, we would be able to sled down the steep inner slope of the emptied pool.

Suddenly, as we sat by the pool, we heard a thunderous sound, as though a massive rock had hit the earth, jolting the ground beneath our feet. I held my breath, and we looked at each other in horror. BOOM. BOOM. BOOM. We'd never heard anything like it. The long thin tendrils of the weeping willows shook. The water in the pool trembled with each explosion. A group of teenagers who were walking by stopped and looked up into the sky. None of us knew what to do. Should we run or lie down? How long it took, I don't remember, but none of us moved until the horrifying sounds that signaled yet another fiasco ended.

When we went home, we learned that Iran was at war with neighboring Iraq. Iraqi planes had raided Tehran's airport and nine other airbases in the country. The next day, Iraqi forces launched a ground invasion and seized the southern city of Khorramshahr, an oil-rich city 622 miles south of Tehran in Khuzestan province.

Khomeini had enraged Saddam Hussein, the president of Iraq, by calling on Iraqi Shiites to stage a revolution like Iran's against Saddam. But by invading Iran, Saddam didn't just intend to punish Khomeini; he also wanted to turn Iraq into a dominant power in the region. He had his eye on the oil-rich southern province of Khuzestan and the Arvand River, a waterway at the head of the Persian Gulf that both countries used for oil exports. With the post-revolution chaos, he thought Iran was weak and even expected the Sunni Iranians in the south to welcome him as their liberator. The Persians, Saddam claimed, had distorted Islam with their Shiite version and discriminated against the Sunni Arabs in the south. His land grab would allow him to set things right.

That night, announcers on state television introduced the air raid siren—a screeching sound that meant the enemy's bombers were nearing. We had no idea what to expect. Iran had never been involved in a modern war except when the British and Russians had occupied the country during World War II. We put duct tape over the windowpanes—vertically, horizontally, and diagonally—to limit their shattering in case there was a bomb nearby or the Iraqi planes broke the sound barrier. Iraqi planes flew over the country almost every night, making it as far as Tehran and bombing civilian areas. The radio warned that any kind of light at night, even the orange ember of a cigarette, could attract the bombers. We installed blackout curtains over our windows. People were prohibited from driving with headlights after dark.

The television showed that the south, the real war zone, was getting demolished, with buildings flattened to rubble and dead bodies scattered everywhere, covered in dust. People fled their homes; the educated upper class that worked for the oil industry came to Tehran and other large cities; others went to smaller towns. Tens of thousands were displaced.

Every time the radar detected Iraqi planes crossing the border, the air raid siren interrupted whatever television or radio program we happened to be watching. The screeching sound screamed from speakers at every street corner. A robotic voice called on people to find shelters, bunkers, basements—anywhere that would be safe from the bombs.

It was terrifying for a ten-year-old like me—and even scarier because the raids were more common after dark. At the sound of the siren, I would rush with my sister and parents down the stairs of our building, which were lit only by the stars or the thinnest slice of moon. We took refuge in the basement, two floors underground, and stayed there until the sirens cleared and the neighbors trickled back to their apartments. Some nights, the Iraqis raided several times. Doctor, our neighbor, brought a carpet, folding chairs, and a table, and stayed in the damp basement rather than lose sleep trekking back and forth to his apartment.

After a week of the raids we got tired of running up and down the stairs and turned our foyer into a shelter of sorts. The foyer was small, with no windows, and was situated against an earthquake-resistant wall. It conveniently led to a bathroom and the kitchen, and we shut the door that opened into the living room. My sister and I knelt on a small carpet night after night and did our homework under the dim light of two old kerosene lamps. Iraqi planes had bombed power installations, and blackouts were common. The city was overrun with refugees from the south, and higher electricity usage was also straining the grid. When the siren sounded, all four of us squeezed under the threshold of the door and in silence and darkness counted the blasting sounds of the bombs as the anti-artillery guns clamored, trying to bring down the planes.

A second siren, a bit shriller than the first one, came nearly ten minutes after the guns stopped roaring. It meant the enemy's planes had flown out of the country's airspace. At that moment, our phone rang. Aunts and other relatives called to find out if we were safe. "Did it sound close to you?" my mother asked our relatives. This was her way of finding out in which part of the city the bombs had fallen. The radio often announced that the anti-aircraft machines had forced the planes to drop their bombs outside the city, in nonresidential areas. We had no choice but to believe them.

After a few months, under increasing international pressure, Iran and Iraq agreed to end the bombing campaigns against each other's cities and limit the war to the south. Even though we were no longer directly under fire, however, the war continued to overshadow our lives. The shelves of supermarkets, once filled with all sorts of imported goods, became empty. The government rationed basic food such as milk, rice, cheese, butter, and sugar. My parents spent hours in queues for a bottle of milk or a small bag of rice. Our family of four was entitled to half a gallon of milk per week. Items such as toilet paper, chocolate, and cereal were nonexistent; we came to view them as luxury goods. My parents hoarded boxes of tissues, canned food, crackers, and anything else that would keep, fearing that the situation might get worse.

For us Iranians, it was a lonely war. The United States had already imposed economic sanctions on Iran after a group of Islamist students had climbed over the walls of the US embassy the previous November, seized the building, and taken fifty-two Americans hostage. The students claimed that this was their way of signaling their resentment toward the United States for overthrowing Mossadeq in 1953. Khomeini endorsed the attack and demanded the return of the shah, who was in the US to treat his cancer, in exchange for the diplomats. The hostage taking became another embarrassing dilemma for many Iranians, representing the chaos the revolution had ushered in.

Iran was isolated and outmatched in other ways, as well. None of the Sunni Arab countries sided with Iran. Ours was a Shiite and Persian state whose leader ranted about exporting his revolution. Because of its isolation, Iran lacked the heavy weapons Iraq was acquiring from its allies. By the time the war had begun, moreover, the Iranian army was already on its knees, the regime having executed many of its senior officers.

Iran struggled to meet these challenges, and in the process the country underwent further changes. The Revolutionary Guards, which was a new force lacking military training that had emerged to defend the revolution, quickly evolved into the shape of an army. Inside the country, the war also stirred strong nationalistic sentiment. No one wanted Iran to lose any part of its territory. We were often told at school that Iran looked like the shape of a cat on the map. Khuzestan, the province Iraq had invaded, was the cat's belly.

The nation rallied behind the regime, determined to fight the invaders. A sea of Iranian men headed south to fight. Even Mohsen, my mother's imprisoned cousin who was an air force pilot, and whose ex-ecution had been commuted to life in prison, pleaded to be allowed to fight in the war, a request that was never granted.

In May 1981, less than a year after the war began, Iranian forces pushed the Iraqis back to the border and liberated Khorramshahr. The battle was so bloody that they nicknamed the city Khoonin-Shahr, meaning the City of Blood.

Saddam called for a cease-fire, but Khomeini was intoxicated by the victory. The war was now a blessing for the ayatollah. Without it, he could not rally his supporters against his opponents at home. Needing to make the war a long-term project to stabilize his regime, Khomeini said that Iran must conquer Karbala in Iraq, more than 346 miles away from Khorramshahr.

By that summer, rifts among political factions had deepened, and Khomeini was openly sidelining all groups that had helped overthrow the shah, with the exception of his own Party of the Islamic Republic. Mehdi Bazargan, the leader of the nationalist party Freedom Movement, had resigned in protest of the US embassy takeover, pointing out that the invasion of a foreign embassy was against all international norms.

Khomeini called the war a "holy defense" and labeled those who opposed the war traitors and the enemy of Islam. He soon banned all political parties except his own. To his followers, he promised a glori-ous fate, particularly if they died on the field of battle. He reminded them that they'd become martyrs, like Imam Hussein, Prophet Mu-hammad's grandson who was massacred in a battle near Karbala in Iraq. Martyrdom was the path to paradise, Khomeini told them. Using this religious rhetoric, he inflamed the masses, readying them to fight and rallying them behind the regime.

Khomeini's followers, bearded men and black-clad women, began purging nationalist and communist figures, anyone who opposed Kho-meini, with zeal. Thousands of young men and women, including teenag-ers, landed in jail and faced the firing squad. Abolhassan Banisadr, who had been the first post-revolution president, fled the country. His foreign minister, Sadeq Ghotbzadeh, was arrested and executed.

As he eliminated his enemies, both real and imagined, Khomeini also increased his already considerable power. His title, *vali faqih*, meaning literally "the learned patron," became emblematic of the state he had in mind for the nation, as though the entire country were made up of immature children who needed a father to guide them.

And so the war continued like a curse, ravaging our lives. The regime announced that a draft would be called to expand the size of the Iranian armed forces. Universities, which had been shuttered a year earlier, remained closed, leaving young men with nowhere to go but the battle zone. The regime banned boys over the age of fourteen from leaving the country so that they couldn't escape the draft. As a consequence, many of our friends and relatives sent their sons overseas before their fourteenth birthdays. Many young men who were already of age had to look for another way to avoid being drafted. My eighteen-year-old cousin, for one, fled illegally to Turkey; disguised as a peasant, he traveled on foot through a rugged, mountainous area among a herd of sheep, led by a human smuggler.

Abbas and Sedigheh came to our home one evening to say good-bye. Sedigheh couldn't complete her PhD, their daughter would have nothing to do in three years after she finished high school, and their son would soon be banned from leaving the country. Abbas would go on to open a carpet store in Paris.

As many of our friends and relatives left, my parents weighed their options. My father was in his fifties, and he'd never worked overseas. We heard from my uncles in Los Angeles that many educated Iranians in the United States had no choice but to work as cab drivers, waiters, or construction workers to earn a living. Getting legal immigration status was complicated. Many doctors in our housing complex were taking their families abroad, only to leave them and come back to work in Iran because they were not licensed to work in those countries.

My parents were not in immediate danger because they'd never had any ties with the shah or any political parties. They chose to stay.

CHAPTER SEVEN

---•◆•---

OUR BODIES,
OUR BATTLEFIELDS

In September 1981, almost a year since the war with Iraq began, Iran's second post-revolutionary president, Mohammad Ali Rajai, introduced a bill in Parliament to enforce obligatory veiling for women. The assembly passed it immediately, and suddenly, just like that, women were required to cover their hair and bodies. I was ten years old, and although I had not reached puberty, the government required girls to cover their hair at school but not on the streets until their bodies showed signs of womanhood. The regime banned women from wearing makeup, perfume, and high heels, prohibiting any effort that involved beautifying oneself.

Under the Islamic Penal Code, anyone who violated the new law was subject to prison, a fine, and up to seventy-four lashes. We knew people who'd been lashed on their backs with a whip. Women who were subjected to lashings could keep their clothes on; sometimes people bribed the person who lashed them to strike gently. But victims often came away with gashes on their backs, which took weeks to heal.

At school, the regime required young girls to dress according to the new code to prepare them for the future. I had to wear a beige headscarf, a bright blue coat called a manteau that hung loosely to my knees, and a pair of matching pants. The coat was shapeless and coarse; the pants had an elastic waistband; the scarf was nylon. My mother taught me to fold the square scarf diagonally and wear it over my head. I couldn't hear clearly with two layers of nylon over my ears and found the knot under my chin suffocating. I had to avoid making any abrupt moves, which would cause the scarf to slip down my head.

To say that this new clothing was a shock to me would be an understatement. I'd attended an American school and was used to wearing T-shirts, skirts, and jeans. When my mother noticed my dismay at the new clothes, she promised that this would be temporary. "The clerics will be gone before you know it," she said. I believed her.

Secular women staged protests, but the regime enforced the veiling law with an iron fist. The Pasdars confronted unveiled women with batons on the streets. Men were also banned from wearing short sleeves because their bare arms were suddenly deemed too sexy. To monitor compliance, hard-liners set up headquarters everywhere: at the entrance of government buildings, department stores, universities, and airports. Everyone, even religious women who wore the veil voluntarily, was subjected to this humiliating scrutiny, and the hard-liners always found faults with people's appearance. The veil became a tool of oppression.

The regime segregated schools and required male teachers to teach only at boys' schools and female teachers at girls' schools. It sent devout Muslims called "morality teachers" to educate us to embrace the new values. These morality teachers were often young and soft-spoken; they wanted to coax us into the regime's ideology. They lined us up in the yard every morning, arms-length apart, and gave us a political brief. They instructed us to wave our fists in the air and chant, "Death to America, death to Britain, death to Israel." All those countries had supported the shah and were now supporting Iraq, they said.

For a brief period when I was in fifth grade, I became the pet of my morality teacher. She called me to help with the class chores during the two-hour session she taught us every week. She asked me if my family supported Khomeini, if we attended Friday prayers, if I had loved ones fighting in the war. I knew how to answer each question: "Yes." I had learned to lie to protect myself and my family.

One day at noon, the teacher asked me to accompany her to the school washroom to perform the Muslim ablution—the ritual of cleaning the arms, feet, and face before praying. She'd taught us how to do it, and as her student I couldn't object. Obediently, I followed her to the newly set-up prayer room. Out of some six hundred students and dozens of teachers, I was the only one with her in the room. We took off our shoes and walked on the wall-to-wall carpet. She handed me a white hood to wear instead of my scarf. I'd never worn one; I put my face into the hole and pulled it over my head. Then I stood next to her and began whispering the Arabic words of prayer. When our prayer was over, she looked at me and said that my prayer was nullified, because I had worn the hood the wrong way. The triangle that was supposed to cover my chin was on my forehead and so my ponytail was showing.

I saw, in that moment, her interpretation of Islam. Her Islam was more about outward signs, such as praying in public, fasting, and covering yourself—to a point that was annoying. It seemed like everything else you did—especially anything that involved fun, such as listening and dancing to music, watching movies, speaking to the opposite sex, or showing your hair—was a "sin." Her religion drew much of its power from oppression, from limitations that it placed on its adherents and those unlucky people who—like my classmates and me—were subjected to it involuntarily.

I knew that Islam did not have to be this way. My mother prayed every day and never talked about it. She told my sister and me that Islam was about inner things, such as being kind, generous, and forgiving. My mother's Islam was pacifist, unlike the one forced on us by the regime. I assumed that most of our teachers—apart from the morality teachers, that is—viewed religion the same way my family did because none of them prayed at school. If they prayed, they did it in the privacy of their homes. You almost never saw shopkeepers close their stores at the call of the prayer and rush to the mosque. The Islam that most families practiced those days was a way of life and about the ethics they believed in. My mother told us that Islam was about being honest and generous—not about rituals and showing off our religiosity, the way the morality teachers did.

As for the white hood that my morality teacher had made me wear during the prayer, I hated it even more than the headscarf. With only a hole for the face, the hood was far more suffocating. The hood couldn't be easily slipped on and off, whereas we could let the scarf slip down over our shoulders as soon as we left the gates of the school, running away like birds released from a cage. We were still young; until middle school we could get away with not wearing the headscarf on the street.

I swallowed my dismay that day in the prayer room, but from then until the end of my time in school, I joined most of my classmates in mocking the morality teachers. We felt disconnected from them. They took down the mirrors in the school restrooms because they thought it was too vain for us to look at ourselves. We joked that the real reason was so that the morality teachers didn't have to see their own facial hair. The women had mustaches and bushy eyebrows, and to save their beauty for their husbands, they refused to pluck out the hairs until they got married. The morality teachers were also brazenly ignorant about the things they banned. One of them preached to us about the cultural dangers of the evil *"auk-band."* She meant a Walkman! (*Auk-band* in Persian means "original packaging.")

Even though we tried to ignore the morality teachers, they continued to play a central role at schools. They required us to knit winter clothes for soldiers in combat and to donate canned food that would be headed to the war zones. They constantly reminded us about the war—the curse that most of us kids distanced ourselves from. Even students who'd joined our school after fleeing their homes in the south rarely spoke about it. Morality teachers at boys' schools were even more intense. When I got together with teenage boys near the pool, they said that their morality teachers encouraged them to volunteer for the Basij, a paramilitary militia group made up mainly of teenagers who embraced Khomeini's call for martyrdom. The morality teachers constantly glorified martyrdom, reminding the boys that they would enter paradise if they died in service of Islam. Eventually some of the boys at my friends' schools signed up and went to the front with little military training. Those boys never returned—not even their bodies.

On days when Iranian forces were launching an offensive, the morality teachers canceled classes and summoned us into the auditorium and the hallways. The entire school sat cross-legged on the hard floor to pray for the soldiers. A live feed from the battlefield blared throughout the school: "Dear listeners," a male voice announced. "Please pay attention. Please pay attention. Our brave brothers, our fighters, the force of Islam, have responded to the call of their country today; they have chosen the path of martyrdom."

Then, as we sat quietly, a morality teacher tried to evoke our deepest emotions with a dirge, delivered in a singsong tone as though she herself was crying. She compared the war to the battles of early Islam and called the operation the struggle of believers against infidels. She described gruesome, pitiful images: men bleeding to death with chopped-off limbs, a headless soldier taking a step to his death, an injured fighter carrying the dead body of a comrade, and a father embracing martyrdom instead of his newly born child. Some of the soldiers were as young as we were, she reminded us.

Her passionate account eventually brought tears to the eyes of many of us. "Pray," she said, "pray for their victory. That's the least you can do while our men are giving their lives." My spirit sank at her words; panic scissored through my body, and I imagined my friends, the boys in our neighborhood, in the trenches, bloody and dead. When would this war end?

From our kitchen window I could see rugged mountains piercing into the sky in northern Tehran. Iran is among the world's most mountainous countries, and Tehran sits near the Alborz mountain range, which stretches from east to west along the southern coast of the Caspian Sea. The highest peak in the range is Mount Damavand, a landmark depicted on Iranian banknotes. Its white cap, permanently covered in snow, is over eighteen thousand feet tall, a volcano that has been dormant for hundreds of years. Damavand has long been a symbol of resistance and pride in Persian literature and mythology. Poets have described it as a source of magical power and heroism against tyrants.

Maybe the rough landscape surrounding our city really did have magical powers, or maybe we just spent too much time listening to adults cursing the regime privately and publicly. But little as we were, we were turning defiant. We were far from the only ones. It seemed that everyone, from cab drivers to people in a line to buy bread, hated the regime. People had overthrown the shah to build a democracy, but this regime had robbed them of that hope, while also robbing them of their personal liberties.

I was ten when the regime banned women and girls over the age of nine from swimming in pools with men, including the one in our complex. At first we ignored the ban and continued swimming. But when I was twelve and starting to develop breasts, I could be lashed if I ventured into the water in my bikini. I sat around the pool with other girls, sweating under a blistering sun in our manteaux and headscarves. We watched the boys with envy as they dove into the water. They could swim until the age of fifteen, the supposed age of puberty. That pool had been the source of our liveliness. Banned from the water, we felt as though we'd been deprived of oxygen.

One night, after darkness had fallen, a group of us girls peeled off our manteaux and headscarves. From every corner of the pool, we jumped into the water. As I dove with my arms stretched over my head, my fingers and hands touched the water first, and then my entire body slashed through it. I blew the air out of my nostrils for as long as I could, cherishing that moment, letting the little bubbles caress my face. When I surfaced, the chlorine-scented air felt like the most calming aroma imaginable. My pants and shirt got heavy and slowed me down, but it only made me swim harder—a battle that, in time, would become emblematic of my constant struggle with the Islamic Republic.

Adults stood by and watched us as we swam. Sometimes they complimented us for our defiance. We did, however, fear the Pasdars, who had a few times entered our complex. We did a few laps and then climbed out and ran home in our dripping clothes.

This was my first public act of rebellion, one I'd learned from older girls. Decades later, the memory of that swim still resonates in my mind with a sense of satisfaction. In the end, we'd conquered the pool—and that victory emboldened us to launch other, greater rebellions.

At school, I wrapped my Bon Jovi tapes in aluminum foil to disguise them as sandwiches and hide them from the morality teachers, who searched our bags every morning, looking for un-Islamic items. If they caught us, they would expel us from school. I was never caught. Instead of practicing revolutionary songs at home, which we were required to recite at school, I stood in front of a mirror and sang Madonna's "Like a Virgin." My friends and I spent hours dancing to pirated videos of "Billie Jean," copying Michael Jackson's moves.

Defiance was epidemic. Hundreds of manteaux shops mushroomed around the country to refashion those ugly manteaux and pants we had to wear. In the early '80s, pleated coats with padded shoulders over tight-fitting pants became fashionable because loose tops and tight bottoms were trendy in the West. School authorities and Pasdars wanted us to wear tighter coats and looser pants. Before the end of the decade, the fashion reversed; our coats tightened and shrunk above the knee, and the pants became radically looser. To punish us, school authorities made us wear a hood instead of the headscarf so that we would show less hair. They banned jeans, claiming they were too Western. But outside on the streets, we wore them; everybody did, men and women. It was one of the myriad small acts of defiance by which we pushed back against the regime. We didn't always win, but at least these little rebellions made us feel that we were in charge of our lives. If authorities caught us defying the rules, they would do their best to break our spirit.

In the spring of 1985, I entered the school building in an ocean of students to take a final exam. Unlike the other girls, I hadn't noticed the principal, who sometimes stood in a corner to survey the students' appearance. She was notorious for having expelled students in the past for not looking proper. Our resentment toward her fueled a rumor that she had been a prostitute under the shah, had repented after the revolution, and was now taking revenge on the students for her own sins. If I'd seen her, I would have pulled my hood over my forehead, looked down, and become as invisible as possible. Instead, I was giggling with my friends and displaying a lot of hair. When I passed her, she pulled at my hood and saw that I was wearing hoops in my ears. With her index finger, she touched one of them. I froze. She glared at me and pointed toward her office. I headed in that direction, consumed with worry. I had to take that final exam or my summer vacation would be ruined, because I would have to take it at the end of the summer.

I bit my fingernails for a good half an hour until the principal showed up. I apologized and begged her to please let me take my exam. In response, she screamed, "Our men are dying while defending your honor, and you dare to beautify yourself!" I cried and said I was sorry. Her mere presence was daunting. Tall and broad-shouldered, she hovered over me in her chador, raising her hand in the air.

Finally she ordered me to rip the stitches off the hems of my manteau and pants with my fingers. I did, until I looked shabby and felt completely humiliated. Then she excused me so that I could use the last fifteen minutes to take my exam. As I marched off, I thought of her hypocrisy: my earrings had nothing to do with the war; it was about her power over me.

Our bodies had become battlefields. The Islamic regime was intent on controlling every dimension of our lives, and we were determined to resist. If we fought fiercely enough, we could push back the boundaries the regime had imposed on us. Indeed, many of the authorities had learned that we were teenagers obsessed with our looks; they had accepted that we fixed our blurry vision with contact lenses and crooked teeth with braces. Even a morality teacher at my school wore braces to beautify her smile. People like the principal wanted to instill the fear of authority in us at an early age.

Yet we mocked the authorities with their own values. One day in high school, a friend stood up to explain that she hadn't done her homework because her brother had been killed in the war. The students covered their faces with their hands and ducked under the tables. We knew that she had no brothers. She raved about her brother's devotion to Khomeini and shed large tears to complete her act. "He is in Paradise now with Imam Hussein," she sobbed. "But I will never see him again." The teacher, a bright woman who taught algebra—and was certainly not pro-regime—twitched the sides of her mouth. She knew the girl was lying, but she didn't dare challenge her for fear of seeming to question the regime's values. Perhaps she wondered what was becoming of us. Why was the regime failing to mold us into the generation of devotees that it wanted us to be? The teachers, like our parents, had grown up under the shah's secular system, but they respected religious sanctities more than we did. What had happened?

During all my school years and at different schools, only a handful of the girls embraced the regime's ideology. The rest of us didn't want to be its walking symbols. And our numbers increased year after year, as it became clear just how much we could get away with.

We had decided not to surrender, or at least not without a fight. To feel human, we needed to retake control of our minds as well as our bodies. We waged the war on both fronts.

CHAPTER EIGHT

———— ·•◆•· ————

MASOUD

At five o'clock every Monday afternoon when I was in my early teens, Masoud rang our doorbell. He would flash a toothy smile when I opened the door. Tall and bony, in his early thirties, he'd walk with long strides into the hallway and then our living room, his black boxy briefcase in his hand. To avoid drawing attention to himself, he always wore a pair of faded jeans and a polo shirt, like most other young Iranian men in the late 1980s. In winter, when temperatures in Tehran dipped below freezing, he would arrive bundled in a navy blue overcoat.

"Masoud" was a nom de guerre. We had no contact information for him; our rendezvous took place at the same time every week. If we weren't home, he'd circle back the following Monday. But for years, my sister, Goli, and I made sure one of us was there to greet him.

Once in the living room, Masoud would place his briefcase on the coffee table, lift its top with care, and then turn it around so Goli and I could peer inside at his precious cargo: rows of neatly arranged Betamax and, later, VHS tapes, labels facing up for easy reading.

Masoud would tap on each tape as he gave us a staccato rundown of what he had to offer. "This is a horror movie, and you won't like it," he said on one visit, knowing what genre of movies we preferred. "*The Color of Money* is great. It won the Academy Award this year. You need to watch it. *Crocodile Dundee* is a romantic comedy. You'll love it."

"Not the silly crocodile man," Goli interrupted. "We've already seen it three times. Anything new?"

"Take *Out of Africa*, with Meryl Streep and Robert Redford. I promise to bring you the Academy Award show next week," he said, knowing how eager we were to see it. The Oscars had been awarded over a month earlier, and Masoud usually had several copies of the show. "The client before you has kept it for three weeks."

Goli picked up an MTV show along with *Out of Africa* and *The Color of Money*. We had to take one more since Masoud only made house calls with a four-tape minimum. We shared the films with a neighbor to split the cost.

We called Masoud a "video-man," a job that the revolution had created after Khomeini banned almost all movies—except a limited few that were reviewed and censored before screening—and shut down hundreds of video stores in addition to banning Western pop music. He denounced movies, especially foreign ones and the Iranian films made before the revolution, as un-Islamic, deeming them a source of Western culture that would pollute our supposedly pure lifestyle. It was part of his effort to turn the country into an island cut off from the rest of the world, an isolated laboratory where he could mold and shape the population according to the precepts of the revolution. Iranian movie theatres could only show "approved" films, movies that presented a tarnished image of the West, such as *One Flew Over the Cuckoo's Nest*, an award-winning movie in which Jack Nicholson plays the role of a criminal who lands in a mental hospital and which was in theaters for over a year. State TV broadcast mostly movies about World War I or II, to glorify resistance and to invigorate us with the same courage that the Allies had in their fight against the Germans. Intimate scenes, such as those in which men and women held hands, kissed, or—God forbid—lay in bed together, were censored. It would take the local film industry until the 1990s to flourish under censorship and rise to international fame.

Watching movies, Iranian and foreign, as well as American television, had been a favorite pastime among the middle class before the revolution. As a young girl I had loved watching *The Six Million Dollar Man*, the American series that ran throughout the mid-1970s and which in the years before the revolution re-ran on Iranian television constantly, dubbed into Persian. When Khomeini came to power and Western media was banned, Iranians' love for it didn't disappear—the ban just caused many people to turn to the black market, and to young vid-eo-men like Masoud.

Video-men were motivated young entrepreneurs who pirated all types of movies and secretly delivered them to people's homes in their trademark boxy briefcases. Their jobs were dangerous; if they got caught, they could be fined, lashed, and jailed. But if the danger was considerable, so too was the demand—and the potential payoff for black marketeers willing to risk their freedom to fulfill it.

In the first year after the revolution, the underground market was overwhelmed by Indian movies, all of them dubbed in Persian. We en-joyed watching Indian women in colorful saris, dancing and singing passionately. They were a welcome distraction from the bloody images of the war on state television. Goli and I became so immersed in these movies that we wrapped ourselves in my mother's shawls as if they were saris, painted a red dot between our eyebrows with lipstick, and then circled around a chair, singing and dancing, mirroring the movements of the women in the movies.

That was a phase, however, and just when the latest Hollywood mov-ies arrived, we were growing tired of Indian films with happy endings. By then, we could pretty much predict the plot in the first few minutes, and American films offered a novelty and unpredictability we couldn't find in Indian cinema. Besides, my mother and her generation were big fans of American and European stars: Sophia Loren, Audrey Hepburn, and Peter O'Toole had been celebrities in Iran. Almost everyone was in love with the French actor Alain Delon and his Persian voice—a perfect, deep pitch that was much sexier than Delon's real voice.

These actors, who spoke Persian in our version of their films, had ruled Iranian cinemas until Khomeini banned them. Before the revolu-tion, Western film stars had looked down over Tehran's streets from big posters hanging outside movie theaters. My mother had followed their stories in *Zan-e-Ruz (Today's Woman)*, a women's magazine that also translated interviews and articles into Persian. She read about Sophia Loren's poverty before she became a star, Elizabeth Taylor's unhappy marriages and her love affairs with Richard Burton, and Natalie Wood's mysterious death. These men and women became household names, especially after Elizabeth Taylor visited Iran in 1976.

As for my sister and me, our favorite movie before the revolution had been *The Sound of Music*. With friends, we each pretended to be one of Captain Von Trapp's seven children. We ran around the pool and sang *"Do do doshab Nakhabidam, Re rooyeh mahat didam,"* meaning, "I did not sleep for two nights, until I saw your beautiful face." The rest of the song rhymed with Julie Andrews's *"Doe a deer, a female deer, Ray a drop of golden sun,"* but was a different lyric in Persian.

We weren't deprived of Western movies for long. By the mid-1980s, first-run American movies were arriving in Iran soon after they opened in the United States. But because of the way the films were recorded—somebody taped them as they played in theatres, then smuggled them into Iran—we could hear the audience booing and bursting into laughter, even see them walking in and out to get popcorn, at times blocking the entire screen. Watching these movies was an adventure in and of itself, because for a long time the cameras that were used to pirate the films weren't mounted on a tripod. So the quality wasn't good; often the sound was barely audible. Throughout each movie our fingers hovered over the remote control's rewind button, ready for the inevitable moment when we missed some crucial bit of dialogue. When we needed a break, we would watch older movies, which were available in versions of much better quality, or MTV shows, which were recorded directly from the American cable program.

Before Masoud, our former video-man, Bijan—another nom de guerre—had disappeared for several weeks. When he finally showed up again, we found out that he'd been arrested. His boxy briefcase had given him away, since government forces on the hunt for video-men sometimes stopped people with briefcases on the streets and searched their bags. Bijan had tried to bribe the men who stopped him, we heard him tell our parents, but they were not the usual kind he could buy off with money or a couple of porn tapes. They were vigilant. They took him to court, and a zealous judge sentenced him to a hundred lashes—delivered with a thick cord to his back—and fined him nearly $900, an amount of money so large that a middle-class family could live on it for over a year. The authorities confiscated the tapes at his home, but luckily the clients had most of his movies. Bijan's gashes took weeks to heal, and in the meantime he worked to replace the tapes he had lost.

Bijan quit being a video-man shortly after his arrest. He had gotten married, and his wife was opposed to his profession, even though he earned several hundred dollars a month, which was considered a high income in those days. "She complains that her relatives keep asking about my job, and she is too embarrassed to tell them that I smuggle movies," he told us the last time we saw him. "No one likes to boast about an illegal job. I always wanted to stop after saving enough money to start a respectable business." And indeed, after introducing us to Masoud, Bijan opened a small sporting goods shop.

Masoud had been in the business for a long time. Several times, when the government forces put up roadblocks, Masoud called and told us that for a few weeks his colleague would visit us. The colleague was a giant man who always wore a long trench coat. He never carried a briefcase, and he walked like a wrestler, his arms swinging back and forth inches away from his body. Once inside our home, he'd pull tapes from every pocket of his coat, nearly a dozen in all.

I could tell that Masoud really loved his job. Watching movies was his passion. He would linger on our couch for a few minutes after we made our selections, discussing specific scenes in the movies we'd just watched. His favorite scene was the opening of *The Godfather*, when Marlon Brando's hand is kissed by each of his "associates," as they file past him one by one. "The way they bow with hesitation, not knowing what's on the Godfather's mind. All that is played out with no words." Masoud repeated this description each time he persuaded us to watch it again.

One Monday, Masoud didn't come. We knew something bad had happened. This time no one called as in the past to say that he'd be back; no one came to pick up his tapes. Weeks went by with no word, then months. A year passed before we found a new video-man. The word came from our new guy and was confirmed by others who delivered movies: Masoud had gone into a coma after a terrible car accident, an all too common circumstance in a country in which, because of reckless driving, there would soon be more deaths on the roads than in the war. His fiancée sat by his side for months, holding his hand, hoping that he'd wake up. Masoud never came out of the coma, the new video-man told us.

A year after the accident, Masoud's fiancée permitted the doctors to pull out the tubes that were keeping him alive. Goli and I wept when we heard the news. He had grown to be like a family member. We didn't even know his real name, but we were bound together by our love of movies, our shared escape from the dictates of the Islamic Republic. For us, as for Masoud, the films were a safe haven where we could dwell for a couple of joyful hours, pretending to live in a free world.

Without video-men like Masoud, our lives would have been bleak. We had only two channels on Iranian state TV, and they were a continuous loop of either war images or clerics preaching. Mostly we kept our TV turned off, except when my parents watched the news in the evening. My mother called our television set a "mullah-vision" (mullah means "cleric" in Persian), since we could rarely turn it on without hearing one speaking.

Still, we found ways to make even state television bearable. Some of the mullahs' talks were so hilarious that my parents watched them for comic relief. One time a senior cleric explained how the jolts of an earthquake might demolish the ceiling in an Iranian home and drop a man from the top floor onto his aunt on the lower floor, impregnating her in the process. The cleric reasoned that the accidental child was legitimate. My parents laughed so hard they teared up. For a long time at parties, adults talked about this cleric in disbelief. How on earth did he come up with such an idea?

Another cleric, who was visiting a rural mountainous region in northwestern Iran, where locals had used short wooden skis as transportation for centuries, tried to reconcile skiing and the Islamic Republic. After the revolution, the clerics had denounced skiing as a sport for the rich, especially because the shah had a passion for it; he had brought modern skiing to Iran, and almost everyone in the country had seen pictures of him with his wife and children in their ski outfits. Now this cleric was trying to put an Islamic stamp on the sport by endorsing traditional skiing. Standing on the snow among the villagers in his clerical robe, turban, and slippers, he cited Prophet Muhammad as a supporter and fan of skiing. Watching him, my sister and I burst into laughter.

Prophet Muhammad probably knew nothing about snow and skiing; he was from Saudi Arabia, where it never snowed.

Such moments of unintentional comedy, however, paled next to Western movies, which opened up a window to a world far larger than we'd otherwise have known. These films allowed us to escape the restrictive boundaries and beliefs of the Islamic Republic, while connecting us to ideas and imaginations far beyond Khomeini's dystopian society. By watching the films, we perfected the English we had learned in school before the revolution, and even picked up slang words; some Iranians taught themselves English from scratch by watching movies again and again. We embraced what we saw on our TV screens—not out of devotion to Western culture, but because the alternative would have been to accept an oppressive ideology. The Islamic Republic wanted the entire population to look and think alike. As the regime had once promised, the middle class had indeed soared after the revolution, but because of that people longed to escape the confines of the Islamic Republic. We craved creativity, novelty, and modernity, all of which the regime vehemently discouraged. We were, in a sense, scrambling to build an identity for ourselves other than the one the regime wanted to impose on us.

How many people watched these pirated movies, I never knew. But their influence went well beyond a certain class or group. More and more homes were getting connected to the electric grid and buying televisions by the mid-1980s, which meant that many more Iranians were able to watch the movies that had been banned by the state. This was, in some ways, an unintentional consequence of the regime's policies; after the revolution, the clerics had approved watching television so that they could reach a wider audience. Television ownership would increase accordingly in the decades to come: in urban areas it grew from 22.6 percent in 1977 to 97.5 percent by 2004, and in rural areas it leaped from 3.2 percent to 89.1 percent. Anyone who owned a television could easily watch movies; they just needed to purchase a video player at an electronics store.

Once people were exposed to Western movies, they began imitating what they saw in them. Many people were looking for a distraction, among them Iranians who had supported the regime but had since lost faith in the system. Although the revolution had narrowed the inequality gap by putting a large segment of the population on a fast track to the middle class, it had failed to offer these newly risen Iranians dignity and a stable economy. Economic growth and per capita income dropped to their lowest points in the 1980s partially as a result of lower international oil prices, as well as difficulty in producing oil in the south because of the war and the high costs of war itself. Those revolutionaries who had already moved up in society were disillusioned to discover that less money was entering the Iranian economy.

One of our pro-regime neighbors reflected this dissatisfaction with the regime, as well as the creeping influence of Western culture. He'd moved into the unit right above ours two years after the revolution; the regime had arrested the apartment's owner and seized the unit. Our new neighbor was a young man with a lush beard, and his wife was the only woman in the complex who wore a head-to-toe chador. When we saw them in the elevator, the couple greeted us with a smile but looked down to avoid eye contact with us, and spoke little.

Our neighbors kept to themselves until they had a son; then, the father began bringing his baby boy in a stroller to the garden. As the baby dozed off, his father watched teenage boys playing soccer. Eventually the boys invited him to play on one of the teams. He became their soccer buddy—the bearded man with his untucked shirt over his unfashionable pleated pants, who stood out among the teenage boys, their hair shiny with gel and the words "Iron Maiden" and "Metallica" inked onto their sleek jeans. When the boys shared their rented videos with one another, he began borrowing them. He even got copies of the boys' heavy metal cassette tapes. Within a few years, his beard shrunk into a trimmed one, his shoes began to shine, and a leather belt adorned his pants. In the elevator, he was no longer shy; he began looking directly at my mother and me and even exchanged a few words with us now and then. We called him by his first name, "Hussein *Agha*" ("Mr. Hussein").

Trends from current Western films were constantly reflected in many people's clothing. When *Top Gun* was released, men started to adopt Tom Cruise's short hairstyle and wear embroidered bomber jackets and Ray-Ban sunglasses, as he had in the film. Street vendors sold fake Ray-Bans at every corner, shouting: *"Einak-eh Top Gun,"* meaning *"Top Gun* sunglasses." Before this Tom Cruise trend erupted, long, rocker-style hairdos had demonstrated defiance of the government; government forces required men to cut their hair short, so anyone with long hair was obviously not a member of the Hezbollah or Pasdar.

The regime did what it could to discourage such Western fashions. Fining people for wearing any kind of sunglasses had always been common, but when the *Top Gun* style came into vogue, the forces shaved men's heads to intimidate them. The speed with which new trends appeared made it difficult for the government to root them out, however. It was impossible to round up hundreds of thousands of people for all dressing the same.

CHAPTER NINE

THE WAR ENDS

I turned eighteen in 1988. Even though the war had been raging since 1980, Khomeini still refused to accept a cease-fire. We tried to ignore the war, but it lingered in our peripheral vision, a relentless source of horror. I often thought that the fighting would never end—that it would continue until I entered adulthood, at which point all the young men I knew would either have died fighting or fled the country. I feared that, like my parents, I would spend my days queuing up for two pounds of rationed sugar or a small frozen chicken; that I would worry about replacing the last box of tissue, the one on which a large X appeared over the Western brand name Kleenex, and on whose opposite side bold Persian letters spelled out *No-Zohur*, meaning "newly emerged." I thought I would grow old and Khomeini would still be alive, still raging against the West and Saddam.

One night in late February 1988, Saddam launched a missile strike on Tehran. The missiles hit the city throughout the night, raising new fears for the first time since 1980, when Saddam and Khomeini had agreed to stop targeting each other's cities. Now it seemed that the agreement had been forgotten.

Early the next morning, the sirens began howling again, signaling yet another missile attack. I was still in my bed, exhausted after a poor night's sleep. My mother was calling me to go to the foyer. I sat up and looked outside at the sky for a few minutes, but then fell back on my pillow. I was tired of running. In my own teenage way, I needed to pretend that the war didn't exist. The missile would kill us anyway if it landed on our building, I thought, and it would happen so quickly that we wouldn't be able to escape. I hadn't moved out of my bed during the night when half a dozen missiles had exploded. I had just counted them, one-two-three-four-five-six, and tried to go back to sleep.

I was still in my bed when I heard a familiar explosion—except this time the explosion shook our twelve-story building, and through the window across from my bed I could see a thick cloud of black smoke swirling up into the sky. The missile had landed only a few blocks from our home. The war had reached our doorstep.

Within moments the siren stopped, and I got dressed and ran outside to see where the missile had struck. Many people in the neighborhood were heading in the same direction. I saw some of my friends, and together we rushed toward the black cloud. As we got closer, I saw that the entire single-level cooperative store at the corner of Hafiz Avenue and Karim-Khan Street was flattened. Fire trucks stood at the corner, but there was no fire; the building had simply been punched down like bread dough. People were saying that the store janitor had been killed. The smell of debris, wafting from bricks and concrete that had turned into dust, filled the cold morning air. The building's thick steel beams were mangled like crooked paper clips; not a single wall remained standing. It was a miracle that the shock waves had not shattered our windows—and we all knew well that, had the missile flown for just a few seconds longer, we would all have been killed.

That afternoon, my family hurriedly packed our bags and left Tehran. The war had entered a new stage. A rumor spread that Iraq was intentionally targeting densely populated areas in Tehran to increase the death toll. It was too dangerous for us to stay. But our apartment was the only home we'd ever known, and as I cast a farewell glance at it, I wondered if we'd ever see it again. Before leaving, my mother quickly rolled up a couple of our handmade carpets, the most precious items in every Iranian household, and placed them under the dining table. "This will limit the damage in case the windows break," she told us. After having seen the cooperative store, I knew that this was a useless effort.

Our evacuation of Tehran wasn't the only traumatic change I experienced during this time. My parents were getting divorced.

Traditionally, divorce had been stigmatized in Iranian culture, but by the late '80s the stigma had lost its strength. Women no longer felt obligated to remain in unhappy marriages. Divorce rates had risen and would continue to do so; by 2013, one out of every four marriages would end in divorce.

My mother was a free spirit who loved traveling. She would ride in the back of a bus for hours to visit a remote waterfall or to see the rose water festival every spring—the ceremony during which rose petals are boiled in big pots in Ghamsar in central Iran to extract their scent. My father was more introverted; he rarely accompanied my mother on her adventures. These differences had now gotten the best of their marriage—but while their separation had preoccupied us before the devastation reached Tehran, it was now the least of our worries. I no longer cared how or where they lived, just as long as they were both safe.

My sister, father, and I headed for the northwestern city of Tabriz, where my father's family lived; Saddam's missiles could not travel that far. My mother flew to Mashhad, another city in the northeast, which was also beyond the range of the missiles. We would not see her for nearly two months.

Every night at my grandmother's apartment in Tabriz, my father sat glued to his shortwave radio, switching from BBC Persian to Israel Radio in Persian to the Voice of America, as we tried to make sense of the events wracking our country. In the south, Iraqi forces were advancing and had retaken parts of Iranian territory. Iran was at its weakest, and the morale of the entire population was low. There was no sign of the ideologically driven teenagers who'd once stood up bravely against the Iraqis; most of them had been killed, while those who might have taken their place were now too disillusioned with the war and the regime to volunteer.

Meanwhile, Saddam continued to pound Tehran with his thirty-foot missiles, demolishing houses and hospitals. Nearly half the city's population had left. One day during Friday prayers three missiles hit Tehran, disrupting the event and rattling the city's remaining residents. We learned that another missile had exploded a block away from our apartment building, but luckily it had hit a piece of state property where no one lived. This time, though, the blast shattered most of the windows in our complex.

The worst, however, was yet to come. On March 16, Saddam began a campaign of chemical warfare, gassing the Kurdish town of Halabja near the Iranian border. The footage, which we saw on state television in Tabriz, showed the most horrifying scenes of the war. Dead bodies lay scattered in the streets of Halabja, their faces disfigured, their skin burnt away to expose the flesh beneath. Mothers sat like statues, still holding their children, all of them having suffocated to death in that position. A newscaster explained that the raid had lasted five hours. A cloud of white, black, and then yellow smoke had risen 150 feet in the air; it smelled of sweet apples. But within minutes, victims had begun blistering and coughing up green vomit. It was genocide: thousands were killed outright; thousands more died gradually and painfully as a result of their injuries. Saddam had started using nerve gas on Iranian troops as early as 1983, and the United States, fully aware of their use, provided him with satellite imagery of Iranian troops. Only a year before the attack on Halabja, in June 1987, Saddam had gassed the Iranian Kurdish town of Sardasht, and now it was rumored that he might use chemical bombs in other parts of the country. Halabja had been seized by Iranian-backed Kurdish fighters; after the gas attack Saddam's troops entered the town and reclaimed it for Iraq.

Saddam ultimately fired 180 missiles at Tehran during fifty-two days, and Iran retaliated by pounding Iraq's capital, Baghdad, with missiles bought from North Korea. Finally, after considerable international pressure, the two countries agreed to once again end the raids on each other's cities. When the cease-fire finally came, at the end of April 1988, we returned home and found in our garden a rainbow of spring flowers. Miraculously, our apartment was undamaged—not even the windows, even though many of our neighbors were replacing their windowpanes.

But the horror wasn't over. A month later, in July, an Iranian civilian airliner, Iran Air Flight 655, was flying over the Persian Gulf, taking its 290 passengers to Dubai. At the same time, an American naval vessel, *Vincennes*, had chased Iranian gunboats into Iranian territorial waters after they'd opened fire on the vessel. *Vincennes* spotted the ascending plane, which had just taken off at the port city of Bandar Abass and was still in Iranian airspace. *Vincennes*'s captain, William C.

Rogers, mistook the aircraft for an F-14 fighter and sent warning radio messages to its pilot. But being a civilian aircraft, the plane's radio was on mode 2—not mode 3, the one the military used. When *Vincennes* received no response, it fired two surface-to-air missiles at the plane. The airliner exploded in the air, killing everyone onboard.

The United States claimed that the downing of Flight 655 was a mistake, but no one in Iran believed it. Iranians felt they were no longer safe anywhere, on the ground or in the air. Khomeini's desire to drag out the war, we felt, had turned Iran into a pariah state. We were under attack from all sides, with no end in sight.

I had no inkling then that just two weeks later I would experience the happiest day of my life. The news, when it came on July 19, 1988, was completely unexpected. My mother called from her new home in Tehran and, in a jolly tone, told me to turn on the TV. A newscaster was declaring that Khomeini had announced he was drinking "the chalice of poison" and ending the war.

I screamed hysterically, stamping my feet on the floor in front of our TV screen as tears of joy streamed down my cheeks. Goli ran out of her bedroom and froze in front of the television screen with a wide smile. The nightmare had ended.

The Iran-Iraq War was the longest conflict of the twentieth century. By the time it ended, half a million people on both sides had been killed or maimed, while nearly five million Iranians had been left homeless. The war had cost Iran $650 billion. But it had finally come to an end, and at that moment all I could feel was joy.

A year later, Iranians received another piece of unexpected news. Listening to the radio over breakfast early in the morning of June 3, 1989, I learned that Khomeini, "the Father of the Nation," had died at the age of eighty-seven. I had been getting ready for school, but now my classes were canceled; schools would be closed for ten days so that Iranians could mourn the ayatollah's death.

I held my cup of tea in my hand, closed my eyes for a few seconds, and imagined the future. It was as bright as the morning light in our kitchen. I was eighteen, a senior in high school. Khomeini and his war had been a dark cloud over nearly half of my young life. A glimmer of hope had finally appeared, and the road ahead suddenly seemed more pleasant.

One of the girls in the neighborhood called a bit later, and we agreed to meet by the pool. Black banners had already been raised at the gates of our complex—more out of fear than genuine mourning, I knew, though I couldn't get worked up over this act of hypocrisy. What mattered was that Khomeini's reign had finally ended.

Summer was in full bloom. The delicate leaves of the weeping willows fluttered in the morning breeze, and the scent of freshly mowed grass wafted up from the lawn. Swallows sang from treetops. My friend and I sat on the bench and watched the water roar from a large makeshift pipe into the pool. Perhaps, I thought, we'll even be able to swim again.

PART TWO

AWAKENING

1989–1999

CHAPTER TEN

AFTER KHOMEINI

The entire country—schools, businesses, and the public sector—was shut down to mourn the death of Ayatollah Khomeini. In Tehran, the Basij—the paramilitary militia—set up roadblocks at every corner to maintain security, and the video-men were reluctant to make their rounds.

Bored, I tuned into state television and watched the live broadcast of Khomeini's funeral service. Hundreds of thousands of people had marched to Tehran from all over the country to bid farewell to the father of the revolution. Ayatollah Khomeini's body was on display under refrigerated glass in Mosalla, the prayer ground in central Tehran. His disciples had held a vigil around the case.

The burial ceremony was two days later, on June 6. Again, I watched it on television. A cameraman filmed from a helicopter, capturing the crowd of mourners who had raced to the cemetery, Beheshteh Zahra ("the Heaven of Zahra"), named after Prophet Muhammad's daughter and located fifteen miles south of Tehran, near where Khomeini had asked to be buried. The crowd was so large that no vehicle could pass through to deliver the body to the grave. The helicopter that had brought the body from Tehran hovered above and slowly lowered the coffin onto a truck. The camera zoomed in on the coffin. The mourners thronged around it, each pushing, stretching their arms, trying to brush a hand over it. After all, the authorities had referred to Ayatollah Khomeini as Imam, like the title used for Muslim saints.

As people flocked around the truck to reach out to the coffin, the wooden box fell off the vehicle and floated away on the hands of the mourners. Realizing that they'd lost control of the ayatollah's body, the guards fired water cannons at the crowd. But the mourners wouldn't let go.

Suddenly, as the coffin bounced over the heads of the crowd, its top came off, and Ayatollah Khomeini's corpse, wrapped in a white shroud, fell out. It was chaos. People pounced on the shroud and tore it off, revealing Ayatollah Khomeini's lifeless legs, bare belly, and white beard before the eyes of millions of Iranians watching the event live on television.

The broadcast disconnected for a few minutes. When the footage returned, it showed soldiers pushing the mourners back. They had retrieved the body and placed it back inside the helicopter, which had landed amidst the crowd. People continued to push ahead to stay close to the coffin. Several men clung to the helicopter's landing gear, falling to the ground one by one as it rose. Five hours later, another helicopter returned the body in a metal coffin. By the end of the day, eight people had been crushed to death.

These were the masses that Khomeini had galvanized; for them his word had been law, but now without him no one could control them. The foreign radio stations my father listened to, Israel Radio, the VOA, and the BBC, constantly proclaimed that the Islamic Republic was faced with a crisis: no one was able to replace him. He'd embodied the power that he had amassed as one individual, and now that he was gone he'd left a power vacuum. No one was as charismatic as he'd been in leading the masses; further, there was no need for such politics anymore. Khomeini's policies, the war, and his hostile rhetoric toward the West had isolated the country and reduced the economy to a shambles. Many in the leadership were eager to reconcile with the outside world and bring the masses under control.

The dilemma of replacing him was partly caused by Khomeini himself, who had fired his successor just two months before his death. Mohammad Ali Montazeri, his expected replacement, was a senior cleric who had become increasingly critical of the ayatollah. The brother of Montazeri's son-in-law, Mehdi Hashemi, had also leaked information to a Lebanese newspaper, revealing that during the war in 1985 the

Iranian regime had used its influence over Lebanon's Hezbollah to secure the release of seven American hostages. In return, senior administration officials under Ronald Reagan had sold arms to Iran, although
Iran had been the subject of an arms embargo. The revelation of the
arms deal was a huge scandal for the Reagan administration, but it also
had enormous repercussions in Iran. The disclosure embarrassed the
regime, which had always portrayed the United States as an enemy;
Ayatollah Khomeini had called America the Great Satan. Now the Islamic Republic appeared to be in bed with the devil.

The regime claimed that it had outsmarted the Americans to get
weapons. All the same, Ayatollah Khomeini banished Montazeri and
executed Hashemi. The ayatollah delegated the task of finding a new
successor to the Council of Experts, a group made up of some eighty
clerics. Khomeini also assigned a group of trusted allies to rewrite the
constitution for his new successor. Knowing that the leader who replaced him might lack his charisma, Khomeini demanded that the new
constitution should give the person extensive authority.

Now, after Khomeini's death, only one man was capable of introducing a new tune into Iranian politics: Akbar Hashemi Rafsanjani. A
soft-spoken cleric with a wispy beard, Rafsanjani had been Ayatollah
Khomeini's confidant. Rafsanjani was closer to him than the ayatollah's own son, Ahmad, who had always appeared at his father's side.
Rafsanjani lived just steps away from Khomeini and had been involved
in developing the political structure of the regime since its formation.
During the war, he had served as commander in chief and Speaker of
Parliament. It had been Rafsanjani who had persuaded the ayatollah to
end the war.

Khomeini had understood the urgency of preparing the regime to
survive his death. "Tell them that they must finish drafting the constitution quickly," he told Rafsanjani while on his deathbed. "You and
Khamenei must stay close," he said, referring to Ali Khamenei, who
served as president. As he died, Ayatollah Khomeini had also reached
for Rafsanjani's hand, squeezed his thumb, and uttered his last words:
"The revolution will thrive if you stick together."

But there were not many revolutionaries left to band together. Rafsanjani and Khamenei were the only remaining members of Khomeini's

inner circle; the others had either perished in the purges or been assassinated by the Marxist Mujahedin Khalgh Organization (known as the MKO), a leftist group that the ayatollah had sidelined but which had launched revengeful attacks against the regime. Khamenei had been injured in one of those blasts, losing the use of an arm. In a sense, he represented the violence the Islamists had endured in their fight with the MKO.

Members of the Council of Experts rushed to Tehran after the ayatollah's death to pick his successor. State-run television showed the clerics sitting on the red leather seats in Parliament, where they'd convened their emergency meeting. The whole country would watch their deliberations. It was a moment of extraordinary transparency for a government that had so often operated in the shadows.

A cleric read Ayatollah Khomeini's final recommendation in which he'd decreed that his successor did not even need to be a *marja*, a senior authority on religious texts and a source of emulation for Muslims. Khomeini and Montazeri had both been *marja*, but Khomeini had decided that he only wanted a successor who could defend the "integrity of the revolution." This was a major compromise for a system that was founded on religious principles—but it was clear that such compromises would be necessary if the regime were to survive.

The council suggested picking a group of clerics to replace the ayatollah, but only half the members—Rafsanjani and Khamenei among them—actually backed the idea. It would be embarrassing to replace him with a group that could garner only a small number of supporters.

At that moment, Rafsanjani did something unexpected. Sitting in the chair reserved for the head of the council (although he did not hold that position), he said that even Ayatollah Khomeini had never liked the idea of a council. What's more, he said, Ayatollah Khomeini had named Khamenei—in fact on three separate occasions—as the best man to replace him as supreme leader.

Rafsanjani was highly respected among the clerics; his words carried great weight. Now he appeared to be signaling that he wished to step aside so that his friend could take the highest position in the land.

The camera showed Khamenei in his oversized glasses, black beard, and black turban, sitting silently in his seat. He was known to be modern. Unlike conservative clerics, he had smoked a pipe before the revolution, socialized with secular poets and writers, and played the *tar*, a traditional instrument. When he was jailed for his opposition to the shah, he had befriended a communist activist, even though other clerics avoided communists because they denounced God. In 1987, Khamenei had even gone so far as to criticize Ayatollah Khomeini's "absolute power." When the ayatollah lashed out at him publicly, saying that he "must not interfere in matters that did not involve him," Khamenei backed down, but his comments had already made him seem like a moderate.

Khamenei seemed like the ideal candidate to become the supreme leader. The clerics were looking for a man who'd serve as a figurehead for the government, occupying a symbolic position while a more pragmatic generation of politicians—including a newly empowered president, the position of prime minister having been abolished in the post-Khomeini constitution—worked to steer the country in a new direction. It was obvious from political debates on television and in the press that the clerics felt the country needed to chart a different course. Khamenei would project a much more sympathetic image than the ayatollah had. He seemed like a free thinker, as well as a compromiser; when he had served as president, Khamenei had even allowed Ayatollah Khomeini to pick the prime minister, Mir-Hussein Moussavi.

The clerics cast their votes: 60 out of 74 voted for Khamenei. The man who had walked into Parliament as president on July 4 left the building as the country's *vali faqih*, its "learned patron." The clerics quickly promoted him from a mid-rank *hojatol-Islam* to an *ayatollah* so that his title would fit his new position. Iran was under a new ruler, and we watched breathlessly to see where he would lead the country—and who would fill out his new government.

A few days after Ayatollah Khomeini was buried, an election was scheduled, and Rafsanjani ran for president. He held a press conference and invited dozens of foreign reporters, who had been allowed into the country to cover Khomeini's funeral—the first time since the revolution that the regime had permitted a large group of foreign reporters to come onto Iranian soil. Ayatollah Khomeini had viewed foreign media with suspicion; this was another dramatic indication of how the post-Khomeini Iran would be different.

I watched the press conference with my mother. Rafsanjani sat on a gilded chair in a chandeliered hall as local and foreign reporters approached a microphone one by one to ask him questions. The television showed an American reporter, Geraldine Brooks of the *Wall Street Journal*, walk to the microphone wearing an *abaya*, the Arabic version of the Iranian chador but with sleeves so that it covers a woman's arms as well as her head. Brooks looked more conservative than most of the Iranian reporters present at the conference.

What happened next was stunning. Brooks asked Rafsanjani about Iran after Khomeini, but instead of answering, Rafsanjani looked at her with a smile and asked, "Why do you wear that heavy veil when a simple scarf would do?"

My paternal grandmother had a drawer full of silk headscarves, all pressed and perfumed, that she matched with her dresses. But the regime had never considered that kind of veil sufficient; many public places had pictures of women in chador, with a note saying that it was the perfect clothing for a woman to wear. Now a presidential candidate seemed to be sending a message to Iranian women, saying that he did not approve of the restrictions we had endured for the past decade. My mother and I looked at each other, each of us wondering what his comment meant for the future.

Rafsanjani's popularity surged overnight. Those few words, spoken to a foreign female journalist, ensured that women voted for him overwhelmingly when the election took place on July 28. He won 96 percent of all votes. When he took office, he called himself the "commander of reconstruction" to rebuild the country after the war. In reality, he was the new architect of the Islamic Republic: a pragmatic complement to the progressive Khamenei, and a powerful executive who would almost literally rebuild Iran in the years ahead.

CHAPTER ELEVEN

MEETING A HAWK

The second group of foreign reporters came to Iran in June 1990, after a devastating earthquake had killed thirty-five thousand people in northern Iran and left half a million more homeless. It was the worst natural disaster since the revolution, and Iran needed international help to rescue survivors and relocate them. A large group of Western reporters arrived to report on the disaster. I couldn't know it at the time, but their presence in the country would change my life.

I had graduated from high school not long after Rafsanjani's election, and had been accepted to Azad University to study English translation. While in school I also worked part-time as an English teacher, as well as taking private French lessons with a French woman who was married to an Iranian.

Many Western reporters had reached out to my French tutor to find translators, and I was thrilled when she asked me and two other friends if we would be willing to work with the journalists. I still remembered Geraldine Brooks's appearance at the press conference with Rafsanjani. He had chosen a foreign reporter to spread his message about the veil, knowing his words would travel farther through Brooks than if they were spoken to an Iranian reporter. Through her, he had sent a signal both to Iranians and to the West that he was a moderate. Journalism, I could see, was a powerful profession—and the idea of entering it in any capacity thrilled me.

I went out with several French and English journalists to interview Iranians, and I also translated newspaper articles. I learned quickly that most Western reporters were more interested in life under the Islamic Republic than they were in the earthquake. They'd been barred from Iran for two decades and wanted to find out what was happening behind the façade that the regime projected to the world. Amazingly, the regime didn't seem to want to stop them; even after the earthquake, reporters continued to visit the country, and I continued to work with them.

One evening in the spring of 1992, *New York Times* reporter Judith Miller called me to ask if I would accompany her to a campaign event for the upcoming parliamentary elections. Ali Akbar Mohtashamipour, a hard-line cleric and fierce opponent of Rafsanjani, was speaking at a mosque. Mohtashamipour was also a member of Parliament and was standing for reelection in April.

So far I had avoided meeting officials or going to government sites as part of my work. If security agents caught me with a foreign reporter, they could accuse me of being a spy. But that night, my curiosity got the better of me; I just couldn't pass up the chance to meet one of the most feared men in the regime.

Mohtashamipour was one of the few survivors of Ayatollah Khomeini's inner circle and represented some of the most traditional and aggressive aspects of the revolutionary regime. He had spent fourteen years with Ayatollah Khomeini in exile in Najaf, Iraq. After the revolution, he served as Iran's ambassador to Syria, and when Israel occupied southern Lebanon, Mohtashamipour founded Hezbollah, a Shiite militia, to fight Israel. With Iranian money, training, and support, Hezbollah soon turned into a powerful resistance movement against Israel and became Iran's military arm in the Middle East, with great influence among Shiite Muslims. (This Hezbollah had no links with the mob-like Hezbollah in Iran.) In 1984, Mohtashamipour became the target of an assassination attempt, presumably by Israel because of his role in creating Hezbollah. A parcel bomb injured both of his hands as well as his face. Mohtashamipour was also a hard-line interior minister under whose leadership in the late 1980s the Komiteh morality police raged some of the worst crackdowns, arresting women for showing a little hair, fining them and lashing them.

Soon I found myself with Judith in the backseat of a cab, heading to the poor southern neighborhood of Tehran where most conservative supporters of the regime lived. Judith was wearing a long raincoat, which worked well as a manteau. I wore a black hood over my head, donned my longest and loosest manteau, and even fastened a safety pin under my chin to make sure that the hood didn't slip back. I had no intention of making a political statement this evening. I wanted to blend in and get as close as I could to Mohtashamipour.

We bounced around in the backseat for half an hour and then walked to the end of a narrow, dead-end alley lined on both sides with shanties. A big pile of shoes scattered outside a mosque indicated where Mohtashamipour was speaking.

Mosques had been hotbeds for pro-regime propaganda since the revolution. None of my family or friends ever went to the mosque for prayers. A handful of upscale mosques are often rented for memorial services in Tehran; otherwise, the government controls and funds the mosques, through which it recruits militia members and rewards its supporters.

I bent over to take off my shoes to go inside when a bearded man approached and said that "sisters"—a religious form of address that hard-liners used for women—were not allowed inside.

After working with Western reporters, I'd learned not to take no for an answer. So I quickly explained in my humblest voice that Judith had come a long way to meet Mohtashamipour and that we would just wait for him outside the mosque.

The guard disappeared inside the building and returned a few minutes later to say that Mohtashamipour would receive us after his talk. The man directed us to a small room in the back of the mosque, where over a dozen women were sitting. Inside the room, another door led to the hall where Mohtashamipour was speaking. That door was wide open, but the threshold was closed off by a curtain. This way, the women could hear the talk, but the men could not see the women. We found two empty chairs, and I quickly began taking notes in my notebook. "My brothers," we could hear Mohtashamipour saying, "this is a sensitive time with an important election ahead of us. Now that Ayatollah Khomeini is gone, we need to make sure that the revolution doesn't derail from the true path that he defined."

He went on for a long time until his voice became hoarse. Then, after the crowd chanted *"Allah Akbar,"* "God is great," signaling the end of his talk, the curtain opened, and Mohtashamipour entered the room with several bearded men at his side. He sat behind the room's only desk, wearing a big smile and a black turban, the latter signifying that he was a descendent of Prophet Muhammad. The women quickly swarmed around him, giving him letters and making requests of him as their member of Parliament.

Eventually the women began to disperse, allowing us to inch forward until I finally got a good view of Mohtashamipour. Unlike my parents, who despised hard-line clerics like him, I felt a kind of awe and wanted to know more about these men who had kept a grip on power. Year after year, my parents had promised my sister and me that the regime would collapse, that the clerics would leave, and that we'd be able to shed our headscarves and swim in the pool again. Alas, that never happened—and perhaps as a result, my views were now different from those of my parents. The revolution had ruined their lives and shattered their dreams. But I had grown up in that system and learned to wrestle with its ideology. Now that I was a young woman, I was eager to get a good look at these men and understand how they had managed to stay in power for over a decade.

When we were finally alone with Mohtashamipour and his guards, he greeted us. "Welcome," he said in English with a strong Persian accent. I assumed he had recognized us from our clothes; we were the only ones not wearing the chador.

Judith began to ask Mohtashamipour questions. Mohtashamipour answered in Persian. Robotically, without taking my gaze off of him, I translated their words for each other. He was only forty-five, I knew, yet the lines around his mouth were deep enough to insert a coin into; I wondered if it was caused by injury or age. I surveyed his hands, which he raised to adjust his big glasses. Parts of his left hand, including his pinky and ring finger, were completely missing. The remaining fingers—his thumb, index, and middle finger—were disfigured, the skin sagging.

At first Mohtashamipour only stole glances at us, pretending not to look. The regime had banned men from staring at women who weren't related to them, and he was obviously tying to abide by this rule. But gradually he looked at Judith when she was taking notes, and then he began looking at me, too—straight in the eyes.

I had begun the conversation by explaining to Mohtashamipour that Judith was American, a correspondent for the most influential newspaper in her country. He nodded his head and repeated the word with a heavy accent: "Amrika." "Death to America" was still one of the main chants at the Friday prayers every week, when the regime presented its foreign and domestic policies to the public; so I knew he was practiced with the word—but I still didn't expect the harangue that followed.

Mohtashamipour broke into a speech about the evils of the United States, repeating the government line that I'd heard repeatedly growing up. America had supported the shah; America had backed Israel and therefore was involved in the killing of Palestinian children and innocent civilians; America had sided with Saddam Hussein during the war against Iran. Judith jotted down everything. Her bangs were showing, but no one seemed to care.

That evening, the journalism bug bit me. I started a journal, writing down all the details I had not written in the reporter's notepad that I'd learned to carry with me. Beginning the day after the interview, I immersed myself in politics. I subscribed to all the major newspapers and made charts, listing the names of the hawks—those members of the regime who were trying to keep Ayatollah Khomeini's hard-line policies alive—and the names of the doves, those who were following in Rafsanjani's footsteps. Mohtashamipour fell into the first group.

Later, I read Mohtashamipour's memoir to trace the roots of his radicalism. In 1954, when Mohtashamipour was a young boy, his father had caught him watching a group of people dancing in the street. The father, an illiterate worker, angrily dragged his son away and called the dancers "nonbelievers who had no respect for God or their country." As Mohtashamipour recalled in his memoir, "His words ripped through me. I developed hatred toward such idle people and later in life realized how they betrayed their country," he wrote. He'd remained so adamant in the opinions his father had planted in his mind that perhaps, I thought, when he served as interior minister he perceived women who showed their hair as *idle people who betrayed their country too*. None of it had anything to do with nationalism; it was all about dominating people's lives with one strict interpretation of Islam.

In the parliamentary election that April, Mohtashamipour lost his seat, as did many other hard-liners. But the hawks did not disappear, nor did the culture they embodied. Rafsanjani tried to bring them under control, but the forces—the Hezbollah—continued to act like bullies. They had roots in the system that Ayatollah Khomeini had founded, and soon his successor would bring them under his own wing. Hezbollah began calling itself Basij, the same name used by the militia that had fought in the war and made huge sacrifices. But some of their members were too young to have fought in the war. The renaming was only a tactic to make them untouchable, now that there was no war and no reason for extreme measures against people.

Ordinary Iranians were caught in the middle of this tug of war between the hawks and the doves. Even though certain rules were relaxed—the veil, for instance, and the mingling of unmarried couples—the militia force harassed people for the slightest infraction. It was as if the regime had shed its oppressive mask but retained its coercive nature.

The Basij, for instance, controlled separate entrances for women at universities and government buildings. The Basij sisters had erected curtains at the entrance and set aside little rooms where they scrutinized women's outfits and even wiped women's faces with a tissue to make sure there was no trace of makeup on their skin. They constantly drew up new lists of banned items, such as sunglasses and knee-high boots, or required women to wear hoods instead of headscarves.

At one point, the sisters decided to ban white socks at my university. As usual, I didn't go out of my way to replace them, and I was caught several times wearing white socks. Finally, they sent me to what they called the university court.

A self-proclaimed judge, a redheaded man about five feet tall, led me and five other women upstairs and into an empty classroom. He pulled a chair into the center of the room and ordered us to sit in a circle in front of him. Immediately, he turned to a voluptuous woman with full lips and said: "Sister, I was behind you when you were climbing the stairs. I cannot explain how you were moving your behind, but you have to find a way to stop it."

"Excuse me?" the woman asked, shocked. Her face went red, and she curled her lips in disgust. The rest of us, too, looked at the man with contempt. His lustfulness was obvious through the veneer of his authority. We were all wearing black hoods and loose-fitting manteaux and pants. There was nothing seductive about any of us.

Sensing our fury, the man cleared his throat and switched to a stern tone. "God has created beautiful things, but one should be cautious not to use this beauty in provocative ways. Women should cover their hair and their bodies to hide their beauty. Otherwise society will slip into corruption. We have lost so many men in the war to protect your honor, and you should know better how to honor their sacrifices."

He began flipping through the pages of a file. "Ms. Fathi. You have been stopped four times for wearing white socks. Can't you understand that white socks draw men's attention to your ankles?"

I clenched my jaw and glared at his downturned eyes. I was incapable of seeing the appeal of my socks, which were completely hidden under the loose cuffs of my pants. But there was no point in arguing with him; he had his own imagination. "*Bebakhshid,*" I said and could almost see the exhilaration in his face at hearing the words "Forgive me."

The man groped into his beard and continued, "This other woman, she continues to wear high heels. The clicking sound of the heels is extremely arousing."

The woman next to him rolled her eyes. "Forgive me," she said.

After going on like this for a while, the man released us but warned that next time we would be expelled.

We got away with certain things, but not everyone was lucky. A few years later, one of the boys in our complex, Alireza Farzanehfar, celebrated his twenty-first birthday. The party was at a different apartment building, outside our complex, and the Basij raided it. Maybe the music was too loud, or a neighbor had tipped them off. The guests were drinking alcohol, smoking marijuana, and dancing—none of which was strange for a private party in Iran, where people had long since learned to separate their private spaces from public ones. Still, the Basij were looking for any excuse they could find to crack down on perceived transgressions, and Alireza's birthday party was an easy target.

When the forces barged in, the guests ran to hide, desperate to avoid the lashes and hefty fines that were the usual punishment for this sort of offense. Women in short skirts and sleeveless dresses looked for their manteaux and scarves.

In the confusion, Alireza slipped onto the balcony. One guard spotted his shadow and followed him. The lights were off, and it was a dark night. No one knows what happened next. Alireza was a skillful skier and had an athletic body; maybe he thought he could dangle from the balcony and jump into the downstairs unit. Or maybe there was a fight. All we learned was that he fell to his death from the eighteenth-floor balcony, and his knuckles were bruised and bloody.

Alireza's family was not even able to open an investigation into their son's death. His father, a close friend of my father's, told my father that government forces had threatened his family into silence. They had another son and a daughter, and the forces had warned them that a fatal accident could happen to any of them if they tried to investigate the matter.

It was frightening to witness the regime terrorizing people so close to my family. And before long, I would get a taste of that terror myself.

CHAPTER TWELVE

THE INTELLIGENCE MINISTRY

One morning in early August 1992, my phone rang. "Is this Miss Nazila Fathi?" asked a male voice on the other end of the line.

"Yes," I said. "Speaking."

"I am calling from the Intelligence Ministry. We'd like you to come in to answer a few questions Saturday at ten AM."

For a few seconds, I held my breath; blood rushed to my head, and my nostrils trembled. I had anticipated this call since the first moment I had gone to meet Mohtashamipour with Judith Miller. Later, I had helped her with a few other interviews and worked with several other foreign journalists. The reporters called me a "fixer" now, a term they used to refer to a person on the ground who translated for them, made appointments with local sources, and introduced them to new stories. It was a role that carried significant risks, as a friend of mine had discovered recently; the police had stopped her while she was interviewing people with a BBC correspondent. They took her to a detention center, where they held her for several hours and threatened to charge her as a spy. She quit immediately.

I knew that I had to avoid the police, but the man on the other end of the line was from the Intelligence Ministry. In some ways, Iranians feared the ministry even more than the police, because its activities were shrouded in secrecy and it could press more serious charges. I had no choice but to accept his invitation.

I racked my brain, trying to figure out how they had found me. I had never stepped inside Ershad, the office at the Ministry of Culture and Islamic Guidance that dealt with foreign journalists. Upon arrival, journalists had to register at Ershad and submit their work agenda, but I had insisted that they refrain from mentioning me in any of these reports. I never attended any government meetings with journalists, either, knowing that doing so would put me on the authorities' radar. Yet the Intelligence Ministry had located me all the same.

The agent told me the address for the meeting, and as I wrote it down, I realized that he was summoning me to the ministry's main headquarters. The regime had inherited the building from the shah, whose own feared secret police—SAVAK—had been responsible for the arrest and torture of dissidents. Many of the people who had gone into the building over the years had never been seen again.

"Come alone, and do not tell anyone about this phone call," the agent said.

"Chashm," I said, "yes," trying to hide the fear in my voice.

After I hung up, I immediately decided to ask my father for advice. I had no reason to hide the meeting, especially from my family. What if the ministry detained me on Saturday? Who would know where I had gone?

I quickly dressed, pulled on my manteau and headscarf, and went to my father's office, which was in our housing complex. Three years earlier, he'd taken a job as the manager of our complex, a position that allowed him to stop traveling to the orchard.

"You've done nothing wrong," my father said after I explained everything. "You were a translator and did your job; that's all. Besides, I don't think they want to discourage you from working. Otherwise, they could simply threaten you over the phone. Go see them, and don't be scared."

His words gave me confidence, but I still wanted to find out what I should expect at the meeting. The Intelligence Ministry was relatively new; Ayatollah Khomeini had opposed its formation for the first five years after the revolution, believing that a formal intelligence ministry—by its very nature a bureaucratic organization—would be incapable of keeping secrets and thus protecting the regime. During those years, the Revolutionary Guards, a force that was accountable only to Khomeini, was responsible for gathering intelligence. The Guards' commanders had also blocked the formation of a ministry, not wanting to lose their grip on intelligence activities.

However, a group of young Islamists who worked at the prime minister's office and had read the SAVAK documents the regime had inherited insisted that the country needed an Intelligence Ministry. Those men had realized that intelligence work required an entire organization rather than a military force, like the Guards, which was also busy fighting a war. One man, Saeed Hajarian, finally persuaded Khomeini that a ministry was necessary to distance the supreme leader from some of the mistakes the regime had made. Innocent people had been killed mistakenly during the purges, he told Khomeini. A ministry, with different layers of bureaucracy, would be able to investigate such blunders and avoid them in the future. In the end Khomeini had given in, and Parliament, headed by the pragmatist Rafsanjani, approved the formation of the Intelligence Ministry in 1984.

Since 1989, the ministry had become the beating heart of the country's security apparatus, an Iranian CIA. And ironically, the ministry had the effect of preserving the worst aspects of the regime, rather than ameliorating them. Even though Rafsanjani attempted to soften the extremism of the 1980s in the decade that followed, there was only so much that he changed. The Intelligence Ministry recruited hard-line Guard members because of their loyalty and experience and turned the ministry into a shadowy organization responsible for the country's intelligence activities. It dealt brutally with dissenters inside and outside the country. Lucky prisoners who were granted amnesty talked about the high number of executions in jails during these years on security charges. Even enemies of the regime who had fled abroad weren't completely safe; just a few weeks before I was summoned to the ministry, a prominent opposition leader, Shapour Bakhtiar, was murdered in his home in Paris. Two Iranians, including a nephew of Rafsanjani, were arrested in Europe for the murder.

After I left my father at his office, I got into my car and drove to the office of an Iranian journalist, whom I will call Shahram to protect his identity. A handful of Western wire agencies had representatives in Tehran, and he was one of them. I had first met him at his home office with one of the journalists I worked with, and I felt I could trust him.

It was a hot day, and when I arrived outside Shahram's building, crows were cawing and swallows were singing in the trees. I had begun to think and act more cautiously since the phone call, and so I parked my 1978 Fiat a few houses away. I hadn't even called Shahram ahead of time, in case the phones were tapped.

I rang the buzzer of his apartment and hurried up the stairs. Shahram was standing at the door of his third-floor apartment with a big smile.

"To what do I owe the pleasure of your visit?" he asked.

In a hushed voice, I explained that I needed to speak to him quietly, thinking that his office might be bugged. Shahram, who was over six feet tall, loomed over me as I stepped into his apartment. Once we were both inside, he sat on a couch and stretched both arms over the back. I sat on an armchair facing him and took off my headscarf to cool off in the air-conditioned room. After nearly a decade of wearing the thing, I still found it suffocating.

Shahram was still smiling, but when I whispered that I had received a call from the Intelligence Ministry and they had summoned me to their headquarters, his face grew serious.

"What should I expect?" I asked.

"Nothing to worry about," he waved his hand in the air. "I'm surprised they haven't called you earlier. They want to know who you are, and they want you to know that they're watching you. Just make sure that you don't do anything you'll regret."

"Like what?" I asked.

"Like giving them information about the people you interview," he said in a low voice.

I shuddered.

"Look, if you want to become a reporter, you have to learn two lessons. First, you must be prepared to become a slave to the news. You have to work around the clock."

I looked around his home office, at the worn-out couch and the wooden desk in one corner. His footsteps had cleared a trail through the thick layer of dust that lay on the parquet floor in both of the apartment's hallways, one leading to his kitchen and another to what I assumed was a bedroom. Near the front door, several piles of newspapers stood against the wall. A telex machine chattered away on a low table in a corner. I had seen one of those at the office of Agence France-Presse and knew that the machine printed reports released by the official Iranian news agency, IRNA.

"The second lesson is that you have to protect yourself and your sources," Shahram continued in a whisper. "You mustn't reveal their identities or what they tell you."

He got up. "Let me go and make some tea," he said. "Then you can come and sit next to me so we can speak more comfortably."

I immediately stood up as well. I'd learned how to deal with flirtatious men; most of them knew their limits and backed off once you ignored their advances. Still, I was disappointed that Shahram seemed to be trying to take advantage of my moment of weakness.

I walked to the door, explaining that I was in a hurry and had to leave. "Let me know how it goes," Shahram said as I closed the door behind me.

Before heading out on Saturday, the first day of the Iranian workweek, I put on my most conservative clothes: a long black coat and a hood over my head. Climbing into my Fiat, I headed toward the address the agent had given me, navigating through Tehran's rush-hour traffic.

Twenty minutes later, in the lush neighborhood of Pasdaran in northern Tehran, I spotted my destination. It was a grey building, occupying an entire block at the end of a dead-end street. At the mere peek at it, my heart sank.

I parked in front of a convenience store. The street was quiet, with a few people walking along the sidewalks. It was an affluent neighborhood with large single-family houses behind brick walls; the hedges were neatly trimmed on both sides of the street. Perhaps, I thought, the shopkeeper would notify the traffic police if I didn't return to move the car. Stores usually liked to keep the parking spot out front free for customers.

Before getting out of the car, I looked in the rearview mirror to make sure that the hood I was wearing covered all my hair. Then I walked up to the front of the building, took several deep breaths, and pressed a round buzzer next to the metal door, which looked like the entrance to a medieval dungeon.

A voice asked who I was, and I answered as self-assuredly as I could, conscious that there was a camera overhead. Then the metal door swung open, and I walked inside.

I was in a dark corridor, in front of a wall of glass behind which a guard sat at a desk. He asked for my bag, and I handed it to him through a slot in the glass. I had emptied the bag at home, leaving only a wallet and driver's license inside.

As I stood there, I surveyed my surroundings. I could see that natural light had never penetrated the thick walls of this part of the building. The walls of the hallways were rough and either had a coat of gray paint on them or were made of concrete. In the gloom it was hard to tell.

The guard returned my bag and instructed me to wait inside a windowless room. I sat on a lone chair with a small desk attached to it, like the ones we had at school. In front of me was a much larger desk with a chair behind it, and another door behind that. The setting looked just like the interrogation rooms I'd seen in movies.

After I had been alone in the room for a few minutes, the door behind the desk opened, and a short man appeared. I had expected to meet a bearded agent, but this man wore only a mustache—which could be a sign that he was a bureaucrat, and not a religious fanatic, or a disguise for a religious fanatic who wanted to blend in as a bureaucrat.

The man perched behind the desk and in a calm voice said that the ministry had monitored me for months as I had been working with Western reporters. Blood rushed to my head, and I wondered what—or who—had given me away. Were there spies among the Iranian intellectuals whose homes I had visited with the reporters? Or perhaps the employee I dealt with at Ershad had told the ministry about my involvement with foreign journalists? I'd met the Ershad worker a few times so I could give him an envelope containing a few hundred-dollar bills on behalf of my journalist colleagues; visiting reporters had learned quickly that if they weren't generous with the officials at the Ministry of Culture and Islamic Guidance, they would likely never receive the paperwork that would allow them to roam the streets and visit simple places such as the cemetery and the bazaar, which they were always eager to see. This employee also arranged interviews with senior politicians, who were normally difficult to reach. Each time we met outside Ershad, he would look inside the envelope and nod approvingly. Taking bribes was common but illegal, and I had hoped that he would keep my secret, since I knew his.

The agent was polite, but I was terrified nevertheless. I had begun to sweat and hoped he wouldn't notice it in the dimly lit room.

"You know that Iran fought a war for eight years with a country that Western powers armed," he said in a monotone. "These reporters may want to misrepresent Iran to undermine the regime. The ministry needs to be vigilant." I nodded, trying to seem agreeable. He didn't sound unreasonable for a security agent.

The mustached man walked toward me and handed me some papers. It was a questionnaire with incredibly detailed questions: all the places I'd ever lived; the names of every school I'd attended; the names of my best friends at every school; the names of all my aunts, uncles, and first cousins; and my parents' occupations, as well as any friendships they may have had with activists at any point in their lives.

It was obvious that the ministry was looking for any clues that might link me to Iranian opposition groups. The regime still feared the Marxist group the MKO; they'd murdered many government officials, and it would be only logical to assume that they might try to make contact with hostile foreign governments through international reporters. But I knew that the ministry wouldn't be able to pin anything on me in this respect; my parents, like most Iranians, hated the MKO even more than the Islamic regime. During the war, the MKO had joined Iraqi forces to fight against Iran. My family, like all the others I knew, was intensely patriotic and regarded the MKO not just as terrorists but also as traitors.

Despite my family's broad dislike of the regime, they'd never done anything that could be perceived as a threat to it, so I felt comfortable answering many of the questions on the agent's form. I put down the names of my aunts, uncles, cousins, and schools. For my father's occupation, I wrote "self-employed" to avoid raising questions as to why he had been laid off from the Ministry of Power. When I reached the section where I had to name my friends, I carefully mismatched their first and last names so that they would not be recognized. I calculated that if the agent discovered it later, I could claim that I'd made an innocent mistake.

I did, however, make several significant omissions. For instance, I left off the name of one of my classmates in high school. She had been five years older than everyone else because she had been an activist and had spent time in prison. My closest friends were the ones I'd grown up with in our complex, and I decided not to mention them either.

When I finished an hour later, the agent collected the papers and said that someone from the ministry would contact me. He excused me, and I left the way I had come in, never learning the man's name.

I went home and called my father to reassure him that I was all right. I was still annoyed with Shahram, but I was relieved that the officials from the ministry had acted professionally, just as he'd assured me they would.

A week later, another agent from the ministry telephoned and summoned me for a second interview. He gave me a name, but from the way he articulated it, I guessed it was fake. In case it wasn't, I will call him Mr. X. Just like the first caller, he insisted that I not tell anyone about the call. I was to show up at an address on Villa Street a few days later, which was within walking distance from my father's home, where I still lived.

The address led me to a small immigration building called the Office for Alien Residents; several Afghan men were sitting inside. A guard asked my name at the front desk and then directed me to a large sunny room on the second floor, where two men were expecting me. One of them greeted me, and I immediately recognized Mr. X's deep voice. He invited me to sit, and then along with the other man, much taller than Mr. X, he sat on the couch facing my chair. I was surprised to find tea and a big platter of pastries waiting on the coffee table that separated us.

Mr. X was polite and serious, but the mood changed quickly after we exchanged formal greetings. The larger agent broke into a monologue, railing against all Western journalists. "They are all spies and liars," he told me, almost yelling. "Only traitors help them."

I was startled but did my best to maintain eye contact with the agent, even though sweat was beginning to dot my upper lip.

Then he picked up a pile of papers and started sifting through them. I glanced and noticed that they were in Persian, with some of the paragraphs circled and the margins filled with notes, also in Persian. "Listen to this," he said and began reading:

> Some 13 years after the revolution that toppled the Shah and his Western-oriented regime, Iran is turning out a growing number of impressive, small-budget, quintessentially Iranian movies. They explore with candor that often borders on bitterness the soaring social, economic and personal problems of ordinary Iranians in post-revolutionary Iran. Overcoming the obstacles of censorship at home and suspicion abroad, these films have increasingly been winning critical acclaim and prizes at international film festivals.

He finished reading and glared at me accusingly. "What lies are these? Who said we have problems? If women don't peel off their clothes in front of a camera, does that mean there are 'obstacles of censorship'?" he asked, stressing the final phrase.

I guessed the piece was a translation of a recent article by Judith Miller. Together, we had interviewed people about Iranian movies that were winning international awards. I wondered if this man was genuinely unaware of Iranians' daily complaints about censorship. And if there was no censorship in the country, as he claimed, why had the authorities recently banned several movies, including one called *The Good Wedding* that portrayed veterans disillusioned after the Iran-Iraq War?

As I sat there under the withering stare of the portly agent, I dreaded what would come from this second meeting. I knew there was a real possibility that I might never be able to work with foreign media again and that I would have to go back to my modest teaching job.

I was no longer hearing what the big guy was saying, until he threw the papers on the seat next to him and Mr. X began speaking. "We've been told that you speak English like a first language and that you are an excellent translator," he said civilly.

I exhaled. Mr. X was complimenting me. As he spoke, I felt a black cloud leave the room. The unnamed agent had leaned back on the couch, had folded his arms, and was no longer looking at me. Mr. X, I realized, was playing the good cop.

For the first time in the meeting, I had a long look at Mr. X. He was short, and his wavy black hair was combed back. Two-day stubble coated his upper lip, like the shadow of a mustache. He had deep-set eyes—hawkish, I thought—and with a makeover, he might even have looked handsome.

"Please have your tea," he insisted. I dropped two sugar cubes in my cup and began stirring. The teacup was made of white china with a shiny golden rim. It looked pristine. After the war ended, people had gone into a frenzy of consumerism, purchasing new kitchen appliances and furniture that were not available during the war. Evidently, the Intelligence Ministry had splurged on new china.

Mr. X reached over to pick up a pastry from the table, and I noticed that his hand was missing three fingers: the thumb, the index finger, and half of the middle finger. Maybe he was a war veteran, I thought.

"You seem like an intelligent woman," Mr. X said. "We think we can trust your judgment in case you come across a suspicious journalist. Sometimes spies disguise themselves as reporters. It is not a secret that the West has wanted to overthrow the regime ever since its formation."

If I hoped to continue working in journalism, I knew that I had to engage in this conversation with Mr. X. Arguing with him wouldn't do me any good; he may have been polite, but he was also powerful, as the other agent had just reminded me. Still, I remembered Shahram's advice and was determined not to sell out any of the Iranians who had risked speaking their minds to the reporters with whom I worked.

The Intelligence Ministry may have distrusted foreign journalists, but I knew that they—and I, to a degree—also served the government's interests. By assisting reporters, I was helping to introduce the outside world to the human face of the Iranian people, thereby changing the international perception of Iran. Ever since the revolution, Western governments and media outlets had demonized Iranians, portraying them as armed men and black-clad women chanting, "Death to America." But there was so much more to Iran than this. There was life beneath the surface; there were ordinary people all over the country who longed for freedom and dignity just as people did in any other part of the world. Even though the regime aimed to stamp out these impulses, it had also realized that, by spreading evidence of them around the world, people like me were helping improve the country's image.

Mr. X was still looking at me as I cradled the china teacup in my hands. "Of course," I responded. "Iran is my homeland too."

CHAPTER THIRTEEN

THE WAR REVISITED

All foreign journalists wanted to visit Ayatollah Khomeini's mausoleum. He was now lying in a sarcophagus within an expansive golden cage located right next to Beheshteh Zahra, the enormous cemetery just outside Tehran. The building that housed his body had the biggest golden dome in the country and was surrounded by four minarets. A foundation run by his family had plans to transform the site into a religious and tourist hub by building a hotel for pilgrims there, along with shops, a university, and other cultural attractions.

The shrine was always my first stop with new journalists. From there we headed to the martyrs' cemetery a few minutes away, where the remains of tens of thousands of Iranian men lay under identical grey stones. It was an affecting sight, one that spoke to the deep losses suffered by ordinary Iranians during the war—while Khomeini's enormous resting place reminded visitors of the influence he'd had over his supporters.

A few months after my meeting with Mr. X in August 1992, he had told me that the Intelligence Ministry had issued my security clearance. I could continue working with foreign reporters, but now, like any other local or visiting journalist, with a work permit from the authorities.

Shortly after receiving Mr. X's call, I met with the director of the bureau for foreign press at Ershad. A chubby and soft-spoken man, he had parked his shoes under his desk and shuffled around his office in rubber slippers. After the revolution, many Iranian men had taken to wearing the slippers to signal their humble roots, but in the early 1990s pragmatist politicians had begun wearing dress shoes to look modern and more presentable. The fact that the foreign press bureau director's footwear had not changed with the times indicated that he was still a traditionalist and that I could expect him to be difficult to work with.

I was pleasantly surprise by the visit. The director welcomed me and said that, with the number of foreign reporters in Iran continuing to increase, Ershad was eager to authorize more translators. At his instruction, a friendly woman in his office issued me a letter that authorized me to work with the reporters. The letter stated the dates and places that I could work; I would have to get it renewed regularly if I wanted to stay on the right side of the law, but more importantly, the authorization meant that Ershad would vouch for me if I got into trouble with the security forces or any other authorities.

On a hot day the following summer, I traveled to Ayatollah Khomeini's shrine with Vincent, a French journalist. He had been authorized by Ershad to interview people at the cemetery and Ayatollah Khomeini's shrine, and I was to act as his translator.

For nearly thirty minutes, we were bounced around in the back of a Peykan, a local version of the 1967 British Hillman Hunter that had been discontinued in Britain but had essentially become the national car of Iran, even though it was the most uncomfortable car you could buy. There was so little leg room in the back seat that even a small person like me felt cramped. Big guys like Vincent had to angle their feet carefully when entering and exiting the backseat to avoid getting stuck. Heat and smoke wafted up from the engine, and the suspension was so poor that it was hard to keep from getting nauseous.

We could have found a more comfortable ride. Nicer air-conditioned cabs—mostly French Peugeots and Renaults—were becoming common in Iran, but I liked our driver, Karim. He was jolly, always cracking jokes, and he knew his way around town. Tall and portly, he would courteously squeeze himself up against the steering wheel to give us more room in the back. A photo of his three-year-old daughter, with frizzy hair and a big smile, dangled under the rearview mirror.

When we arrived at Ayatollah Khomeini's shrine, Vincent and I woozily extracted ourselves from Karim's Peykan and showed the guards our papers. Then we removed our shoes and, barefoot, stepped inside the mausoleum.

We entered a gigantic plaza where people were picnicking on hand-woven carpets as kids slid down the complex's marble ramps, screaming with joy. Although Ayatollah Khomeini's tomb sat in the center of the pavilion, a festive mood dominated the place. Partly this was due to the shrine's location; it was close to several towns that had once been slums, but the lot of their residents—most of whom were regime supporters—had improved after the revolution, and many of them made frequent trips to the mausoleum to celebrate Khomeini.

Back outside the shrine, I showed Vincent the shops selling souvenirs with Ayatollah Khomeini's picture on them: posters and postcards, decorative plates, and framed pictures. Ayatollah Khomeini's eyebrows were knitted in a frown in nearly all the photos. Only in one photo did he smile, flashing his teeth at a small boy, perhaps a grandson, who was running toward him. Another photo showed him in white pajamas and a skullcap, carrying a tray with a teacup on it.

Afterward, Karim drove us to the martyr section of the cemetery. As we entered its gates, Karim asked if I knew my way around the martyrs' section.

"Not really," I said, not quite understanding what he meant. To me, the martyrs' section was just a vast monument to all the people who had lost their lives during the war. It stood in stark contrast to the rest of the cemetery, which was green, bushy, and decorated with marble gravestones. By contrast, the martyrs' section was lined with rows of faded grey stones and had a somber air. There was something depressing about seeing row after row of graves of boys who'd died so young, often for nothing more than a concept of patriotism and the promise of reaching heaven. Some graves had aluminum frames over them, containing pictures and personal belongings.

My response seemed to trigger something in Karim. He pulled over and said he'd come with us.

I scanned the engravings on the graves as I passed them. Most of the people buried in the block where we found ourselves had died in the same year, 1985, and almost all were young; some of them would have been my age had they still been alive in 1993. On a photo inside one aluminum frame, a seventeen-year-old boy smiled at me. He was standing in a trench, leaning against some sandbags. A note in childish handwriting was pinned next to the photograph: "Mother, forgive me if I never return. I have chosen the path of God. My last wish is for you not to leave Ayatollah Khomeini alone."

I lifted my head to look for Karim. I saw him in the distance; he was bending over, filling a large soda bottle with water. He strolled to a grave, knelt down, and began cleaning the horizontal stone with the water. Then he put his hand on the stone, closed his eyes, and seemed to say a prayer. People normally did that at the grave of loved ones. After he had finished, Karim moved to another plot and did the same thing.

Vincent walked away after I translated a few more notes, pinned inside the aluminum frames over the graves, which the men had written to their families before their deaths. So I headed toward Karim to ask how he knew the men who were buried here. Maybe they were friends, I thought, or cousins, or neighbors.

I waited for Karim to finish his prayer. He looked calm, as though this was a ritual.

"How did you know him?" I asked.

He looked up. "They were both part of my unit," he said. "I knew many of these men."

"Were you in the army?" I asked, trying to figure out how Karim could have gotten involved in the war. He looked older than the men who were buried here.

"I was with the Basij," he responded.

This took me aback. The Basij was a volunteer force, very different from the Revolutionary Guards or the army. Men who didn't join the Basij entered a mandatory draft at the age of eighteen and underwent three months of training, after which they had a better chance of surviving than those who joined the Basij. Unlike army or Revolutionary Guard units, the Basij were often sent to the front without much training, and sometimes even without uniforms.

I had thought of Basij members as die-hard regime supporters, and Karim didn't seem anything like that. In the car he had told us jokes about the clerics and blamed the revolution for his economic misfortune. Why, I thought, would someone like this have volunteered for the Basij?

"I was fourteen when I signed up," Karim explained. "I regretted it almost immediately. My mother was furious and said that she would never forgive me if I died. But I had no choice! You know how it is in the neighborhoods in south Tehran; everyone else enlists, so you just follow them. Call it adventurousness or foolishness. Almost all teenage boys around me volunteered.

"I was lucky. I served six years but spent most of that time in hospitals. Every time I went to the front, I was injured and sent back. It was God's will that I stayed alive. Now I am considered 30 percent disabled because of the shrapnel in my body. "

Karim turned around and looked in the distance. "We, the Basij, were always on the front lines. If there was a military operation, we would go first, and the Revolutionary Guards and the army would follow us. Before military operations, a preacher spent hours filling our ears with glorious stories about martyrdom, saying how seven beautiful virgins would usher us into paradise if we died. It's funny, isn't it? When you are alive, you can't even get a date—but in death, there's more than one virgin for every man.

"I tried not to listen. None of us had gone to the war to die—not me, not my friends. But the preacher stirred up all sorts of emotions in us. Some of the kids got dreamy-eyed and high—completely brainwashed. They spoke about martyrdom as if it were something glorious, something that didn't involve death.

"And then one time during an operation, we reached a minefield. The commander yelled, 'We are surrounded by the Iraqis and need to cross the minefield. There is no time to clear it, or we'll all die. We need volunteers.' I was a coward, but a couple of these young guys raised their hands. I don't know where they found the courage, but they stepped forward and dove onto the mines. The next kid stood on the dead body of the man before him and jumped, until they built a bridge for us. Then we stepped on their remains and crossed the field." He looked at the grave, his hand still resting on the stone.

I had a lump in my throat. It was one thing to get killed in a battle and another to kill yourself for the sake of your fellow soldiers, as these young men had. Despite the ideology that had clouded their minds, there was a kind of nobility in what they'd done. They hadn't died in vain; they'd given their lives willingly, in order to save others.

No wonder Karim looked older than his age. He never finished school; he was not capable, even though the government had put in place university quotas for war veterans and disabled people. The memories still haunted him. Even the ones who went back to school were never the same. They simply couldn't shake their minds of the war—and after hearing Karim speak about his experiences, I could fully understand why.

Later, as Karim drove us back to Tehran, I was explaining to Vincent the difference between the types of Basij—the ones who had fought in the war and the ones who flexed their muscles on the streets—when Karim interrupted me. "Tell him these new ones are hooligans," he said, anger in his voice.

One hand on the wheel, he reached over to grab a folded paper from the glove compartment and handed it back to me. It was a copy of his marriage certificate. "These idiots have stopped me with my wife and my daughter so many times that I carry this piece of paper," he said. Unmarried couples could still get lashed for hanging out together.

In that moment, I could see how Karim, who came from a traditional family and had fought in the war, could despise the regime's moralistic straitjacket as much as I did, even though I came from a much more Westernized family and, on the surface, had little in common with him. But our conversation made me wonder why so many other traditional Iranians had become disenchanted with the regime as well. Education levels and per capita incomes were both steadily rising; people at all rungs of society seemed better off than they had been a few years before. What else could be shaping our perceptions?

CHAPTER FOURTEEN

THE WALLS COME CRASHING DOWN

One afternoon in August 1992, shortly after my first meeting with Mr. X, I had returned home to find rolls of cable unspooled around our apartment and two men fumbling with the cords. One of the technicians, Ali, was explaining to my father why it had taken them so long to come to our apartment building. There were not enough technicians to meet the high demand.

My father explained to me that Ali and his colleague were installing satellite television in our apartment. Not long before, a few of our neighbors had asked to mount satellite dishes, large aluminum devices eight feet wide, on the roof of our building; with a fist-size device called LNB installed in its center, a dish could access television programs beamed via satellite. Since then, almost everyone had asked to connect their television sets to the antennas. My dad explained that Ali was connecting ours to all three dishes on the roof, each aimed in a different direction: one toward Asia, another toward the Persian Gulf, and a third toward Europe.

Immersed in work and my studies, I had been unaware of this new technology. It was a particularly busy time for me; after the war, many families wanted their children to study English because it meant they could have access to better education abroad in the future. The institute where I taught was packed with students from every social class. I had half a dozen private students in addition to my pupils at the institute, and I often had to cancel all of my classes to work with journalists. I barely had time to watch the movies we rented at home, let alone think about channel surfing.

I was still wondering if we really *needed* satellite television when Ali handed me the remote for the cable receiver and asked me to test it, adding casually that we now had more than two hundred channels. The very idea bewildered me. I was only used to three state channels, the third of which had launched only recently.

I began flipping through the channels. Flashing before my eyes in clear, crisp colors were an embarrassment of options: the BBC news channel, MTV, a movie channel called Star Movie, programs in French, German, Turkish, Korean, and other languages I'd never even heard of. And the languages, the music, the sound effects—they were all crystal clear, completely unlike the stifled background noise that passed for soundtracks in the pirated films on which I had grown up.

"Let me show you something else," Ali said, taking back the remote. "If you press this button, you get two hundred or more radio stations." He pressed the menu and the long list danced in front of my eyes: we had National Public Radio, dozens of rock, jazz, and classical music stations, as well as French, Persian, and other radio stations.

Suddenly, my father's shortwave radio seemed completely irrelevant. In truth, it had been on its way out anyway; over the years he had come up with a system of tapping on the radio whenever authorities jammed programs broadcast from Israel, Washington, DC, or London. The pounding helped to slightly adjust the knob, which brought back a low muffled sound—just an approximation of the broadcast, really, and one that worked only for a few minutes before he had to strike the radio again. Years of thumping had loosened the screws, and the radio was falling apart.

I too had had my share of disappointment with our limited media options in the decade since the revolution. I craved Western music, especially rock music when I was a teenager, but it was impossible to get in Iran—legally, at least. I tried to record music off of radio programs, but the intense jamming made it impossible. I ended up relying on the street vendors who stood idly on the sidewalk in downtown Tehran, their hands tucked in their pockets, whispering "latest Persian/English tapes" to passersby. This was an imperfect system, however, since apart from risking arrest I also had to worry about quality control. I learned to buy from the regulars, those who were always hanging out at certain corners. Otherwise, I might end up with a Persian music tape instead of a Nirvana record, or an old album instead of a new one.

The satellites atop our building changed everything. Now BBC Persian, my father's favorite radio station, echoed loud and clear from the television. A jazz station, simply called Jazz, rocked our apartment. Just by pressing a button we could turn our television screen into a window looking anywhere in the world. Suddenly the walls that had isolated us from the rest of the world came crashing down, and nothing could stop us from getting a peek into the lives of other people in other countries—or in satisfying our hunger for music, TV shows, news, or any other sort of media under the sun.

Ali told me that he had been a video-man but switched to selling and installing satellite equipment just a few months earlier. Demand was high, and the equipment was plentiful, as it was flooding the country from the Persian Gulf in the south. No ban was in place—at least, not yet.

The high demand for satellite TVs spoke to something fundamental about Iranians: we, like people in many countries of the world, are obsessed with the latest technology. We also have a burning desire to know more about international culture, politics, and current events— all things that, after all, Persia helped to shape for centuries. And in the early 1990s, after more than a decade of isolation, many of us were willing to spend good money to reconnect with the outside world.

For a couple of days after Ali left, my sister and I did nothing but watch TV. We devoured everything from soap operas like *The Bold and the Beautiful* to movies we'd previously watched with barely audible sound, like *A Fish Called Wanda*. For the first time, our television set became a source of entertainment for us, rather than a reminder of the barriers separating us from the rest of the world. Now we could be anywhere on earth in seconds. One minute we could watch *Dynasty* and be in Denver, Colorado; the next minute we could stand in front of 10 Downing Street in London, watching British prime minister John

Major in his oversized spectacles. We Iranians felt like citizens of the world once more, and television was nothing less than our passport.

A few months after Ali set up our satellite TV, a worker named Jamal was in our kitchen replacing the old linoleum floor with new ceramic tiles. As the economy continued to pick up, my father, like many home-owners, was dizzy with renovation, getting rid of old furniture, tiles, cabinets, and carpets, as though removing them would distance him from the memories of the past decade.

Our television was playing in the background—we often left it on—when I walked from my bedroom into the living room and found Jamal kneeling on the floor, holding his muddy hands in front of his chest to avoid dirtying anywhere. He was watching *Baywatch* and seemed hypnotized by the images of women lifeguards in bathing suits. I asked him if he knew the program, and without taking his gaze off the screen, he said he was a fan.

Jamal's answer surprised me. Based on his profession I'd guessed he was a member of the working class, and I had thought that satellite television was more common among the middle and upper classes—not only because the equipment cost upwards of $200, but also because I assumed that many religious families were reluctant to watch the uncensored programs for fear of introducing "immoral" influences into their traditional households. What if men's wives wanted to copy Western women and shed their headscarves?

But Jamal explained to me that one of his neighbors had satellite television and hosted viewings of the most popular shows, selling tickets to other people in the neighborhood. Every week *Baywatch* fans, mostly men, crowded into this neighbor's living room and watched the show over tea and crackers.

"But you don't speak English," I said. "How do you understand what they are saying?"

"You can follow the story," Jamal replied. "It's not too complicated." He was planning to buy a satellite dish too. "The programs are not so bad," he said. "There are cooking programs for my wife, and the children can learn English or Turkish." (Since Turkey sits just over Iran's northwestern border and its national language is close to Azari, spoken by Iranian Turks in northwestern Iran, many Iranians want to learn to speak—or at least understand—it.)

Before long I noticed that the images, the plotlines, and even the educational opportunities that had entranced Jamal were leaving their mark on Iranian society. Furniture stores, for instance, began importing modern furniture like the type we saw in foreign TV shows; furniture decorated with gold paint had long been a common sight in Iranian homes, but suddenly even state television was replacing the classic furniture in its studios with boxy red and blue sofas.

The programs introduced color into our lives. Women replaced the dead colors the regime had imposed on us—the color of soil, sand, and dried weeds—with vibrant reds, yellows, and greens. Many women copied Pamela Anderson, the actress who played one of the lifeguards on *Baywatch*, and shaved their eyebrows, replacing them with a thin arched line drawn on with pencil. Even young men who for years had avoided growing facial hair because they didn't wish to look like the bearded, pro-regime men now sported trimmed strips of hair on their chins or jawlines. The Basij called the new beards "satellite styles" and harassed anyone who wore them. But this didn't stop most of the young men who favored them. They were eager to look like people in the rest of the world, and they were willing to endure the heckling of hard-liners in order to do so.

As I traveled around the country for work—something I was doing more and more those days—I noticed that the aluminum dishes continued to sprout on rooftops, even in smaller towns and villages. No place in the country, it seemed, was immune—but the invasive, transformative power of satellite TV paled in comparison to the next technology that was about to hit Iran.

I first learned about the Internet in 1995, after I met Mohammad-Javad Ardeshir Larijani, a conservative politician. A cleric by training, he had discarded his robe and turban when he had gone to study mathematics at the University of California, Berkeley, before the revolution. The experience seemed to have changed his mind in other ways, as well, for in 1992, as head of the Institute for Theoretical Physics and Mathematics in Tehran, he authorized Iran's connection to the World Wide Web. A year later, Iran officially became the second country in the Middle East to connect to the Internet, and although it would take another two years for commercial Internet to become available, when it hit Iran in 1995—the year I met Larijani—it would almost literally reshape the country.

Bringing the Internet to Iran was a daring step for a regime that had been obsessed with limiting exposure to outside ideas and influences—but as Larijani explained it, it made perfect sense. Sporting a bushy beard and a pair of thick glasses, he argued that the Internet was necessary in this day and age so that Iran could keep up with scientific progress in the world. It was clear that after the war, Iranian politicians vied to develop the country and introduce the nation to all the new tools that were becoming available in more developed countries. In his perfect English, he raved that the Internet was expanding quickly. Commercial Internet service still cost hundreds of dollars a month, but all universities and some thirty thousand other subscribers were connected to the Internet. The regime restricted access to porn websites, but this was practically the only kind of censorship it had enforced. The challenge confronting the government, Larijani said, was to offer Iranians faster and cheaper service—not to waste time and money telling them what they could and couldn't do online.

That year, I subscribed to an email service offered by the Ministry of Telecommunications for $100 a month. It was a text-based service on a black screen with white letters that blinked as you typed. The computer dialed a local number, and while it was connected to the web, I could send and receive emails, including attachments. I was very proud of this service, since many of my friends who had immigrated to the States didn't have personal email accounts yet.

Email access transformed my career. I began reporting, and sent my interviews by email to the correspondents I knew. The local color, the interviews, and the in-depth information I offered these publications—none of which had representatives in Iran—were so valuable that *Time* magazine and the *New York Times* both hired me as their stringer, a term referring to a non-staff reporter. A few years later the *New York Times* would hire me as a contract reporter. I quit teaching and became a full-time journalist; for me it was a dream come true that became possible partly because of my access to email.

I wasn't the only person in Iran who felt their life had changed because of the Internet. That year, I found out through a journalism assignment that the clerics in the religious city of Qom had fallen in love with the Internet too. Two hours south of Tehran, Qom is the center of Shiite Islam in Iran; since the country is nine-tenths Shiite, the city has an enormous significance in the religious lives of most Iranians. The city is dotted with golden and turquoise domes, and it houses the shrine of the sister of the eighth Shiite Imam, Fatimeh Masumeh. Only in Qom could you see clerics confident enough to zip past on their scooters, their cloaks ballooning behind them. People resented the clerics in general because of their political leadership after the revolution. When the clerics made the nearly hundred-mile trip northward to Tehran, where they were a minority, they often changed into ordinary clothes, and the powerful ones hid behind the tinted windows of their bulletproof vehicles to avoid people's hateful glares. Taxi drivers often boasted about how they would pick up a cleric waiting for a cab in the shade and drop him off a few feet down under the scorching sun, claiming that they'd picked up the wrong passenger.

The seminaries were traditionally wealthy and could afford to connect to the Internet. Senior clerics received money in forms of alms and religious taxes and received further funding from the government after the revolution.

By the time the Internet arrived in Qom, traditional biases against technology had already lost strength, and younger clerics were eager to use new gadgets in the service of Islam. These clerics owned television sets, if not satellite television, very much different from their predecessors, who feared that radio, television, and even newspapers might pollute their minds. The new generation regarded the Internet as a tool just like these other technologies—and this tool, they knew, could expand their influence in the Islamic world.

Political leaders had always vied to make Qom superior to Najaf in Iraq. Perhaps the epicenter of Islamic education the world over, Najaf was located in a nation that had historically been the motherland of Shiite Islam. Recently, Qom had been catching up; years of political turmoil, war, and persecution of Iraqi Shiites under Saddam Hussein had already taken a toll on Najaf. Still, in order to supplant Najaf as the capital of Shiite Islam, Qom needed all the trappings of a modern center of learning—including the Internet.

Being forward thinking, Khamenei had funded the Computer Research Center for Islamic Sciences in Qom as early as in 1988, when he was still president, so that the city's clerics could digitize Islamic texts and connect to the Internet. If the web could give the regime a voice in the virtual sphere, he felt, why not embrace it? Shiite Islam is a flexible religion that favors adaption and has long proven capable of changing its traditions according to the needs of time. Through the Internet, the clerics could demonstrate this flexibility yet again—while also disseminating their influence among Shiite Muslims throughout the world.

And so it was that, when I visited Qom, I found myself in what had been one of the country's first Internet centers, where I saw clerics walking around in their socks in a carpeted room and perching in front of boxy monitors. To make themselves more comfortable, some of the clerics rested their turbans on the desk next to the monitors they were using, giving them a slightly more relaxed look. They translated books into English, Arabic, and Persian, digitized them, and posted them online. They also had an email system to respond to all sorts of questions from lay Muslims around the world.

Proud of the inflow of emails, one young cleric hopped behind a computer to show me some of the queries he and his fellow clerics were receiving. One was from a twenty-four-year-old married woman who needed advice on how to cope with her husband's inability to satisfy her in bed; another was from a forty-four-year-old man, married with children, who had fallen in love with a younger woman at work; and yet another was from a German woman who'd converted to Islam and was searching for a Muslim husband.

Sex is important in Shiite Islam, for both men and women, and clerics are not shy about discussing it. But I was surprised to see that most of the questions they were getting via email focused on love or sex rather than religious obligations. The cleric wrote to the first woman, the one who was sexually unsatisfied in her marriage, and told her that she needed to speak to her husband about the issue and buy him books that could teach him the tricks and secrets of lovemaking; such books were widely available at bookstores in Qom. He referred the German woman to another cleric, whom I suspected might be a matchmaker. As for the married man, the young cleric told me that he needed to consult a more senior cleric before he could answer his question properly. According to Islamic law the man could marry the young woman in a temporary or permanent polygamous arrangement, but most Muslim women, even here in the city of Qom, were less interested in those kinds of marriages than they were in dedicated, one-on-one partnerships. Marriage is considered a sacred institution in Iran, a pillar of a chaste society, so the young cleric had to be careful not to give the man the wrong advice and risk ruining one relationship—much less both.

I was fascinated to see that people had started to communicate more freely—women as well as men—and that even in the traditional city of Qom people were taking full advantage of the rapid technological changes sweeping the globe. Indeed, the Internet was growing faster in Iran than in any other country in the Middle East. By 1995, some thirty thousand people in Iran had Internet access—the largest number in the Middle East except for Israel.

The Internet could be a tool, as the clerics in Qom had discovered, but, like satellite TV, it could also be a great leveler, bringing down traditional barriers and reducing old norms to rubble. In the years ahead, the new dynamics that these two technologies had introduced to our country would expedite the metamorphosis of Iranian society—to the great excitement of some and to the great dismay of many others.

CHAPTER FIFTEEN

NESSA MOURNS

It was an early morning in March 1995, a few days before Nowruz, the Persian New Year, when our doorbell rang. I was standing at the window in the kitchen, listening to the sparrows chirping in the trees. The trees had burst into pink and white blossoms, completely blocking my view of the pathways that linked the buildings in our apartment complex, where in colder months I often spotted a friend or a neighbor passing by. But the blooms were also a welcome relief, signaling the end of frosty mornings and the beginning of spring.

I went to the door, looked through the peephole, and saw our former maid, Nessa, holding two fat bags. She'd stopped working for us shortly after the revolution. Her daughter, Roya, had managed to secure her an apartment, and Roya had also gotten a job as a school principal and was able to support her mother.

I opened the door, and Nessa strode in, just as she had a decade ago, except now I saw that her bony shoulders were slightly slumped. "How are you, my darling?" she asked me, just like the old days, as though she'd seen my gradual physical transformation from the age of eleven to twenty-four. She let her chador and headscarf slip to her shoulder, revealing her hair. Once a lustrous black, it had devolved into a stringy gray ponytail.

It was common for domestic workers to drop by like this to get money, even after their formal relationships with their employers had ended. When I was young, my parents' wet nurses had visited us

regularly until both women finally passed away. With no pension or social security stipend like what one would find in a traditional job, workers like them had no choice but to depend on their former employer's
generosity once they were too old to work.

Nessa announced that she'd brought us fresh herbs to make *sabzi-
polo-mahi*, the traditional Nowruz dish of saffron rice brewed with
chopped aromatic herbs and topped with fried fish. Before I could say a
word, she went to the sink and began removing bundles of cloth from
her bag. As she unfurled the cloth on the counter, the aroma of cilantro,
dill, chives, scallions, and parsley wafted into the air. She explained that
she'd minced them the day before but wanted to wash them at our place
so that they would stay fresh. She scooped the herbs in her hand under
the running water, letting the flow carry them through her fingers and
into the strainer.

It was clear from the size of the pile collecting in our sink that Nessa
needed extra income on the eve of the New Year. The working class,
whose lot had improved after the revolution, had run out of luck after
Ayatollah Khomeini's death. Rafsanjani had tried to steer the country
away from the rationed food economy that was introduced during the
war; instead he embraced capitalism after Khomeini's death. Shortly
after the war ended in 1988, oil prices shot up too, helping the economy
to expand. But oil prices fell in 1992, and—along with corruption and
mismanagement, which had always plagued the country—deflated Rafsanjani's efforts to reform the economy. Inflation spiked, and the poor
were the first to feel the squeeze.

We made small talk, and Nessa told me that Roya had two teenage daughters, but Nessa rarely saw them because Roya and her husband were busy. Iran and Parvin, her two other daughters, worked at
a beauty salon in Tehran. The two-hour commute was hard, but Nessa
was happy that they had jobs. As for her young son, now sixteen, he'd
quit school and was looking for work.

"You know, my darling," she said, "life is hard these days. People
cannot afford to be as generous as they used to be, and I need all of
them to bring money to the table."

"Do you still support the regime?" I asked out of curiosity, but
quickly regretted it when I noticed Nessa's facial muscles tense. She

closed her eyes, wrinkled her nose, and with the back of her hand wiped a tear from her cheek.

"Did you hear what happened to Ahmad?" she asked, referring to Ayatollah Khomeini's son. "They poisoned him; they murdered him." Her voice sounded strangled, as if a knot were growing in her throat. "If I were there with him, or if only somebody had given him some lime juice, it would have neutralized the effects of the poison."

The news of Ahmad's death had emerged the day before. According to the official version of the story, he had suffered a heart attack in his sleep at the age of forty-nine. But a rumor had already circulated that he'd been murdered.

"They poisoned his opium," Nessa went on. "They could have saved him, but instead, they let him die."

Khomeini had three daughters, but Ahmad was his only remaining son; Khomeini's eldest son had died before the revolution. When the ayatollah had been alive, Ahmad was in charge of his modest home-office—a room furnished with just a bed. The room was attached to a balcony from which Ayatollah Khomeini addressed his supporters as they stood in the small yard beneath it. In photos and television footage of the ayatollah, Ahmad always stood at his side. He coordinated the affairs of his father's office and had a level of influence over him that many in the Iranian regime would come to resent.

It was Ahmad who fell out with Montazeri, his father's successor, and persisted in trying to fire him until Ayatollah Khomeini finally dismissed Montazeri a few months before his death. To make sure that Montazeri remained alienated after his father's death, Ahmad published a series of letters in a booklet called *Ranj-nameh*, meaning "the letter of pain," depicting the cleric as a traitor.

There were speculations that Ahmad might succeed his father as the head of the Islamic Republic, but he never appeared to be a commanding figure in the regime. He often had a distant look on his face, and his black turban was frequently tilted back, showing a black fringe of greasy hair curtaining his forehead. People nicknamed him Ahmad Heyran, meaning "Bewildered Ahmad."

Rumor had it that Ahmad was hooked on drugs—which in Iran at that time could mean anything from opium to heroin or cocaine.

Opium has roots in Iranian culture. One doctor who treated drug addicts once told me that opium to Iranians is what champagne is to the French. Many Iranians smoked it, and for a more intense high some even swallowed balls of opium. When educated Iranians returned from the West in the mid-nineteenth century, they looked down on the practice and viewed opium abusers as addicts. But although the revolutionaries viewed addicts as criminals, arresting and executing many of them, traditional clerics never endorsed or banned opium; some even smoked it themselves.

Both teasing Nessa and repeating what I'd heard, I said, "Some people say Ahmad was on cocaine, not opium, and they killed him with bad cocaine. Do you think the lime juice would have worked on that too?"

"Oh yes, it's the best antidote," Nessa replied, showing off her knowledge of traditional medicine. "But Khamenei and Rafsanjani wanted to get rid of him, so even if the lime juice worked, they would have found another way."

Ahmad had been close with Khamenei and Rafsanjani when Khomeini was alive. Ahmad even facilitated Khamenei's ascent to power by backing Rafsanjani's claim that the ayatollah had wanted Khamenei to succeed him. But Khamenei and Rafsanjani subsequently infuriated Ahmad by sidelining him after his father's death. Ahmad's only job became running his father's mausoleum and collecting its income. Feeling evicted from Iranian politics, he gradually broke away from the two men.

In the weeks before his death, Ahmad had publicly slammed Rafsanjani and Khamenei. Unlike Khomeini, who ruled from a modest home-office, Khamenei had installed himself in a large compound in downtown Tehran and had hired a large staff. He had set up a modern bureaucracy to oversee the government's activities. Instead of relying on the poor as his support base, and on the clerics who had appointed and elevated him to his supreme position, Khamenei had invested in the Revolutionary Guards. Fearing that he might never command the respect of the older clerics, he sidelined them and rewarded younger clerics and Guards members with posts.

As president, Rafsanjani had moved quickly to reverse Ayatollah Khomeini's foreign and economic policies. He mended ties with almost all of the countries Iran had alienated itself from in the immediate aftermath of the revolution. A satirical magazine called *Gol Agha* published a cartoon of Rafsanjani's foreign minister bending over a map with a magnifying lens, mocking his efforts to reach out to other world powers. Khamenei only blocked Rafsanjani from improving ties with Israel and the United States. Like Khomeini, he depicted those two states as the enemies of Iran.

Rafsanjani also imported goods to fill the empty shelves of Iran's supermarkets and invited foreign companies to develop Iranian oil fields. Investment security became one of the slogans of his government to encourage entrepreneurs and industrialists to invest without the fear that the regime might confiscate their businesses like in the early days of the revolution. To rebuild the country, he borrowed funds for the first time since the revolution, racking up foreign debt to $30 billion. But his free market economic policies caused an unofficial inflation rate of 40 percent, which took a toll on poor people like Nessa.

Only a week before his death, Ahmad had made inflammatory remarks about his old friends. "Corruption and bribery are rampant because of mismanagement," he'd said. "The gentlemen constantly blame the United States and Israel for the country's problems. Did the United States send you around the world to beg for Western aid?" Knowing that Ahmad had crossed the line, state media refrained from covering his remarks. Only one weekly, *Omid*, published the entire speech. Everyone knew that, despite his goofy appearance, Ahmad could be a fierce opponent to those who crossed him.

Now, with Ahmad silenced, people like Nessa felt deprived of an advocate within the regime. "I am on my way to the shrine before going home," Nessa said, referring to Ayatollah Khomeini's mausoleum, where Ahmad was to be buried next to his father. "Now that Ahmad is gone, Rafsanjani and Khamenei will do whatever they wish," she sighed.

Nessa tossed the herbs in the plastic sieve several times, then left the strainer on the counter. I paid her generously. As in the past, she put the bills in a small handmade bag that hung around her neck. She tucked the bag into her bra, where it would be safe from pickpockets, then pulled her chador over her head, and wiped her eyes again. "There is nothing left of Ayatollah Khomeini," she sniffed. "Ahmad was the only one who reminded us of him. Now it's all over."

Three weeks after Ahmad's death, gasoline prices soared, and bus fares doubled. The hike was part of the wave of inflation sweeping the economy that mostly harmed lower-income families, who had benefited from price-control and food-rationing policies that were enforced during the first decade of the revolution.

Angry workers, many of whom took buses from a shantytown on the outskirts of Tehran into the city for work, protested when they were faced with higher fares. They marched to the nearby town of Islamshahr, picking up jobless workers and smashing the windows of government buildings along the way. As the crowd grew bigger and angrier, the local police appealed to Tehran for help. The government dispatched the Revolutionary Guards. To disperse the protestors, the Guards first beat them and then opened fire on them. Some ten people were killed. The news of the protests, and the brutal way they were dealt with, sent shock waves through the country. The protests reflected the new socioeconomic displeasure with the regime.

When I visited Islamshahr a few weeks later, the streets were quiet, and people were hesitant to talk. A few residents whispered in my ear that the government forces had shot at people from inside a helicopter hovering above them. The Guards had returned the next day to arrest hundreds more people. Residents believed that the forces had taken photos of demonstrators and then came back later to pick them up—a strategy that, true or not, intimidated the people as much as the shooting.

The protest was the first anti-government revolt since the revolution. Ironically, its perpetrators had been lower-class supporters of the regime, the same people who'd fought in the war and who still paid homage to Ayatollah Khomeini—people like Nessa. They'd been the backbone of the revolution. The events of that spring showed that another autocracy was in the making, one that no longer sought its mandate from Khomeini's supporters.

But with less public support than it had enjoyed under Khomeini, this version of the Iranian autocracy would have to tighten its grip even further if it wished to hold onto power. Although the regime had subdued the demonstration in Islamshahr, dissent didn't disappear. Instead, it simmered beneath the surface and soon emerged in other forms.

CHAPTER SIXTEEN

A FORCE FOR CHANGE

I settled into the front seat of the Peugeot next to Faezeh Hashemi, Rafsanjani's daughter and a recently elected member of Parliament. As her long slim hands rested on the steering wheel, her chador slipped down on her shoulder, revealing a checkered headscarf underneath.

Hashemi, thirty-seven, had refused to be chauffeured to Parliament like other legislators; instead, she drove her own car. I was planning to sit in the balcony to watch her in the assembly and later follow her to another meeting for a profile on her I was assigned to help write. In the back seat, her assistant read her schedule: "Nine to twelve, Parliament's discussion; one thirty, meeting with the Olympic Committee board members back at your office; three, meeting with the new director of the Shiroudi sports complex; five, meeting with women's swimming team."

Hashemi wiped the sweat off her forehead with the back of her hand and looked at the car's digital clock. We were stuck in traffic, and she was late for Parliament's morning session. Inching forward, we reached an opening in the cement blocks that split the express bus lane from our side of the road. Hashemi leaned forward and looked carefully, then made a sharp left turn, veering into the bus lane. A gust of wind blew into the car as she pressed her foot on the gas pedal. Her assistant fell silent in the backseat, and I reached for my seatbelt (seatbelts weren't obligatory in Iran yet) with my eyes glued on a bus coming toward us. Undeterred, Hashemi sped up and glanced into her side mirror. Reaching for the gear, she shifted it and steered the car farther left, letting the oncoming bus streak past us. At the intersection, a white-gloved officer waved at her, and the car lurched to a stop. I finally unclenched my jaw and relaxed my hands, which I had balled into fists. Hashemi rolled down her window and waited for the officer.

"May I see your driver's license and registration?" he asked politely. Hashemi could get a ticket and lose her driver's license for several months for what she'd done. She reached for the documents behind the sun visor and handed them over.

I craned my neck to see if the officer recognized Hashemi. Her campaign posters had been all over the city a few months earlier, and her picture still appeared in magazines as the top candidate in the parliamentary elections. Hashemi was rumored to have received more votes than the former Speaker of Parliament, a much older man and a cleric. Some publications had even suggested that Rafsanjani, her father, had concealed his daughter's real votes. It was too embarrassing to admit that a young woman was the most popular politician in the Islamic Republic. In the official tally she came in second, with slightly fewer votes than the older cleric—an injustice that must have riled Hashemi, given the nature of her platform.

Hashemi had made her debut in politics by challenging conservative clerics who opposed women's right to exercise in public. Using her standing as Rafsanjani's daughter, she argued that there was nothing wrong with fully covered women exercising. An increasing number of old and young women already crowded parks to jog or play volleyball or badminton. But the Basij often harassed and intimidated them to discourage women from exercising.

As part of her campaign to defend and expand women's right to exercise, Hashemi built a bike path for women, increased women's access to sports facilities such as golf courses and tennis courts, and set up the first women's soccer and, eventually, rugby teams since the revolution. She also founded the Islamic Women's Sport Foundation, through which she held games in Tehran involving Iranian athletes and Muslim women invited from other countries. She became the godmother of women's sports. In 1998 she would launch the country's first women's daily newspaper, *Zan*, meaning "Woman."

That day, the officer recognized her after reading her name. "Ms. Hashemi," he said in a scolding tone. "Please don't violate traffic regulations again."

"Yes, sir," she replied. He handed back her papers without issuing a ticket, and we drove off.

I was more comfortable around Hashemi than the other Islamist feminists who had become vocal in the 1990s. With her, I didn't have to worry about my headscarf slipping and revealing my hair. Many of these feminists dressed in the same style as pro-Khomeini women had in the early days and, like the morality teachers at our schools—the Islamist feminists—criticized other types of dress.

Hashemi was a tomboy: she was always in jeans and a long-sleeved button-down shirt, and her chador often slipped down on her shoulders in a traditional way. Hashemi's station in life had enabled her to be more transgressive than many other women could afford to be. The hard-line media often attacked her for wearing jeans, but it had little effect. Hashemi told me that, when she was a university student, the authorities had harassed her for not wearing a hood and a manteau under her chador—but being Rafsanjani's daughter, she could get away with it.

Back then, Islamist feminists were still determined to set themselves apart from secular feminists. Another well-known religious feminist of this era was Shahla Sherkat, a journalist who published a monthly magazine called *Zanan*, meaning "Women," the first true feminist magazine in post-revolution Iran, launched in 1998. Sherkat didn't wear the chador, but she often fidgeted with the folds of her hood over her forehead, as though she was nervous that a rebellious strand of hair might defy her will. Her small frame was always hidden under an oversized black manteau.

I always covered my hair and tried to look proper when I met with Sherkat for an interview—but still, when I showed up for one meeting, she glared at my dress and asked me to leave. I'd worn a loose, ankle-length, cotton dress to avoid having to swelter in pants in Tehran's

90-degree heat; restrictions had loosened by this time, and most women wore short, tight-fitting manteaux over tight pants, but while my dress was not as fashionable or as revealing as theirs, it was not the button-down manteau that the regime favored, either.

I was annoyed by her attitude and felt she was promoting the regime's dress ideology, which was more about enforcing their inequitable social order than promoting chastity. I told Sherkat that I'd worn the same dress to Parliament and the president's office. The sisters who checked our outfits at the entrance had even liked it. "If my dress is good enough for the president, it should be good enough for you," I told her.

Sherkat listened to my protest and then sent me away anyway. "They'll shut down my magazine," she grumbled. I was offended but reasoned to myself that she had a bigger battle to fight than our disagreement over my dress.

Sherkat had been a regime woman in every sense. She had been an ardent supporter of Ayatollah Khomeini during and after the revolution and had worked for the state-run daily *Kayhan*. But over time she had become disenchanted with the regime, as had many of its other supporters. Disillusioned with political developments, she and a few male colleagues had left *Kayhan* in 1992. Together they rented a small apartment, where Sherkat began *Zanan* magazine and the men started *Kiyan* magazine.

Zanan focused on women but avoided the word "feminism." In those days, the term still carried a strong Western liberal connotation. Sherkat's *feminism* was constructed around women's problems rooted in Iranian culture and politics, and she and other activists were seeking indigenous solutions to them. Indeed, her face would turn purple if you called her a feminist. "I am an advocate of women's rights, not a feminist," she'd retort. But that changed too over the years, as did her clothing style.

Kiyan, the journal founded by Sherkat's male colleague, was a political-philosophical magazine that argued that Shiite Islam—the country's official religion—was compatible with democracy and human rights. These journalists had learned that it would be sheer folly to confront the regime outright over their philosophical differences with it, considering how it had crushed opposition in the past. They believed in grassroots change, educating people, enlightening society, and changing the system from within. By this time Iran's population had swelled to sixty million people, 60 percent of whom lived in the cities, compared to less than 50 percent in 1979. The majority of people were between the ages of fifteen and twenty-four, and education levels were growing rapidly. Literacy had risen from 56 percent before the revolution to 77 percent in 1996, and within twelve years, it would reach 99 percent.

Journalists like Sherkat were committed to informing their readers in order to help them shape their government according to their own opinions and desires. People still remembered the instability of the early days of the revolution and knew that institutional breakdowns like the one that had occurred in the late 1970s could provide extremists with the opportunity to seize power. These men and women had no intention of allowing that to happen again. They no longer sought to solve Iran's problems with a revolution, but rather *evolution*—reforming the system.

Like Sherkat and her colleagues, many of these reformers had risen from inside the regime. The men who ran and wrote for *Kiyan* had been the founders of the revolution but had since morphed into more mature, seasoned thinkers. Their leading author was Abdolkarim Soroush. He had been the architect of Ayatollah Khomeini's Cultural Revolution, which had purged hundreds of students and professors from universities in 1980. Soroush, a philosopher by training, had gone to Germany later in the 1980s to complete his studies. After he returned to Iran, he advocated the idea of religious democracy in his writings in *Kiyan*. In a few years, he would even become known as an opposition member and one of the most liberal Islamic thinkers. He argued that faith and freedom could coexist with, and even complement, one another. The essence of the Koran's sacred text remained constant, he wrote, but Muslims' interpretation of it needed to vary according to the needs of their times. Religion was the pathway to building a political system, but it needed a popular mandate to survive. He went so far as to say that there was nothing divine about the clerics' monopoly of power in Iran. "Justice cannot be religious," he wrote. "Religion must be just."

Men and women like Soroush and Sherkat were perhaps idealists whose beliefs had once driven them to ruthless pragmatism but who were now swinging back in the other direction. Intoxicated by the victory of the revolution, they had resorted to extreme measures to found their ideal society. Some of their colleagues had helped wipe out the opposition, had (in many cases) joined in the attack on the US embassy in Tehran, and had supported a bloody war—all actions that left deep scars on society. As government officials, some of them had travelled; many of them had gone to study in Europe, while others completed their graduate studies inside Iran, devouring books and slowly accumulating ideas about democracy, freedom of speech, and human rights. They cherished these notions, nurtured and embraced them as though they had always belonged to them. But in reality they would become as disaffected as any of the regime's former supporters. As one of these reformers told me bluntly, they had realized that the country had moved from one brand of tyranny to another. People had not only failed to gain political freedom but also lost personal liberties they'd enjoyed under the shah's reign.

The 1990s were the formative years for Iranian society that led to an awakening. Soroush's writings stirred a conversation within Iran about the role of religion in the country's politics. "The faithful have given the right of legislation to God and therefore the laws of a religious society are divine," he wrote. "But understanding those laws and making them compatible to their lives is not a right that people can give up. That's why human dealings with Sharia (Islamic law) are similar to their dealings with nature. Even though they are surrounded by nature and belong to it, they venture to exploit it and have even built technology, ignoring nature's rules and limitations in order to make progress. Nature and Sharia may both be strict, but they embrace various guises with colossal benevolence." Islamic law, in other words, was at once immutable and placid, unyielding but adaptable. Men could change it if they were willing to strive mightily enough.

Some intellectuals backed Soroush, while others criticized him. He garnered a huge following at universities, where students and academics were once again resuming their historical role as activists. But while he was controversial, Soroush helped to ignite arguments that would reshape Iranian politics—and would begin a dialogue that would, in time, offer the country a pathway out of its political gridlock. In a few years, he would resume a life in exile and beome known as a liberal Islamic scholar.

Sherkat had worked closely with these former colleagues. When I first met her a year earlier, in 1995, she'd just moved to an apartment above the office of *Kiyan*. Often, on my way up to her office, I'd see her standing in a cluster of men, conferring with them with remarkable ease. Like them, she belonged to a class that the revolution had empowered—and she wasn't about to let them forget it.

Backsliding had become a fact of life for many Iranians. The clerics had reinstated a system of Islamic law after the revolution, reversing the secular legal system that Reza Shah, the shah's father, had introduced in 1926. To modernize the country, he'd taken the courts from the control of the clerics and built a legal system modeled after the ones in Europe. But whereas the shah's legal system had forbidden cruel and unusual punishments, along with other ostensibly backwards practices, the post-revolution penal code sentenced sinners to lashes and thieves to having their hands amputated, along with other eye-for-an-eye punishments. Adultery brought the death sentence by stoning. The civil code determined that the value of a woman's life was half that of a man's life. When young men died in the war, the law gave the custody of their children to their paternal grandfather.

The laws that pertained to women's rights, particularly, had no relevance to the lives of Iranian women, representing half of the population. The middle class had swelled, and if not empowered by the regime, women were more educated and capable than the previous generation of women. They felt dehumanized by the law's making the value of the lives of two women equal to the value of the life of one man, and by its depriving them of the right to get a divorce or to keep custody of their children.

In her magazine, Sherkat explored these issues and exposed the gross injustices of Iran's legal system. She wrote about women who were victims of battery, a practice that, according to some interpretations of the Koran, the holy text endorses. Women needed their husbands' permission to work outside the house or to travel. Without a notarized letter from their husbands, women couldn't even get a passport. Sherkat began a public conversation about these issues by asking what good female cabinet ministers or members of Parliament were as long as their husbands could subvert the will of the Iranian people by barring their elected officials from leaving the house in the morning.

Zanan challenged the government's stance toward women in other ways, as well. Once, it quoted the conservative Speaker of Parliament, Ali Akbar Nateq-Nouri, as saying that "women's most important endeavor must be their struggle as homemakers," right above a quote by an open-minded cleric, Mohammad Khatami: "This must be the year that women will have a dominant presence at universities." Next to those contrasting comments, the magazine published the news about the appointment of Iran's first female professor of aircraft engineering. Women were making progress, despite what officials said.

Iranian women's desire for progress and education had started with the wave of modernization in the nineteenth century. During that period upper-class women had founded movements to promote education and health care services for poor women. They took part in debates over Iranian economic and foreign policy, as in 1891, when the king's wives boycotted the smoking of tobacco, joining the tens of thousands of Iranians who were protesting the king's decision to sell the country's tobacco industry to a British firm. In 1906, women staged demonstrations alongside men, paving the way for the Constitutional Revolution and the founding of Parliament. In 1979, women were part of the nationalist, leftist, and Islamist groups that toppled the shah.

But despite women's historically central role in Iranian politics, the country's traditional society always expected women's demands to serve the interests of the larger community. If women demanded more rights, they were singled out as outcasts who challenged the prevailing religion and culture. And while women did win significant gains during the nineteenth and twentieth centuries, their achievements were fragile and easily shattered.

Women's struggles had finally led to some changes in 1963, when the shah granted them the right to vote and stand for elections; he also enforced the Family Protection Law, which limited polygamy and slightly improved divorce and custody laws. But the 1979 revolution reversed those laws immediately, with the exception of women's newfound right to vote and stand for public office. Women retained some hard-won rights but lost many others in the revolution—while also losing many of their traditional protections and privileges. In 1980, women in senior positions were horrified when the regime arrested the first female education minister under the shah, Farrokhroo Parsa, put her in a bag, and executed her.

Many secular women lost their jobs and left the country after the revolution, but many others stayed and continued the fight—among them a trio of secular women who would inspire young Iranian feminists like Hashemi and me. "The Three Musketeers" was the name given to these three secular feminists, who remained active after the revolution and went on to play a vital role in sustaining and expanding the Iranian women's rights movement under the conservative, repressive Islamic regime.

One of the Three Musketeers is Shirin Ebadi, a petite, rotund lawyer who would eventually win the Nobel Peace Prize in 2003 for her human rights activism. Ebadi was a judge before the revolution, but shortly after taking power the Islamic regime demoted her to an administrative position, charging that women were too emotional to adjudicate objectively. Ebadi quit and founded a law practice in the basement of her apartment building, where she fought against discriminatory laws. The daughter of a lawyer, Ebadi is a tremendously strong-willed woman and took cases that no other lawyer dared to accept. I got to know her well when I spent a few months translating her book, *History and Documentation of Human Rights in Iran*, from Persian into English.

Mehrangiz Kar is the second Musketeer. Also a lawyer and a writer, Kar got her law license just a few months before the revolution, after which she donned a chador and worked pro bono to learn the nuts and bolts of the new laws. The first day she entered the courthouse, the sisters at the entrance scrutinized her outfit for a while and then declared that she smelled of perfume. "Stand outside for ten minutes and perhaps the smell will evaporate," they ordered her. On another day, a judge in a clerical robe and turban spotted Kar whispering to her male client in his courtroom. Some conservatives demanded that women not speak to men who weren't their brothers, husbands, or fathers, and the judge exploded at Kar for her transgression. "How dare you speak to a strange man in my court," he yelled. "Get the hell out or I'll have you kicked out." She resigned as the man's lawyer but continued her work on behalf of other clients. Her subsequent victories in Islamic courts would make her the most popular lawyer among defendants on death row.

The third pioneering activist is Shahla Lahiji. A publisher, she publishes books by women and about women. If Ebadi and Kar are violins, Lahiji is a bow. Without her, no one would be able to hear the two other women. It was Lahiji who published their books and gave them a voice. Standing over six feet tall, she cuts a distinctive figure in Iran's literary and political circles.

For decades religious and secular women in Iran had been sharply divided, but as the revolution receded in the 1990s, their differences shrank. Religious women had long viewed Sharia as sacred, but when it became the law of the land after the revolution, it slowly became demystified. Religious women found it harsh, especially to members of their sex. By the early 1990s, as education levels among religious women increased, the gap between them and secular women diminished further. Both groups demanded respect for women in family and in society—and sometimes even fell back on Islam itself to further their mutual goals.

Lower fertility rates in the 1990s also helped narrow the gap between secular and traditional women. Government measures to encourage people to have fewer children, providing free vasectomies and birth control, led to a decline in the number of children in villages and cities. Families became smaller after the number of births per mother dropped from seven to two over a period of fifteen years. As mothers became more educated, they invested in human capital, raising children who benefited from free education from elementary school to university.

Sherkat used religion, the same tool that had empowered her, to promote greater rights for women. She, Hashemi, and other religious women travelled to Qom, knocking on senior clerics' doors and asking them to reread the Islamic law in favor of women. After all, Shiite Islam favors change according to the needs of the times. Such lobbying campaigns occasionally proved successful. One senior cleric, Yousef Sanei, even decreed that the value of a woman's life should be equal to that of a man's life. He reasoned that in the old days women hadn't contributed to household economies as much as they did in the present, and so their modern worth should be raised accordingly.

The regime resisted the demands of these and like-minded women for several reasons. Women had become the walking symbols of the Islamic revolution in their headscarves and manteaux, and what would be left of the revolution if its symbols challenged it? Giving in to their demands would also show that the regime was willing to compromise, and both Ayatollah Khomeini and his successor, Khamenei, saw compromise as a sign of weakness. Deeper factors were also at play. A chauvinistic culture persisted in Iran—a culture that referred to women as *namous* ("honor") and required men to shield their *namous*. In practice, this meant holding women back from full participation in society, keeping them within the confines of the household and not delegating any responsibility to them other than simple chores.

But human events sometimes undermined these long-standing cultural and institutional barriers to women's rights. The story of a nine-year-old girl named Arian Golshani, for instance, served to chip away at custody laws in Iran. One evening in late 1997, Arian's battered body arrived at the hospital. Arian's father, her stepbrother, and her stepmother had been torturing her for months and finally had beaten her into a coma. The doctors found old fractures and burns all over her body; the latter were even on her scalp and around her genitals. Despite her father's addiction to opium, he had retained custody of Arian and her younger brother; according to Iranian law at the time, girls belonged to their father after the age of seven and boys after the age of two.

It was this law, as much as her family's cruelty, that became the subject of international controversy after Arian died of her injuries two days later. *Zanan* wrote story after story about the case, while Ebadi represented Arian's mother in court. She claimed that she'd appealed to a judge to look at her children's bruised bodies, but he had refused to see them, saying that he would have no power to rule against the law.

Arian's story shocked the nation, but it took several years of campaigning for feminists to secure the legal reform that would prevent tragedies like hers from happening again. Hashemi brought the case before Parliament. *Zanan* published works by female Muslim legal scholars, as well as arguments by secular activists like Ebadi and Kar. None of the women dropped the subject until a watchdog agency called the Guardian Council—a body made up of six clerics and six lawyers who examine Parliament's laws to make sure they don't violate the constitution or Sharia—signed off on an amendment to Iranian custody law in 2002. According to the amendment, a mother can now keep both girls and boys until the age of seven, and keep custody of her children if she can prove that the father is unfit to care for them.

Cases like Arian's revealed just how great an influence *Zanan* had in Iranian society. Newspaper stands carried huge stacks of the magazine, and old issues were scattered around hospitals and doctors' waiting rooms. The magazine created a truly national Iranian feminist movement and fostered a countrywide dialogue about women's issues in the 1990s, and by early in the next decade Iran would experience an outpouring of novels and movies about women. The magazine and Sherkat, its founder, were testaments to the fact that the Islamic regime had changed Iranian women in much more profound ways than had the secular regime of the shah.

Much of this development came down to simple economics. Even though the country had experienced steady economic growth from the mid-1950s to the mid-1970s because of oil revenues generated by the shah's economic policies, traditional women had gained relatively little from these improvements, and most remained relegated to the domestic sphere or relatively menial jobs like housekeeping or work in the country's carpet or agriculture industries. Only after the revolution, when the majority of the population agreed to send off their daughters and wives to study and work in what they believed was a religious society, did women gain access to the same economic opportunities and benefits enjoyed by Iranian men. Young women attended school instead of becoming service workers or manual laborers. And as women became more educated, more and more of them qualified for jobs in modern, urban sectors of the country's economy. Literacy rates among young rural women between the ages of fifteen to nineteen rose from 19 percent before the revolution to 86 percent in 1996.

Technology accelerated these changes. Starting in the mid-1990s, satellite TV and the Internet exposed Iranian women to new cultures, broadening their minds and raising their expectations for their own lives. Perhaps unsurprisingly, Parliament banned satellite TV in 1994, but the aluminum dishes continued to mushroom on rooftops, streaming the outside world into Iranians' living rooms and shaping the attitudes and opinions of many Iranians, men and women alike.

Iran's societal transformation was not without its contradictions, and nowhere was this clearer than in the relationships between men and women. As the Iranian king had learned in the late nineteenth century, marriage offered women a unique opportunity to level an uneven playing field. I had come to understand the very same thing as my relationship with a young Iranian man had deepened and become more serious over the course of the early 1990s.

I'd met Babak Pasha in 1991, right after he returned to Iran from San Diego, California, where he had lived for eleven years after fleeing the war. An only child, he had returned to help run his father's business. Our first date was an evening picnic at the top of a hill, the city stretched out beneath us, the lights twinkling as far as Ayatollah Khomeini's shrine. It was perfectly romantic—that is, until the realities of Iranian life intruded on our bliss.

We had just bitten into our sandwiches when a white SUV lurched to a stop in front of us and three Basij members leaped out. "You bastard," howled one of them at Babak. "How dare you bring a woman up here?"

Babak's face, which I thought looked like Robert Downey Jr.'s, turned pale. Before I could get a chance to offer the small lie I had planned for just such an eventuality—*Oh we are in a temporary marriage, and are getting married on the next Islamic holiday*—Babak apologized and said that we were on a date. Having lived in a free country, lying hadn't become engrained in his character the way it had become a self-protection impulse in me.

It was the wrong answer. The men drove us to a detention center, where our parents came and fetched us with their property deeds as collateral so that we would show up at court a few days later. On the day of our trial, my father testified that we were getting married—an uncommon show of support from an Iranian father whose daughter was dating. Only his intervention allowed Babak and me to escape a sentence of sixty lashes each.

Lying provided Babak and me with brief periods of liberation, but after a while the lies became frustrating and dehumanizing. We longed for normalcy in our romantic lives, but if we weren't married, we couldn't travel or live together. Even when we were driving together, we often had to sneak into side streets to avoid the morality police.

The trouble was that our generation was deeply ambivalent about marriage. Women were beginning to rethink their relationships with men. Some of us were daughters of mothers already empowered under the shah; others who were coming of age were daughters of women empowered under the Islamic regime. Faced with an increasing number of empowered women, young men were postponing marriage, too; most of them simply had no idea how to deal with the stronger women of our generation.

So I did what many other Iranian women had taken to doing in their romantic relationships: I took matters into my own hands. After we had been dating for five years, I proposed to Babak. He accepted.

Large, extravagant weddings are common in Iran, but Babak and I decided to have a small ceremony, although we planned to embrace all the celebratory traditions. I wanted to wear a dreamy off-white wedding dress and to be married sitting at the *Sofre-yeh Aghd*, an elaborate wedding spread that was a Zoroastrian tradition observed throughout the country. On an embroidered fabric is placed a large mirror—the mirror of fate—with lit candlesticks on its sides. The spread is decorated with plates of painted eggs (a symbol of fertility), coins (a symbol of wealth), and honey, herbs, rice, and bread (symbols of growth and prosperity).

On our wedding day we sat at the *Sofre-yeh Aghd* while our family and friends stood behind us, holding a sheer cloth over our heads as someone rubbed two cones of sugar together over the fabric. A cleric, the man who had also performed my in-laws' wedding ceremony, solemnized our union with the marriage verse from the Koran.

I was glad to have this ancient custom be a part of our wedding, but Babak and I both abhorred the financial traditions that often went hand in hand with it. Before many Iranian weddings, the couple's parents, or sometimes the elders of their families, gather and negotiate a dowry that the bride brings to her husband's home, as well as *mehrieh*, the money or property that the groom vows to pay the bride, and *shir-*

baha, an amount that he pays to the bride's mother for having raised her. The bigger the numbers, the higher the value of the bride—so naturally, most women asked for *mehrieh* of hundreds or even thousands of gold coins. Newspapers reported stories about families who borrowed money at astronomical interest rates or even sold one of their members' kidneys in order to afford a better dowry. A large number of young men landed in prison every year because they couldn't afford the colossal amounts they'd vowed upon marriage to pay as *mehrieh*. One man was jailed after he fell out of love with his wife and she demanded what once had seemed like a modest *mehrieh*: four pounds of fly wings. One newspaper jeered that he'd need to hunt flies for the rest of his life.

To be sure, there was a practical reason for absurd customs like these: because the law gave men the right to engage in polygamy, divorce their wives, and retain custody rights, women's families often felt the need to tie young couples together with financial obligations. But I was a progressive, working woman, and I had no intention of having a price tag slapped on my forehead. So I asked Babak to sign an optional twelve-article amendment to the marriage certificate that feminists had managed to add to family law, giving some limited rights to Iranian brides. The amendment allowed women, at the time of divorce, to ask for half of the collective wealth they and their husbands had earned after marriage; it also allowed wives to file for divorce and gave them the means to limit their husbands' ability to marry other women.

Babak understood and supported my request for a prenuptial agreement, and it did nothing to dampen the joy of our marriage. Our wedding was on a rare misty day in Tehran, after an October shower had washed away the trees' yellowing leaves and a cool breeze danced restlessly in the air. We'd picked the date carefully; it was right after summer's blistering heat and before winter's freezing cold.

I let the wind caress my skin and play with my hair. I had refused to wear a headscarf and manteau on my wedding day on the street. In retrospect, my insistence was petty, but I was by no means the only woman in Iran who defied this rule on my wedding day—and for some strange reason, the regime looks the other way on this one occasion. It was the first time in my adult life that I'd appeared in public without covering my hair, and would prove to be the only time I would ever do so in Iran.

CHAPTER SEVENTEEN

REFORM

I voted for the first time in my life on May 23, 1997, at the age of twenty-six. I had gone to a polling station with Scott McLeod of *Time* magazine to cover the presidential elections but took advantage of being there to cast a ballot myself.

After waiting in line with Scott by my side, I took out my birth certificate—a red jacketed booklet like a passport—and handed it to an election official to get a ballot in return. I wrote "Mohammad Khatami" in my clearest handwriting, folded the ballot, and dropped it in a large white box.

The Islamic Republic has long boasted that it is a democracy and derives its legitimacy from the vote of the people. It holds separate elections for Parliament and president at regular four-year intervals. At that time, Iranians could vote starting at age fifteen, and elections are always on a Friday, the weekend day, so that more people can go to the polls. Still, this being Iran, there are limits to what is allowed in these ostensibly free elections. For instance, not everyone who wants can run in the elections; the regime vets each candidate and bars the majority from participating.

After we walked out of the polling station, I called my sister on my cell phone. "Goli," I said. "Hurry. The polling stations are starting to get busy. You may end up having to wait in line."

My sister replied that she was waiting for my father to get ready. "I don't think he'll vote if I don't take him with me," she told me.

I hung up and called my mother. An early riser, she'd already voted. It was the first time she—as well as my father—had voted since the 1979 referendum that Ayatollah Khomeini held to determine the shape of the post-revolution government. He had given voters the option of choosing "yes" or "no" to the question of whether Iran should have an Islamic republic, explaining that the difference between it and a republic was that there was no tyranny in an Islamic republic. My parents were among a few of their friends who had voted no. Ayatollah Khomeini's regime claimed over 99 percent of the country voted yes. Years later, however, former officials would acknowledge that the regime had tampered with the votes.

That day, Scott and I drove around Tehran to check the polling stations. Lines had begun appearing by eleven AM. Young and old, women in chador or in headscarves that revealed their hair, all waited, clasping their birth certificates. I had never seen such crowds.

To get a sense of how people were voting, we stood outside the stations to conduct exit interviews. Most people told us that they were first-time voters and were voting for Khatami, just as I had. The cleric whom *Zanan* had quoted as demanding that Iranian universities increase their rosters of female faculty, Khatami combined a respectable religious background with outspoken progressivism that made him seem to many like the most electable of all the candidates on the ballot.

Around noon, I called Babak to urge him to vote. "I'm keeping my birth certificate clean," he said. People who disliked the regime as much as he did took pride in not voting. By going to the polls, they argued, that would only be endorsing the regime. I tried to persuade him that this time was different, but he didn't budge.

Babak and his parents, like many other Iranians, had adopted a kind of political nihilism after the revolution. I had tried to persuade Babak's parents to vote, but they looked at me with mocking smiles, as if I were a fool. His parents had initially supported the revolution and had even backed Ayatollah Khomeini until he returned and launched a wave of violence. Since then, they'd tried to stay out of politics.

Shahin, Babak's mother, had never fully recovered from the scars of the revolution. She had attended university in the 1960s, even though her father and brother had opposed her pursuit of a higher education.

Her father had married off her older sister in an arranged marriage before she could even finish high school. Shahin had married her cousin and earned her master's degree in psychology. Then she taught psychology at a college. But the Islamic regime demoted her, as it did many other women. At the age of thirty-six, Shahin was assigned to teach Persian literature at a remote high school two hours outside of Tehran. She taught for a few more years, always hiding under a heavy black headscarf and manteau to avoid further humiliation. The revolution had robbed her of her lifelong accomplishments. Gradually, the commute and the constant intimidation at work wore her down. She lost her passion for teaching and, broken and depressed, applied for early retirement. Her arched eyebrows and high cheeks began to sag. Once full of hope and aspiration, she was now a shell of her former self. Babak never forgave the revolution for taking his youthful mother away.

Babak's parents had lost their faith in the Islamic Republic, but Khatami had stirred hope among many other people. A philosopher by training, he was neither corrupt, like most Iranian officials, nor part of the shadowy violent network that had dominated the country during the early years of the revolution, as a number of senior clerics had been. He had, however, played a role in the revolution itself, and for two years in the late 1970s he had led the Islamic Center in Hamburg, a mosque founded in Germany by Iranian émigrés in the 1950s and an institution that became a rallying point for theological opponents of the shah in the 1970s. In 1980 he returned to Iran and served as a member of Parliament. Later he became minister of culture but resigned in protest of what he considered to be a repressive cultural environment in the country. For five years he headed the National Library, where he authored two books and refined his political ideas. A large group of religious intellectuals backed him and called him a reformer.

As a politician and public intellectual, Khatami had introduced a new strain of political thought into the public discourse without challenging Khamenei directly. He argued that the constitution, not the whims of individuals, should be the foundation of the state. He criticized the regime's religious ideology, being quoted in *Zanan*, "It is not right to confine religion within dark and tight boundaries and exclude a majority of citizens, including thinkers and intellectuals." His campaign slogans were "The rule of law" and "Iran, for all Iranians," and he went as far as inviting Iranians in exile to return to the country. "They must not be afraid because of their political views," he said of these dissidents. "They should know that we have laws in this country."

Khatami even adopted a respectful rhetoric toward the West—something that was unheard of in a political environment in which opposition to America and its allies had long been taken for granted. "The West has a large and unique civilization that is spreading," he said. "We must not be intimidated by it, nor should we remain passive. We need to understand it and connect with its collective culture and values. Understanding and studying the West has always been important to me."

Such pronouncements had raised hopes that Khatami would be able to restore Iran's lost respect in the international community. In April 1997, just a few weeks before the election, a German court had issued an international arrest warrant for Iran's intelligence minister, Ali Fallahian. According to the court, Fallahian was behind the 1993 assassination of Iranian Kurdish leaders living in Berlin. Iran's gunmen had opened fire on the activists at a restaurant called Mykonos. The case became known as the Mykonos Incident and turned into an international sensation. The German judge also implicated Khamenei and Rafsanjani in the killings. Several European countries recalled their ambassadors from Iran in protest. By the eve of the election, the Iranian people were more eager than ever to shed such infamy—a sentiment that surely drove support for Khatami, with his apparent friendliness toward the West.

Khatami's differences extended to his appearance and dress. When he spoke in his eloquent Persian, you could almost see his brain whirring behind his eyes. His neatly wrapped black turban indicated that he was a descendant of the Prophet Muhammad, but unlike other clerics who mumbled the Koran in their speeches, he quoted philosophers from Plato to Jean-Jacques Rousseau. His grey beard was slightly brown above and on the sides of his mouth, as though he dyed it regularly. While other clerics shuffled around in *nalein*, clerical slippers, Khatami wore polished dress shoes.

Khatami's rival was the establishment candidate, Ali Akbar Nateq-Nouri, Speaker of Parliament, whose real votes in parliamentary elections had been less than those of Faezeh Hashemi's votes. During his campaign Nateq-Nouri kept repeating the old themes of the revolution, such as animosity toward the West and the need to build a chaste society in Iran. His chances of winning women's votes had melted fast after he told *Zanan* magazine that women's most important endeavor was their struggle as homemakers. Still, Nateq-Nouri was popular among certain subsets of traditional Iranians and officials close to Khamenei. Their public support for him led to speculations that Khamenei himself favored Nateq-Nouri too.

Many people believed that the regime would rig the votes to get Nateq-Nouri into office and retain its grip on power. The satirical magazine *Gol Agha* published a cartoon on its cover with the caption "You write 'Khatami,' but they read it 'Nateq,'" suggesting that Khatami's votes would be counted for his rival. Perhaps sensitive to such overt displays of distrust in the regime, Rafsanjani vowed at the Friday prayers a week before the election that his government would honor the will of the Iranian people. His daughter, Hashemi, was campaigning for Khatami too.

As Scott and I drove around Tehran on Election Day, the huge crowds we saw at each polling station suggested a large national turnout. I called local reporters in Iran's other major cities—Isfahan, Shiraz, and Tabriz—and learned the turnout was high there as well. No one had seen such crowds since the revolution.

Eager to find an articulate Nateq-Nouri supporter, we drove to a lush neighborhood in northern Tehran with narrow winding streets. Called Jamaran, this was the area where Ayatollah Khomeini had lived. If Nateq-Nouri supporters would be anywhere, we thought, they would be here.

We stopped at a bakery where the smell of *sangak*, Persian flatbread made in a furnace on hot pebbles, wafted in the air and reminded us of our hunger. As we stood in line to get bread, we noticed a young man in his early twenties walk out of a polling station across the street and stand behind us. I introduced Scott and myself and asked if the young man would tell us whom he had voted for.

"Nateq-Nouri," he said, poker-faced.

Scott's eyes sparkled. "Why?" he asked.

"Because Ayatollah Khamenei wants him to become president," the man said. "I would never defy my leader."

Scott looked relieved. Perhaps our search for a conservative spokesperson had come to an end.

"The Islamic Republic was founded on certain values," the young man continued, "and without those, there will be nothing left. Only Nateq-Nouri can protect the regime."

Scott took notes as I translated, and the young man went on. "Look at that car." He pointed to a woman driving it as Persian dance music blasted from the car's windows. Her hair was raised in a beehive with a scarf sitting loosely on top of it. "Nateq-Nouri would put an end to such obscene appearances."

"So you don't like Khatami's ideas about more political and social freedom?" Scott asked him.

The young man looked at Scott for a few seconds and then burst into laughter. "I got you!" he said, slapping his thighs. "Why on earth would I vote for Nateq? Of course I voted for Khatami."

Scott, always good humored, was amused, and two older men in the line began laughing too. I was surprised at how well the young man had mimicked the party line so often heard on state television—and heartened, too, that these decaying ideas were becoming a source of open mockery. It seemed a sign that Iran's increasingly educated and informed population had learned to think for itself.

It was almost evening when we arrived at Scott's hotel, the Sheraton, which had been renamed Homa after the revolution. Since a man and a woman who are not married to each other cannot accompany one another to hotel rooms in Iran, I waited for Scott in the lobby while he went to fetch his laptop.

While I was waiting near the front desk, Mr. X, the intelligence agent, walked past me and whispered: "Please meet me outside the rug store."

I was surprised that Mr. X wanted to speak to me right there inside the hotel. He had summoned me several other times since I had first met him in 1992, but we always met at the same immigration office. I got the impression that he was the only person responsible for meeting with Iranians working for foreign media outlets, because—as I discovered

after comparing notes with other Iranian reporters and translators—
he questioned all of my colleagues too. During our meetings, Mr. X
continued to warn me that I should not tell anyone about our meetings, which I ignored; for my protection, I spoke to my colleagues about
them. Yet my nervousness and fear of revealing too much information
never disappeared, even after I learned that Mr. X was more interested
in my analysis of the issues I covered rather than the people I interviewed. After all, I had concluded that my phone was tapped and they
already knew whom I was interviewing. But for example, like when I
told him that unemployment had caused the 1995 protest in Islamshahr,
he even nodded in agreement. The regime had accused the exiled opposition of instigating the riot. I spoke in an objective and nonaccusatory
tone and found that Mr. X was eager to hear my opinion even though it
was different from the government line.

I walked to the far end of the lobby, through a hallway, and toward
the carpet shop at the hotel. Mr. X was standing outside the store. In an
urgent voice, he asked, "Who are people voting for?"

"Khatami," I said. "Almost everyone we spoke with voted for him."

His face brightened. "Really?" he asked. For a brief moment, I saw
the human face behind his bureaucratic mask. I had imagined this face;
once, during a telephone conversation with Mr. X, I'd heard the voice of
a little girl in the background. "Daddy, daddy," she had called, reminding me that he had a life too. Mr. X had never revealed his politics, but
if my impression on this day was correct, and my answer had made him
happy, he was not alone in his sympathies. It would turn out that the
majority of the Revolutionary Guards also defied their commanders
and voted for Khatami.

"Thank you," said Mr. X. He walked away, and I returned to the
lobby to find Scott.

The next morning, the news confirmed what our informal polls had
indicated: Khatami was in the lead. In truth, I was surprised. Like everyone else, I had been sure that the regime would not allow the people
to deny its man the presidency. But it seemed that the unimaginable
had occurred. People had stood up to the system and won.

When the final results were in, Khatami had more than twenty-one
million out of some twenty-eight million votes. Some 80 percent had

participated. It couldn't have been more obvious or dramatic just how much the electorate had changed since the previous election, when the turnout had been 50 percent. A host of factors—urbanization, better education, access to information, and women's empowerment—had transformed the Iranian psyche. Iranians had rejected the passivity of the past two decades and decided to redefine their relationship with the state. They had embraced Khatami's notion of strengthening Iranian democracy, and had turned out en masse to prove that, without their consent and participation, the regime lacked legitimacy—that in the Islamic Republic of Iran, both the words "Islamic" and "Republic" had to count.

Rafsanjani had also played an instrumental role in Khatami's victory. His interior ministry had held fair elections, in the process all but ensuring the humiliating loss of the regime's favored candidate. Although Rafsanjani had elevated Khamenei to power less than a decade before, the supreme leader would never forgive him for this betrayal.

Six months later, on November 29, I was having a late lunch with a colleague in the lobby of his hotel. The staff had clustered around a small boxy television, watching Iran's soccer team play against Australia. Soccer draws more fans in Iran than any other sport, and for the past several days everyone in the country had been glued to their radios and televisions as they followed the World Cup qualifying games.

Sitting in the lobby, we watched the hotel staff despair: as the game neared its end, the Iranian team was down a point and seemed as if it would be trounced. But suddenly, in the final seconds, the Iranian team scored a goal, tying the match and qualifying Iran to compete in the World Cup for the first time since the revolution. The hotel lobby exploded, the hotel staff leaping from their seats and screaming joyously.

We finished our lunch, *chelo kabab*, rice with kabab, and stepped out to catch a taxi—but the traffic on the main Valiasr Avenue had completely stopped. People had turned off their engines and poured out from their cars, many of which were decked in Iranian flags. We walked up the street, watching the spectacle. Drivers were honking their horns in celebration, and people were singing and dancing in the street—some of them, even, on the roofs of their cars. Bus roofs had turned into makeshift stages teeming with men and women who flung their arms over their heads and sang with joy. Women took off their headscarves and waved them in the air, defying the long-standing ban on showing their hair. Other rules quickly went by the wayside, as well, including the ban on alcohol consumption by Muslim citizens. One man emerged from his house in his white sleeveless undershirt carrying a gallon of vodka and paper cups.

For five hours, the authorities lost control of the capital. I saw several young men throwing a police officer in the air, the man obviously drunk with joy as he was hoisted aloft over and over again. Nearby, a young man stood atop a police car, waving the Iranian flag. Farther down, in Valiasr Square, a large crowd surrounded several young bearded men, clapping and chanting in a singsong tone, "Basij must dance! Basij must dance!" Newspapers reported that the revelry was repeated all over the country.

The traffic never moved that afternoon, and I could not go home. I stayed out on Valiasr Avenue, watching the outburst of energy, and then walked to my father's home, which was in the neighborhood, and waited until the traffic began to disperse in the evening and Babak could come and pick me up.

But the celebrations—and the transgressions that flowed out of them—weren't over. A week later, thousands of women broke through a police barricade to enter Azadi stadium and welcome the soccer team back to Iran—thereby defying another ban that had barred women from going to stadiums since the revolution. I went inside with the throngs of women and watched while they cheered and screamed as the soccer players entered the field.

The players returned home as heroes, and not just because they had made it into the World Cup. Their victory—along with Khatami's election—had made Iranians feel that they were once again a part of the international community, and had imbued many Iranians with a sense of national pride that they never thought they would feel again. Overnight, soccer became a potent political vehicle, not just because it unified Iranians but also because it justified many demonstrations of personal freedom that would have been speedily quashed under normal circumstances.

The sheer size of the outpouring was likely all that prevented the government from cracking down on these infractions and restoring order. The celebrations were massive, involving some 60 percent of the population under the age of thirty. Suddenly, all of the nation's soccer fans—many of whom had previously had nothing else in common— had turned into a force for change. All they wanted was to celebrate, but in so doing they effectively reestablished a culture of joy in public—a practice that the Islamic Republic had denied them.

Iran's World Cup qualification marked an unlikely turning point for the country's civil society. From then on, whether their team won or lost, tens of thousands of people took to the streets to celebrate its performance. It was as if their ability simply to come together in such massive numbers gave them confidence. At times the regime tolerated them, and at other times its forces clashed with them. But whatever the outcome, one thing was clear: a battle of sorts had begun. There would be no turning back.

CHAPTER EIGHTEEN

THE REGIME STRIKES BACK

At first, Khatami kept his promise of reforming the system. After assuming the presidency on August 2, 1997, he appointed two liberal politicians to lead Iran's key ministries, the Interior Ministry and the Ministry of Culture and Islamic Guidance. Both men had once been hard-liners but had become more moderate as the revolution receded, and they would play a vital role in reforming Iranian politics during the Khatami years.

The new interior minister, Abdullah Nouri, had been a trusted ally of Ayatollah Khomeini in the early days of the revolution. As a sign of how much his thinking had changed since that time, his first step as Khatami's minister was to issue permits for demonstrations, implementing a constitutional right that the regime had forbidden.

The culture minister, Ataollah Mohajerani, was a liberal intellectual who helped to loosen Iran's rigid restrictions on speech and media. Mohajerani favored a free press, and many activists became journalists as they openly discussed reforming the Islamic Republic in dozens of new publications. Mohajerani also lifted the ban on pop music, held concerts, and encouraged filmmakers and writers to produce more work. Filmmakers made movies about social and political repression, and these films attracted huge audiences. A comedy called *Marmoulack* (*Lizard*) became a box office success; it depicts a thief escaping from prison in a clerical robe. People liked the fake cleric because, unlike regime clerics, he praised beauty, love, and Western culture.

But Khamenei felt threatened by Khatami's reform agenda. Khamenei's job as supreme leader was to safeguard the revolution, and he feared that giving even an inch in this respect could pose a threat to his rule. Like Ayatollah Khomeini, he viewed compromise as a sign of weakness, and so he fiercely contested any attempts at reform. First, as commander in chief, he refused to hand over control of the security forces to Nouri—a common transfer of power in the past, but one that Khamenei withheld this time. Activists began holding legal demonstrations, but security forces attacked these gatherings and broke them up. Then Khamenei used the judiciary, whose head he had appointed, to shut down publications that crossed him and to jail reporters who challenged him.

In November 1998, as this power struggle raged on, a series of murders shocked the nation. The bodies of Dariush Forouhar and his wife, Parvaneh Eskandari, both dissidents the regime had long tolerated, were found in their Tehran home. Forouhar had been a member of the Religious-Nationalist Party, which Ayatollah Khomeini had alienated after the revolution. He was stabbed to death behind his desk. Parvaneh's body lay on their bed; she had also been stabbed. They had treated their would-be assailants as guests. Plates of fruits and pastry were still on the table when police found their bodies.

A week after the couple's murder, Mohammad Mokhtari, a writer, left his home on December 3 to buy groceries and never returned. It took the police a week to identify his body, which had been found the next day near a cement factory in the suburbs of Tehran. That same day, Jafar Pouyandeh, a translator, went missing. He had last been seen in downtown Tehran on December 8, screaming for help as two hefty men grabbed him and shoved him into a car. His body was found a week later.

Newspapers called the killings "chain murders," because they seemed to be linked to one another. Pouyandeh and Mokhtari had not been dissidents, nor did they even have much of a following. Still, their murders appeared to be politically motivated. People speculated that only someone linked to the regime would kill people so brazenly, while newspapers hinted that the plot was aimed at dislodging Khatami by incriminating his government. Everybody wondered whether the killers would be caught, and when—and where—the chain would end.

Around this time, my apartment went under surveillance. It wasn't the only sign that I was on the government's bad side. I was working full time for the *New York Times* now as its stringer in Tehran. But while I was the only Tehran-based journalist for this renowned international publication, Ershad, the bureau responsible for dealing with foreign media at the Culture Ministry, refused to give me the necessary credentials.

The government had already attempted to keep me from doing my job—and now, with the surveillance, I suspected that the regime wanted to intimidate me as well. Three cars, each with two men inside, staked out our house in shifts. They blocked our driveway, and we had to ask them to move their car every time we needed to get in or out of the garage. They took notes when they saw me, as if to make it clear that I was the reason they were there. They had walkie-talkies, which I took as proof that they were government forces, since no one else was allowed to use the devices.

The men terrified me to the point that I pleaded to Shirin Ebadi, the human rights lawyer who would later win the Nobel Peace Prize, for help. But she told me that there was little she could do. She herself had received death threats, and I already knew that her name was on the "death list"—an ominous list of eighty dissidents and public figures (including the four victims of the chain murders) that I had received via fax, as had many other journalists. Many activists, she said, had locked themselves in their homes, feeling vulnerable and helpless. Along with fifty other intellectuals, Ebadi had written a letter to Khatami, appealing to him to use his power as president to find the murderers. She advised me to carry my cell phone with me wherever I went and to avoid going out alone.

It's unclear whether or not Ebadi's letter had any effect on Khatami, but the murders were aimed at signaling his inability to run the country and in some ways made Khatami determined to end such lawless behaviors. A few weeks later, Khatami's government issued a statement announcing that the culprits were a "rogue group" at the Intelligence Ministry. Four people were arrested, and the intelligence minister, who had been handpicked by Khamenei, resigned. Investigative journalists would soon claim that the group had killed more than eighty people over the years, including Ahmad Khomeini, Ayatollah Khomeini's son. They used a variety of means such as car crashes, shootings, staged robberies, and injection of potassium to stimulate a heart attack. Although poisoned opium wasn't named as one of their tools, Nessa's suspicions did appear to have been vindicated. Reporters wrote articles and books to detail the killers' crimes, revealing that the victims ranged from dissidents to unknown figures such as a flight attendant and, in one instance, an elderly religious woman.

Exposing the regime's brutality was an accomplishment for Khatami but an embarrassment for the regime. Khatami's revelations confirmed widespread speculation that the regime had been eliminating its opponents, and led many people to suspect that there was more than just a "rogue group" behind the killings—suspicions that were only reinforced when Saeed Emami, the ring leader behind the murders, died in prison under mysterious conditions. He had swallowed hair removal cream, although it was unclear whether he had committed suicide or was forced to swallow it. Even after his death, it seemed likely that the real perpetrators of the killings remained at large, and no one could be sure if the violence had ended. The heavy air of horror in society continued to linger. It was clear that Khatami could name no one else beyond the four agents who had been arrested.

The line dividing the good guys from the bad remained blurred—so when Mr. X summoned me to a new location in December, I panicked. "It will be easier for you if we meet closer to your home," he had explained over the phone. My knees shook when I arrived at the new rendezvous point and found it to be at an apartment building, on a quiet dead-end alley, where the units were rented for short stays. The concierge handed me a key and instructed me to wait inside an apartment.

I searched the two-bedroom apartment in a panic. I lifted the bed skirt of a queen-size bed and pushed back the shower curtain in the bathroom. The place smelled stale, dusty, and airless. I went into the kitchen and opened the drawers. A kettle was on the stove. In one of the drawers, I found a small knife with a yellow rubber handle. Feeling utterly defenseless, I dropped it in my manteau pocket.

I went back into the living room, which was furnished with a sofa and four brown matching armchairs set around a television. Pouyandeh and Mokhtari, I knew, had been strangled with ropes thrown around their necks, so I pushed one armchair against the wall and sat down right before Mr. X turned his key and opened the door.

The second I saw him, I let go of the knife in my pocket, and I ended up taking it home with me. He and his buddy were both hidden behind boxes of fruit and pastry, as though they were planning to have a feast, not looking like murderers at all. I would learn later that Mr. X would summon another colleague to that place, and she would feel as terrified as I did that day. But within a half hour she too left the rendez-vous unscathed.

Time passed, but the chain murders remained a source of tremendous controversy in Iran. The regime went after journalists who continued to write about the killings, and also targeted Khatami's close aides. The mayor of Tehran, Gholam-Hussein Karbaschi, who had played an instrumental role during Khatami's election, was jailed on charges of mismanagement and corruption. Nouri, the interior minister who had become increasingly popular, resigned under pressure and began publishing a reformist newspaper, but was soon jailed on charges of insulting religious sanctities. Then Khatami's opponents in Parliament impeached Mohajerani, the culture minister.

The turning point came in July 1999, after the authorities shut down the daily *Salam*. The newspaper had published a letter penned by Emami, the death squad's ring leader, before his arrest and death in prison. Written to the intelligence minister, the letter contained details about the law that had limited the freedom of the Iranian press, and highlighted Emami's influence on and close ties to the intelligence minister—something the minister had vehemently denied.

Student activists staged a demonstration at their dormitory to protest the closure of *Salam*. Later that night, when some of the students were asleep, the Basij and the security forces raided the dormitory. They broke into the rooms, beat the students, pulled women out of their beds by their hair, and tossed several men out of the building's windows. Until four AM, they wrecked the dormitory. When I visited the scene the next day, I found the students' furniture crushed; doors, windows, and bookcases smashed into pieces; mattresses torn down to their metal springs; and some of the rooms burned up. One man, Ezat Ebrahimnejad, was visiting his friends at the dormitory and was killed. Another man was blinded; many more were injured and arrested.

The violence enraged the student community nationwide. Iranian law banned the country's security forces from entering university grounds in the first place, and their brutality was simply beyond the pale. It was clear that the attack was aimed at intimidating the student community, and equally clear that the students would not be cowed so easily.

The Office for Fostering Unity, a pro-reform student body, called for more protests. The Office had been set up by Islamist students to monitor student activities in the early days of the revolution, but its members were elected, and students had since voted reformist activists into the organization's leadership, turning the Office into one of the most powerful wings of Khatami's reform movement. The Office had branches and bureaus at every single university around the country.

I found over a thousand ordinary people outside the closed gates of Tehran University the next day. People had come to show their solidarity with the students. Dozens of shopkeepers had pulled down the shutters of their stores—mostly bookstores—and now stood outside the university. Inside the campus, several hundred students chanted "Death to the Dictator"—a clear reference to Khamenei—in unison with the protestors outside. Their voices echoed in the air. Then they joined each other in singing protest songs from the early days of the revolution.

> My childhood friend, my pal, my companion;
> The nightstick strikes our head, you are my cry and my pain,
> Your name and my name are carved on this blackboard;
> Our bodies are still scarred by the blows.

The Basij and the police, known as the security forces, both controlled by Khamenei, stood off to one side. On a handheld speaker, a policeman began asking people to leave. The protestors sang louder to drown out his voice.

Only your hands and my hands can tear down this wall;
Only you and I can end this pain.

This show of defiance did not go unpunished. Without warning, the security troops and the Basij descended on the crowd assembled outside the university's walls, attacking the singing civilians with clubs and chains. The security forces, distinctive in their olive green uniforms, howled to scare the protestors, but often they raised their clubs without actually bringing them down on anyone. However, the young Basij members, who were always more brutal than their counterparts in the security forces, struck many of the protestors so hard that they fell to the ground, whereupon the security forces dragged them away and locked them inside black cages installed in the backs of pickup trucks nearby. Protestors chanted "Taliban get lost," comparing the Basij to the repressive political movement that was then emerging in neighboring Afghanistan.

As the security forces shot tear gas to disperse the protestors, I ran inside the gated campus. I found my way to the university's mosque, which the students had turned into a makeshift hospital staffed by some medical students. Two men carried in an unconscious woman who had fainted from the intensity of the tear gas. Dozens of other people were bleeding from their heads, arms, and legs. They were in bad shape, but in a sense they were lucky; rumor had it that government forces were snatching injured protestors from hospitals and imprisoning them.

The size of the demonstrations swelled over the coming days, spreading to Enghelab Street outside Tehran University. Students in other cities soon followed Tehran's lead. The unrest forced the merchants in the bazaar—the traditional heart of the economy in any Iranian community—in Tehran and several other cities to close their shops. By the fifth day, the protests had reached eighteen cities. The brutality at the dormitory and the mass arrests that had followed only further enraged the students, and emboldened them to take drastic measures that would have been inconceivable under normal circumstances.

On the sixth day of the demonstrations, a few hundred students in Tehran began marching south toward Khamenei's office. Until then, they had limited their rallies to university neighborhoods in the capital, but the violence of the past five days had obviously pushed them over the edge. Alarmed by the march, the head of the Revolutionary Guards, Rahim Safavi, who also controlled the Basij, called Khatami's office, warning that if the students passed Jomhouri Street, the last intersection before Khamenei's compound, the Revolutionary Guards would fire on them. To heighten the threat, twenty-four senior Revolutionary Guards commanders issued a public letter, declaring that they would intervene to restore order if Khatami failed to do so.

Khatami sent Saeed Hajarian, the reformists' strategist and a member of Tehran's city council, to speak to the students. Hajarian caught up with the students at Jomhouri Street. "At one corner stood the Guards and at the other corner were the students," recalled Hajarian later. "I pleaded with the students in every possible way and finally directed them back to the dormitory." That night, a deputy interior minister slept at the dormitory so as to deter the government security forces from attacking the students again as they slept.

But the students wanted more from Khatami. He had said that the attack was "the price he had to pay for unveiling the truth behind the murders"—and indeed, the pressure seemed to be aimed at undermining Khatami. The students had been the driving force behind his election. In many ways, Khatami had given them the courage to speak up and demand change. But he had remained silent after the demonstrations spread around the country. During the protests, the students had chanted, "Khatami, where are you?" They expected him to side with them and to use this moment to end the lawlessness of the Basij—a militia force that for years had derived its power by creating chaos. In a democracy, the students felt, there was no need for a militia like the Basij, whose members had become known as "plainclothesmen"—a description that revealed their murky roots and intentions. Seven people had been killed, hundreds injured, and over a thousand people jailed.

On the evening of July 13, the same evening that the deputy interior minister stayed at the dormitory, state TV read a statement by Khatami in which he distanced himself from the students. The statement said the demonstrators were "attacking the foundations of the regime." I froze in front of the screen, incapable of understanding his decision.

Khatami had twenty-one million votes behind him—a number that no one had garnered in the history of the Islamic Republic. The regime couldn't kill millions of its own people. Had he stood up for the rights of the students and resisted the internal pressure that Khamenei and other elements of the regime were putting on him, the Iranian people would have backed him. Why did he give in so easily?

The students, understandably, felt betrayed; their leader had abandoned them, and without his support they were more vulnerable than ever. As student activists were arrested en masse and tortured, the opposition's momentum evaporated. In its place, disillusionment spread.

The events of the summer of 1999 were vital to the reform movement in one way: they revealed that the constitution was a major obstacle to democracy. This was the same constitution that Khatami had repeatedly called the pillar of democracy and the one that Rafsanjani had helped redraft after Khomeini's death. While this version of the constitution defined the authority of the supreme leader, it gave too much power to him. Khamenei alone controlled the Revolutionary Guards and the Basij, as well as the state media and the Guardian Council—the body that vetted election candidates and bills passed by Parliament. Even the Council of Experts, which theoretically had the power to choose a new supreme leader, seemed irrelevant because its candidates were first screened by the Guardian Council. Khamenei had final approval over appointments to other key positions, such as the ministers of intelligence, foreign affairs, interior, and defense. He appointed the head of the judicial branch, the body that administers and enforces the laws, as well as members of an arbiter body, the Expediency Council. No one could challenge Khamenei under the current constitution. He'd become more powerful than Ayatollah Khomeini had been.

Reza Khatami, the president's brother, told me that summer that Khatami had never expected to win the presidency in 1997. Like everyone else, he'd thought that Nateq-Nouri would be elected. He'd only intended to use his candidacy as a platform to garner a big audience for his newly launched magazine, *Aeen*. In the magazine, he was planning to introduce new, progressive political ideas. "He wasn't prepared for the responsibility that was almost dropped on his shoulders," his brother told me.

When he was in office, Khatami came under enormous pressure as a result of a combination of factors: the gruesome murders of dissidents, the elimination of his allies, and the daily crackdown against his supporters. The pressure would have paralyzed even the most iron-willed and well-planned administration. And Khatami's government, as his brother made clear during our conversation, was certainly not that.

According to Khatami's brother, the president's mother, his siblings, and even his nieces and nephews accused him of showing weakness. To be sure, he knew that his popularity had plunged; he knew what people wanted and knew exactly what was going on in society. "But he says that we have no other choice," the younger Khatami said. "For now, our thoughts are the most lethal weapon."

I personally saw Khatami as a philosopher, not a politician. His goal in July 1999 was to avoid further bloodshed. Khatami feared that the unrest would unleash more violence, and he was determined to avoid that possibility, even if it meant appearing to betray his ideals and those of his supporters. Several months before the attack on the dormitory, in response to the students who criticized the slow pace of reform, he said, "I never promised to eliminate your opponents. In a civil society, people are entitled to their beliefs. If there is going to be change, people should bring it. I am still loyal to the principles I raised about tolerance, freedom, and social justice. But they need to become norms in society. I am not going to resort to violence to establish them. If anyone opposes the constitution, even that can change."

Despite his weakness, Khatami remains a progressive and influential figure in Iranian history. He laid the groundwork for a buildup of moderation in the nation's politics. In the years following his ostensible betrayal of the 1999 student protest movement, his rhetoric about democracy and popular will has become mainstream, and many other clerics and politicians have adopted his stance on reform. But none of this changes the fact that, at the time, his compromises were seen as a concession to tyranny—by many students, and also by me.

That summer, I got a peek at the flaws of the reform movement and sadly discovered that many of its members weren't fully committed to its promise of inclusiveness. Khatami had talked about repairing Iran's ties with the West, and many of his followers seemed to genuinely desire more normal relations with the outside world. But when it came to taking practical steps toward mending ties with the international community, Khatami and his government faltered.

Three years had passed since the *New York Times* had introduced me as its reporter on the ground and applied for my press credentials. Ershad had rejected the request on the grounds that Iranian reporters who worked for Iranian state media in the United States were not allowed to work freely. This was true partly because those reporters traveled for unknown reasons on diplomatic passports, and the passports put them at great disadvantage because Iran and the United States did not have diplomatic relations. As for me, without a press card, I could not attend press conferences, cover official events, or even have a byline; any of these routine aspects of professional journalism would allow Iranian authorities to charge me with working illegally.

After Khatami's elections, I had been optimistic that I would finally get my credentials. The new director of Ershad was a reformist bureaucrat named Hossein Nosrat. A short, dark-skinned man with a trimmed beard, he had worked as a foreign correspondent for the state-run IRNA news agency and later served as a press aide to Iran's United Nations mission in New York. He was the darling of foreign reporters. A chain-smoker, Nosrat was on a first-name basis with many well-known American journalists. He watched CNN at his office instead of Iranian channels and considered himself an expert on American politics and media, constantly comparing O. J. Simpson's trial with similar Iranian ones, or the obstacles that the Clinton administration faced with Khatami's setbacks at home. To facilitate working conditions for Western journalists, he made a point of being reachable on his mobile phone around the clock.

But despite his many positive qualities, Nosrat somehow managed to anger many Iranian women who came in contact with him. Even Ershad's female employees rolled their eyes and complained that he was dismissive of them. He refused to speak to a colleague who complained to him that Mr. X had interrogated her in a hotel, where she sat with two male agents in a room with a king-size bed. "I don't want to hear about it," my colleague quoted him as saying. "Come back only if you are capable of settling your issues." When I asked him about my press card, he came up with a new excuse for withholding it. He said that the Intelligence Ministry had not issued a security clearance for me, and that anyway he personally did not approve of a woman being a reporter for the *New York Times*. "The paper needs to nominate a mature man instead of a young woman," he told me, as my face burned with rage.

Nosrat exposed me to a kind of sexism I'd never experienced before. The regime discriminated against women, but it never labeled us less competent than men. Its sexism was often hidden beneath a veneer of religious justifications; it would claim that women were too desirable to be at certain places at certain times, for instance, but not that we were unworthy. We had learned how to fight against such prejudice; I could always persuade senior clerics in Qom, who normally refused to meet with women, to receive me in a chador, for example. Even the regime itself had gone against certain traditions pertaining to the female sex. Officials had, for instance, set up seminary schools to train female clerics for the first time in the history of Shiite Islam. Women started becoming clerics or even *marja*, authorities on the Koran.

The regime, I knew, needed women to spread its ideology—so I was totally unprepared for Nosrat's contemptuousness. Even though he played an important role in improving the country's image in Western media as he dealt with foreigners, perhaps he was unaware how insulting some of us found his remarks. Having lived abroad for many years, he was Western in his head, but his feet were stuck in traditional Iran. He adopted a Western guise when he was in contact with Westerners, but with Iranians he reverted to his own traditional values—values that, as was clear from the ire he managed to incite in his fellow Iranians on a daily basis, were no longer relevant. However, he was not alone; a few other reformers had angered feminists with sexist comments, but in Nosrat I had my first up-close encounter with this particular shortcoming of the reform movement—one of several that ultimately disillusioned many of its supporters.

As Nosrat dashed my hopes for a career in journalism, my husband and I decided to leave the country in August 1999. He was in the process of becoming a Canadian citizen and needed to move there in order for his paperwork to go through. I had applied and been admitted to a master's program in political science at the University of Toronto, and was ready to move on with my life and work.

Little did I know then that Iran would move on too. What I'd seen in the 1990s had only been the infancy of the country's modern civil society. It would grow and mature in the years to come, as ordinary Iranians reaffirmed their commitment to reform the country and secure the freedoms that had been withheld from them for so long.

The king's wives in the 1890s. These women joined hundreds of thousands of angry Iranian smokers in boycotting tobacco, which eventually forced the king to cancel the tobacco concession he had granted to Great Britain. (Golestan Palace Collection)

Reza Shah, the founder of Pahlavi dynasty, and his five children. The British forced Reza Shah from his throne in 1941. His eldest son, the future Mohammad Reza Shah, stands second from left. (Etelaat)

The author in 1978. I wore T-shirts and shorts before the revolution, and was free to swim in the pool at our housing complex. (Author's collection)

After the 1979 revolution the Islamic regime required all schoolgirls to cover their hair with a headscarf. (Author's collection)

Iran's first president after the revolution, Abullhassan Banisadr (forth from left) and Dariush Forhour (third from right) laid wreaths of flowers on Mossadeq's grave after the victory of the revolution. Banisadr fled the country in 1981 after he fell out of favor with Khomeini, and Forouhar was murdered in his Tehran home in 1997. (Etelaat)

Mohammad Mossadeq (seated, right), the former Iranian prime minister and a nationalist whom almost everyone in the country regarded as a patriot. A court sentenced Mossadeq to three years in prison on charges of treason and then exiled him to his village. He died in 1967, perhaps more of a broken heart than old age. (Etelaat)

Supporters of Mohammad Mossadeq and Ayatollah Khomeini staged anti-Shah demonstrations in Mossadeq's hometown, Ahmad Abad, in the years leading to the 1979 revolution. (Etelaat)

The Iranian army helped Britain and the United States orchestrate a coup against the democratically elected government of Prime Minister Mohammad Mossadeq on August 19, 1953. (Etelaat)

Mohammad Reza Pahlavi, known as the Shah, ruled Iran from September 16, 1941, until his overthrow on February 11, 1979. (Etelaat)

Faezeh Hashemi, the daughter of former president Akbar Hashemi Rafsanjani, served as a member of Parliament from 1996 to 2000. An ardent feminist, Hashemi favored more rights for women. In 2011 she went to jail for her activism during the 2009 uprising. (Author's collection)

Iranian women were not only allowed in the driver's seat but also had to change our own flat tires in a country where AAA and similar services do not exist. Here I change a tire with a friend, Pooneh Ghodoosi (right), in the middle of the night on Valiasr Avenue. (Author's collection)

After religious feminists appealed to him, Grand Ayatolloh Yousef Sanei, a pro-reform cleric, issued a ruling saying that the value of a woman's life should be considered equal to that of a man given the modern woman's education and contributions to the household economy. (Author's collection)

The reformist president, Mohammad Khatami, was elected in a landslide in 1997 and served for two terms until 2005. (Hassan Sarbakhshian)

The author at age twenty-one, returning from Shemshak, a ski resort in northern Tehran. (Author's collection)

The regime faced some of the worst demonstrations since the revolution in July 1999, after government forces attacked a student dormitory, killing one man and injuring many others. (Hassan Sarbakhshian)

The regime arrested hundreds of demonstrators during the protests in July 1999. (Hassan Sarbakhshian)

Every year on February 11 the regime celebrates the anniversary of the 1979 revolution. At the government's urging, massive numbers of Iranians participate. Here crowds are assembled in Azadi Square; the Azadi monument (*Azadi* means freedom) is behind them. Pro-democracy protestors staged massive rallies here in 2009. (Author's collection)

Mohsen Kadivar at his Tehran home in 2000, after spending eighteen months in Evin Prison for calling the regime despotic. He is currently an associate professor of Islamic Studies at Duke University. (Author's collection)

Students held demonstrations around the country to stop a death sentence for Hashem Aghajari, a history professor at Tarbiat Modares University. One man is holding a white banner that says, " November 9, 2002 = the Middle Ages," indicating just how archaic many Iranians feel their country's system is. (Hassan Sarbakhshian)

Members of the Office for Consolidating Unity, the student movement that was the backbone of the reform movement, staged a sit-in to protest the mass disqualification of presidential candidates in the run-up to the 2005 election. *From right:* Ali Afshari, Mehdi Aminzadeh, Abdullah Momeni, Majid Haj-babaee, and Javad Razavi. Momeni would be in jail from 2009 to 2014 for his role in post-election protests. (Aminzadeh's collection)

Saeed Mortazavi, a notorious judge, was behind the closure of over a hundred pro-reform publications and the jailing of many reporters and activists. The Canadian government has also accused him of having been involved in the death of Iranian-Canadian photojournalist Zahran Kazemi. (Hassan Sarbakhshian)

Mir-Hussein Moussavi served as prime minister during the 1980s but retreated from politics after Ayatollah Khomeini's death. He ran in the 2009 presidential race, and his supporters believed that he was the true winner of the election. He and his wife, Zahra Rahnavard, have been under house arrest since 2011. (Hassan Sarbakhshian)

Ahmadinejad supporters at a rally in Tehran a few days before the 2009 presidential elections. (Author's collection)

On June 15, 2009, hundreds of thousands of Iranians poured into the streets to protest incumbent President Ahmadinejad allegedly stealing the election. The protests rocked the country for six months as Iranians demanded en masse that the government hold new elections. (Hassan Sarbakhshian)

Chayan's fifth birthday and the last family photo taken at our Tehran home before we boarded a plane, a few weeks later, to begin a life in exile in 2009. (Author's collection)

PART THREE

THE DECADE OF CONFRONTATION

1999–2009

CHAPTER NINETEEN

THE REFORMERS
SPEAK OUT

During a visit to Tehran from Toronto in the summer of 2000, I met with the new Ershad director, Hossein Khoshvaght. He had just replaced Nosrat. I wanted to find out if I should consider going back to journalism in Iran after completing my master's degree, or if I should look for other jobs instead. Would Khoshvaght be more supportive of female professionals than Nosrat—which is to say, would he even countenance the idea that I had a future in Iranian journalism?

A wall-mounted air conditioner was humming in Khoshvaght's L-shaped office as the new director, sitting behind his desk, welcomed me with a warm smile. Khoshvaght was the son of a senior conservative cleric, Azizolah Khoshvaght. Khoshvaght's sister was married to Khamenei's son. But I knew that none of those ties had defined his politics. He was a former journalist and an advocate for freedom of the press.

Still, I was in no mood for pleasantries. Having waited for several years to get credentials, I was extremely frustrated with Ershad, so I immediately began complaining about how I felt Nosrat had discriminated against women. I told Khoshvaght that as a woman, I could do everything that a man could do and even more. I had skied with Rafsanjani's daughter (albeit on segregated slopes), I had been invited to Khatami's mother's home in the city of Yazd, and I had dined with female members of Parliament in their homes. My access to these women was possible only because I was also a woman. The stories about them had presented the human face of Iranians to international readers in the pages of the *New York Times*, and no male reporter could have met them under the conditions I did.

After I finished speaking, a young woman in a bright green manteau brought my file into the office. Paging through it, Khoshvaght said it was unclear who had blocked my press card. All the papers were there, including my security clearance. He promised to get back to me in a few days.

The next day, I got a call from Ershad telling me that my press card had been issued. From that moment on, I began filing stories for the *Times* under my byline for the rest of that visit during the summer of 2000. Through the Internet I had kept abreast of events in Iran. Online activism was generating information and shaping public opinion. Earlier in 2000, Windows software had enabled Persian speakers to type Persian fonts online for the first time (until then Iranians had used the Arabic font, which was slightly different). The number of Persian language weblogs had surged to one hundred thousand, which put Persian as the most common language for blogging in the world after French and English. Discussions that couldn't be published in newspapers appeared online. That year, Montazeri, Ayatollah Khomeini's banished successor, also published his memoir online from his home in Qom, where he had been under house arrest; the document confirmed rumors that Ayatollah Khomeini had ordered the execution of over three thousand political prisoners in 1989. This was the country's worst massacre of the past century—and for the first time, ordinary Iranians could read all about it.

Writing from my home that summer before returning to Toronto, I filed stories about the increasing friction between the reformist forces, led by Khatami, and his opponents, led by Khamenei. Khatami was pushing for reform, meaning more political and social openness, but Khamenei felt threatened by it. The country was divided: the president ran the country, but his opponents controlled the jails and courts. That past winter, reformist politicians, including Khatami's younger brother, had won the majority of the seats in Parliament. Everyone was eager to see which side would prevail. Hope for change was high.

That summer, I paid a visit to Zahra Eshraghi, Ayatollah Khomeini's granddaughter and the wife of Khatami's younger brother. She worked as an advocate for women's rights at the Interior Ministry. This alone was a sign of just how far the country had come since the revolution—but as I found when I met with Eshraghi, that was just the tip of the iceberg.

When I arrived at the ministry, I found the doors to all the other rooms in the long hallway flung open except for Eshraghi's. A hand-written note on her door asked visitors to knock before entering.

I complied, and a woman in a black hood opened the door. I explained that I had an appointment. When she let me inside, I found the thirty-six-year-old Eshraghi unveiled, her blond hair raised in a bun and a pony fall extension attached to the top of her head. She wore a pants suit instead of a manteau, along with high-heeled cowboy boots. Eshraghi offered me a seat on the couch, and as she sat down next to me, the scent of her perfume wafted over me. Before coming up to her office, the Basij sisters at the entrance had scrutinized my clothes, checked if I wore any makeup or perfume, and decided that they disliked my pink manteau. Only after I spread my black scarf over my chest did they let me enter the building. How had Eshraghi managed to get past them in this getup?

Seeing the surprise on my face, she explained that she drove to the ministry in a headscarf, with the chador draped over her shoulders. Only when she approached the ministry did she pull the chador over her head. She took the elevator in the indoor parking area, where the sisters could not see her, and then she took off the chador when she was inside her office.

Eshraghi's disapproval of the chador, which had always been the flag of the revolution, signaled her disapproval of many other revolutionary values. She also loved music and singing, even though her grandfather had banned it for the entire nation. "I have always been under a lot of pressure because of my family," she said. "I could not pursue my passions. Instead of studying music, I studied philosophy. I can never stop wearing the chador entirely because of who I am." Who she was, indeed, was revolutionary royalty: in addition to being the granddaughter of Ayatollah Khomeini, she was also the daughter and daughter-in-law of senior clerics. All three of these men—her grandfather, father, and father-in-law—had passed away, but their shadows still fell over her life.

But these days, Eshraghi said, she was mostly disappointed in her brother-in-law, the president. She blamed him for not acting more courageously. "Reform is crucial for the country," she told me. The revolution had been meant to install a democratic system in Iran. Her grandfather, she said, had never wished for the country to become what it was today. It had been Khalkhali, the chief justice who had presided over the vicious purges after the revolution, who had laid the cornerstone for the violent and repressive regime that had emerged since 1979.

Like Ayatollah Khomeini's other grandchildren, Eshraghi wanted to clear his name by distancing him from the bloodshed of the previous decades. Yet almost everyone in his family had refrained from entering politics, perhaps out of sheer disillusionment. Hassan Khomeini, Ahmad's son, was the only one in the public eye. He was in charge of the mausoleum, but he never interfered in politics. Another grandson, Hossein, became a dissident, traveling to the United States and speaking against the regime—but then returned to Iran and remained quiet. Eshraghi was one of the family's few members who had braved the political arena in Iran.

Eshraghi was living proof that the generation of Iranians who had grown up after the revolution had different aspirations from those of their parents, no matter whose sons or daughters they were. They didn't share the grievances that had turned many of their parents into revolutionaries, but they had grown up with a set of grievances all their own. They, like their parents, knew repression and were shaped by it.

Later that summer, at a student event at Shahid Beheshti University, I saw where the winds of dissent were blowing. The university is located near the notorious Evin prison, where thousands of people had gone to the gallows, and where many of the regime's critics are still incarcerated. Built forty years earlier, Evin is isolated by a sprawling wall that disappears into the distance—a testimony that Iranians' struggle for freedom has not ended yet.

That day, a Sunday in August, students at the university were celebrating the release of dissident cleric Mohsen Kadivar, who had served eighteen months in Evin for calling the regime's rule a form of religious despotism. Relying on Shiite sources of scholarship, Kadivar argued in one of his nine books, *Theories of State Based on Divine-Popular Legitimacy*, that *velayat faqih*, the position of supreme leader, is neither religious nor rational in Shiite Islam. He called the position "a minor jurisprudential hypothesis," an insulting reference to Khamenei, who aspired to be the leader of Shiite Muslims around the world.

When I arrived at the university, the hallway was crowded with young men and women who could only hear what was happening in the auditorium through the speaker system in the hall. I managed to get inside the auditorium after a student activist fetched me and snuck me through a back door. Several hundred students had filled the seats, and many crammed together for space on the stairs. I stood near the front row, where Kadivar, age forty-one, sat in his white turban and black cloak.

The students were clapping and cheering. Whereas they had once chanted, "*Allah Akbar*," cheering had become the new language of protest. When the speaker Hashem Aghajari took the podium, the students rocked the auditorium with applause and chants of "Freedom of thought must be liberated." Young women in tight manteaux waved their fists in the air and chanted, "All political prisoners must be released."

Aghajari, a war veteran with a thick mustache and large spectacles, limped to the microphone on his artificial leg. He had lost the limb, as well as a brother, in the war. Once an Islamist, Aghajari had also evolved into a moderate man; he was now a history professor.

Addressing the crowd, Aghajari said, "Religion has performed badly when it has gone along with power." Referring to Ayatollah Khamenei's position, he said, "Those who believe *vali faqih* is a kind of divinity on earth, that it cannot be criticized or judged by the law, need to engage in debates with Islamic intellectuals and let the voters choose." The audience roared with applause after every single sentence. "Governments that suppress thinking in the name of religion," he continued, "are neither religious nor humane."

I had heard similar comments voiced in private, and newspapers and bloggers had begun to cautiously float these notions. But now, in the auditorium, it felt as if ideas that had been bottled up for so long had suddenly been released. The students' enthusiasm showed how thirsty they had been for them.

"It is time for the institution of religion to become separated from the institution of government," Aghajari declared. "It is true that religion opiates the masses."

I looked at Kadivar, the black-bearded cleric whose release from prison we were celebrating. He had a fixed smile, his elbows leaning on the armrests as he gazed at Aghajari with an aura of relief. Kadivar had expressed these same ideas about religion and the state in his writings about Khamenei's rule two years earlier, and he must have been heartened to see his argument championed by so many people. Kadivar's ideas, I reflected, had been just like a balloon he had tested by releasing it and seeing if it would remain afloat. A few others had done the same and had landed in prison, like him. But in the time that I had been away and he had been locked up, the sky had become full of balloons just like his. No one knew what direction they would ultimately fly in, but they were innumerable, and more of them were being released every day.

This was a relatively recent development. A few years earlier, religious intellectuals like Soroush and Khatami had started a conversation about a religious democracy. They argued that Islam and democracy could coexist, claiming that Islam by its very nature embraced freedom. Activists seized upon the term "religious democracy" and constantly referred to it as an alternative model of government to the theocracy of the current regime. But no one explained exactly what a religious democracy was, and Khatami himself had proven unable to translate his liberal ideas into concrete policies.

Disillusioned with the idea of a religious democracy, Iran's students were now embracing the call for separation of mosque and state. People were weary of the interference of religion in their lives. They'd moved beyond Khatami and Soroush's stale ideas.

It was clear that summer that the flame of the revolution had completely died. If even a man like Aghajari, who had sacrificed so much in defining the war of Ayatollah Khomeini's regime, was claiming that the regime's mix of religious and political power had turned toxic, who was left to defend it? Khamenei, it seemed, was struggling to shore up a system that felt archaic, even irrelevant. The majority of the population could no longer identify with its values and now wanted to change its basic structure. But this threat, I soon discovered, would make the regime more dangerous than ever before.

CHAPTER TWENTY

NO FEAR OF
AUTHORITY

O ne evening in May 2001, while I was back in Iran on assignment,
I was watching television and saw a student leader I knew. Ali
Afshari had just spent more than nine months in solitary confinement;
he had lost weight since I had seen him a year earlier, speaking passionately at a student rally. Now, at age twenty-eight, he spoke in a forcibly
loud voice as another man questioned him.

"I apologize to the supreme leader," he said, his gaze avoiding the
camera.

"What were your intentions?" the man asked.

"We wanted to cast doubt on the religious government," he said,
referring to the student movement. "We wanted to question Ayatollah Khomeini's views and create tension in society. Ultimately, we were
planning to eliminate the position of the supreme leader."

The next day, newspapers charged that Afshari had made false confessions under duress. It certainly would not have been the first time;
the regime had intimidated many dissidents in front of the camera since
the early days of the revolution, making them confess false crimes and
apologize for them to the nation. After their release, many of these dissidents had admitted that they had only done so under torture.

Afshari's confession, however, served a new purpose. Khatami was
running for a second term, and it was clear that, by humiliating Afshari

on national television, the supreme leader's regime aimed to intimidate the student movement, the backbone of the reform movement that was campaigning for Khatami.

Afshari's friend, Mehdi Aminzadeh, age twenty-four, told me a few days later that he had refused to watch Afshari's confession. The two were members of the pro-reform Office for Fostering Unity. The Office had branches and members at every single university around the country—a nationwide network with an unmatched ability to mobilize young Iranians.

Just a year earlier, the students had used their networks and sent five of their leaders into the 270-seat parliament. Now, emboldened by their victory, they were determined to reelect Khatami. Even though his fellow reformer had been broken before the eyes of millions of people, Aminzadeh resolved to keep up their work. He traveled around the country and urged people to vote for Khatami.

Khatami was running against nine regime candidates. The watchdog Guardian Council had weeded out all pro-democracy hopefuls. Khatami was the only candidate who was calling for more political and social openness. "Society needs freedom like it needs air," he'd said during one of his televised debates a week before the election, seeming to wipe a tear from his cheek when he spoke about the pressures his government had faced during its first term.

The pressures on Khatami had only grown in recent months. In the latest attacks, in March 2001, a member of the Basij had attempted to assassinate Saeed Hajarian, Khatami's advisor and the official who in 1999 had persuaded student demonstrators to avoid further confrontation with the regime. The bullet had struck Hajarian in his neck, leaving him severely disabled; he would never speak or move easily again.

Despite these setbacks, the students urged their fellow Iranians to back Khatami for a second term. Without him, activists could lose the relative freedom of expression they'd enjoyed since 1997, when Khatami was elected. Khatami may not have been perfect, but it was clear that— for the moment, at least—he was the best option available.

In his capacity as president, every Monday Khatami met with Khamenei—the man who had the final word on state matters. The students called these meetings "the strategy of bargaining from above":

Khatami negotiated and reasoned with Khamenei. In the meantime, civil society, including the student movement, needed to put the right pressure on Khamenei *from below* so that he would cave in to Khatami's demands. The students believed that with a second term, Khatami would be able to put reforms on an irreversible course.

Activists like Aminzadeh had a reason to be hopeful—until many of them discovered that the regime didn't take well to pressure. Just a few days before the elections and a few weeks after Afshari's televised confessions, Aminzadeh received a summons. When he showed up in court, he found himself before Saeed Mortazavi, the infamous judge who had shut down nearly one hundred newspapers and jailed dozens of activists. Mortazavi sent Aminzadeh to wait in the hallway; he stood there for five hours.

Finally, Mortazavi summoned Aminzadeh and informed him of a vague charge against him: he had, the judge said, been accused of insulting sanctities in a student publication. Aminzadeh had neither written for the publication nor been involved in it in any other way. The charge, he knew, was merely an excuse to put him away before the elections.

Mortazavi set a bond of fifty million rials, equal to $5,500. Aminzadeh had five other sisters and brothers; his father had a small farming company. Hiring a lawyer to get him out of jail would be a burden on the family. Nevertheless, Aminzadeh asked if he could call a family member to pay the bond.

"No, no," Mortazavi said, Aminzadeh told me later. The judge crossed out a line on the paper in front of him. "We need you to answer some questions immediately. I will increase the bond to a billion rials. You are going to prison now."

Aminzadeh had grown up in a religious family in a small town called Baft and later lived in Sirjan in central Iran. His father had supported Ayatollah Khomeini in the early days of the revolution, and his uncle had fought in the war, losing a son in the fighting. Like many Iranians, Aminzadeh's father had gradually lost his faith in the revolution and often argued with his brother, who despite his loss continued to support the regime.

Aminzadeh's life experiences had conditioned him for a life of political activism. Growing up, he listened to the BBC Persian radio with his father every night. When he scored well on the national university entrance exam, he applied to study civil engineering in Tehran, the capital and the center of politics. Upon arrival, he joined the Office for Fostering Unity. During the protests in 1999, he visited hospitals to count the injured and the dead.

He was aware that his activism might earn him time in prison, and as his guards led him out of Mortazavi's courtroom, he was relieved to hear that they were taking him to Evin prison. These days Evin was safer than Eshratabad, a detention center controlled by the Revolutionary Guards, who were openly going after activists since Khatami's election. After Khomeini's death, the Guards' power had appeared to diminish, but it was clear now that Khamenei had brought the force under his control and was nurturing them. Aminzadeh knew that Afshari and eighteen other activists had been held at Eshratabad. No inspectors were allowed to visit Eshratabad, and horrible stories about it had already leaked out. Prisoners could not use the toilets except at arbitrary times, sleep deprivation was common as a form of torture, and some of the prisoners were held in solitary confinement for nearly a year. Many of them had developed severe health problems.

A number of officials in Iran's government opposed the Revolutionary Guards' handling of the prisoners at Eshratabad. Members of Parliament had pressed the judiciary over the detentions, arguing that the Guards couldn't legally detain anyone. Finally Khatami's Intelligence Ministry had stepped in, taking some of the prison-bound activists to Evin to save them from the clutches of the Revolutionary Guards. Fortunately for Aminzadeh, he was among this group.

That day, Aminzadeh was taken to section 209 of Evin and led to a three-by-six-foot solitary cell. The space was tiny, with only a small sink standing in a corner and a barred window that looked up into the sky. Aminzadeh was given three blankets: one to sleep on, another to cover himself with, and a third to roll up for a pillow.

Spared from the Revolutionary Guards, Aminzadeh's first prison experience was milder than he had expected. Two interrogators politely questioned him from ten AM to three PM. The meals were surprisingly nourishing and tasty: rice with barberries, barbequed chicken, minced kebab. One dish, fried fish from the Caspian Sea, was so good that Aminzadeh could still recall the taste years later.

After a month in Evin, Aminzadeh was released, and only then did he learn the results of the presidential election: Khatami had won with over 76 percent of the vote. Some eighteen million people had voted for him. It was an enormous margin of victory—and a tremendous concession by a regime that had once declared that 99.9 percent of Iranians favored it.

Aminzadeh felt invigorated by the news of Khatami's reelection, and along with other student leaders he decided to step up his activism to help give a boost to the reform movement as a sympathetic administration entered a second term.

But even as the activists' efforts and Khatami's victory seemed to signal that the reform movement was revitalized, the regime kept trying to wear it down. In a humiliating gesture, a court acquitted the men accused of the attack on the dormitory in 1999. Then, in July 2001, the judiciary pressed charges against ten reformist members of Parliament, despite the fact that, as legislators, they were legally immune from prosecution for their statements on the floor; eventually the court sentenced four of them to jail. At the same time, the watchdog Guardian Council was also rejecting legislation crucial to reformers, including a bill that defined political crime in order to stop arbitrary arrests and another aimed at promoting freedom of speech.

This tug of war between the regime and the reformers wasn't entirely new, but this time there proved to be a crucial difference. This time, the Iranian people would use technology, not just protests and other forms of direct action, to join the fray.

That fall, in my home in Tehran, I was folding my laundry and watching CNN around four fifteen PM when the images of one of the Twin Towers in New York flashed before my eyes; a dark cloud was whirling into the air from a pitch black hole in one of the towers. I had gone up to the rooftop of one of the towers just a few years earlier during a visit to New York and had sipped coffee at a café just below the buildings. Now people were running through those same streets amid smoke and debris. I held my breath, knowing that the terror before my eyes was happening right then; people, dots on the screen, were jumping to their deaths to escape the heat and the smoke inside the building. I watched a second plane smash into the South Tower. Within moments the first tower crumbled down; its thundering sound echoed in my head as though the building around the corner had collapsed, as though thousands of my own neighbors had perished. The live broadcast of this unspeakable human suffering had erased borders and nationalities, nullifying the distance between our two countries.

Many other Iranians, including government officials, also watched the tragedy play out on live television. Authorities immediately worried that the West might accuse Iran of plotting the attacks; for years, the United States had blamed Iran for sponsoring terrorism through its proxy force Hezbollah in Lebanon.

The Iranian government moved quickly to formulate a response, in the process showing just how far its foreign policy had come since 1979. Khatami publicly condemned the attacks. A reformist member of Parliament, Ahmad Bourghani, hurried to the US Interest Section at the Swiss embassy in Tehran with a wreath of flowers and signed a memorial book there.

As evening approached on September 11, thousands of people gathered in Mohseni Square and held a candlelight vigil for the victims of the attacks. In the silence, one woman whispered to me that her niece lived and worked in Manhattan and the family had not heard from her all day. People rushed to quiet a woman who broke into a sob in a sign of mourning. The scene was a testimony that despite the regime's anti-US propaganda, Iranians didn't feel animosity toward Americans.

In the aftermath of 9/11, it became clear that there was wide support within Iran for a more active and responsible foreign policy. Khatami spoke to Tony Blair of Britain twice in the first week after the attacks. At the Friday prayers three days after the attacks, regime supporters did not chant their usual slogan of "Death to America." They acted not out of respect but out of concern; they wanted to avoid further inflaming tensions with America during this sensitive time. In his first speech after the attack, Khamenei even refrained from calling the United States "the enemy" the way he had for nearly two decades. "Islam condemns the massacre of defenseless people, whether Muslims or Christians, anywhere and by any means," he said. Suddenly, the regime had begun looking outward, toward the West, in a way it hadn't for decades.

At the same time, Iran also came under increasing international pressure over its nuclear program. The shah had initiated the program before the revolution with plans to build twenty-three nuclear power plants in Iran, two of which were already under contract with a German venture by Siemens AG and AEG in the southern city of Bushehr. The company, however, ended its cooperation with Iran after the revolution, and the program was put on hold until after the War with Iraq. In 1995, Iran signed a contract with Russia's Ministry of Atomic Energy to finish the incomplete German reactors in Bushehr. But Iran's nuclear program had remained on the West's radar after the revolution to ensure that the regime would not divert its facilities into a military program. Iran had an ambitious missile program and was trying to enrich uranium—a process that can be used for both producing nuclear fuel for reactors and making nuclear warheads, if the uranium is enriched to high levels. International concerns peaked over Iran's program in 2002, when an exiled opposition group, the National Council of Resistance, revealed that Iran was building two secret nuclear sites, one of them a uranium enrichment facility in Natanz in central Iran. Iranian officials argued that the programs were peaceful and aimed at becoming self-sufficient in producing nuclear fuel. Yet the West warned that it would impose sanctions if Iran refused to halt its enrichment activities, and Israel threatened an attack on the facilities.

Activists on the ground didn't care about the debate over Iran's nuclear program. In their minds, the fight for democracy came before the regime's ambitions to become a powerful country in the region— possibly by having nuclear weapons or reactors. And if the 9/11 attacks proved one thing to reformers and the opposition abroad, it was that television was an enormously powerful tool for shaping opinions internationally and domestically, and for uniting people all around the world behind building a democratic Iran.

Those opposition members who had fled abroad had learned to reach out to people inside the country through satellite TV. The regime had banned satellite television shortly after the technology had first appeared in the 1990s, but the aluminum dishes had sprouted on rooftops across the country anyway. I had even seen the grey dishes over mud houses in the town of Zabol near the border with Afghanistan and Pakistan, 926 miles away from the capital. It was hard to estimate how many Iranian households had satellite television, but the programs aired on it certainly had a wide reach.

In October 2001, Zia Atabay, an Iranian journalist turned activist in Los Angeles, capitalized on the heavy viewership of World Cup–qualifying soccer matches that month to make a political plea. Sitting alone behind a desk, he urged people to demonstrate in the streets against the regime. Along with another opposition channel called Pars TV, Atabay floated the idea of overthrowing the regime and installing in its place the son of the former shah, who was currently living in exile. They suddenly had high hopes after the US invasion of Afghanistan that month and the toppling of the Taliban. Talks of returning the former Afghan king to his country had intensified, and Iranian royalists were hopeful that perhaps they could return the shah's son to Iran too.

Before one World Cup–qualifying match in Bahrain, Attabay urged viewers to celebrate in the streets after the Iranian team won and "let the religious establishment of the Middle East hear" peoples' voice for freedom. When the team lost, Attabay told viewers that the players had been instructed to lose and urged people to head out into the streets anyway in a show of protest. I went out after the game ended at midnight and found cars had already blocked Africa Street near my home and were honking their horns in a singsong tone that had become a sign of protest. People had come out on foot to watch them.

I roamed the streets and watched women take off their headscarves and dance on top of cars. The crowds stayed out until the early morning hours. The Iranian news agency reported that people had gathered in fifty-four different neighborhoods in Tehran. Newspapers reported that the security forces arrested seven hundred people for chanting anti-regime slogans.

These acts of defiance continued throughout the rest of October, with people in Tehran and other large cities demonstrating after every game. The Basij and the security forces arrested hundreds of people in an effort to discourage them from reappearing on the streets again. According to the government, most detainees were young, between the ages of thirteen and seventeen—in other words, all of them were born and raised after the revolution. They were different from my generation: we had defied the regime but never rebelled against it, perhaps because we had witnessed the brutality that had followed the revolution itself. But these younger Iranians were just as frustrated as we were with Khatami's slow pace of reform, and they were eager for some kind of alternative leadership. They had glimpsed the weakness of the regime, and they had dared to act—and in truth, they were beginning to seem stronger and stronger by comparison.

The protestors' displays of strength would peak over a year later, in November 2002, after a court issued a death sentence for Hashem Aghajari, the history professor I had seen call for the separation of state and religion at Shahid Beheshti University two years earlier. He had been charged with apostasy for saying in a speech that people should not follow their religious leaders unthinkingly, as the regime demanded. Aghajari refused to appeal the sentence and wrote a letter from prison saying, "I should have died when I lost my leg defending my country, but I have lived two decades. If the death verdict is right, let them carry it out, and if it's wrong, my death might help the judiciary to revise its laws."

University students rose up immediately; they believed that, if the regime executed Aghajari, it would go after them too. Protests broke out in cities across Iran, from Tehran to Hamedan, Tabriz, Kerman, Orumieh, Isfahan, and many other places. I went to a demonstration at Amir Kabir University, in downtown Tehran. At its lush campus, some five thousand students sat cross-legged on the ground for six hours, listening to speakers and cheering in defiance. "The regime must understand that we are the last generation that engages in a peaceful conversation with it," said one activist in a passionate tone. "The next generation would opt for other alternatives."

Classes were canceled for five days. Finally, Khamenei ordered an appeals court to review Aghajari's death sentence. The students had won, forcing the regime to back down. Their momentum seemed to be growing. And then, suddenly, it ground to a halt.

On July 9, 2003, I was at a press conference at which student activists at the Office for Fostering Unity told reporters that they were canceling a big protest. They had been planning to demand the release of dozens of activists—among them Aminzadeh, who'd been arrested for a third time. But members of Parliament had asked the students to give them time to negotiate the activists' release.

Pressure on the students had intensified in recent months. Tehran had been wracked by waves of protests since April, when the government had suggested that it might privatize state universities. Free public education had been one of the last promises to all Iranians by the Islamic Republic, and now it was poised to be snatched away. Satellite television programs fanned the unrest by urging people to demonstrate in solidarity with the students. For two months, crowds poured out into the streets every time the students set a date for demonstrations. Protestors would gather at major intersections in the evenings and chant anti-regime slogans. By July, the initial crowds of five thousand had swelled to over fifteen thousand.

That day, after the students announced that the latest protest had been canceled, they hastened to clarify that they were not withdrawing their demands for the release of their friends; rather, they said, they were pursuing that goal through what they called "civil channels," on the advice of their representatives in Parliament. After a short question-and-answer session, the press conference ended.

As I emerged from the building in which the conference had been held, I was behind three of the students when several stocky men in black suits swarmed around them. Two men grabbed the student closest to me; one of them twisted both his arms behind his back, and the other one punched him in the stomach. Together they dragged the student over to a black sedan and shoved him into the backseat. I saw the bloody face of another student in the back of a second car. Two other men pulled away the third student. The street was busy; people stopped on the sidewalk to watch, and shopkeepers hurried outside to see what the commotion was all about. But no one said or did anything, and the cars sped away.

It all happened in the span of a few seconds. The rest of the students from the press conference had been trailing a few steps behind us, and now I saw they had leaped back inside the building and were pushing the door shut as two men tried to force their way inside. Finally, the students managed to shut the door.

I stood on the street with a friend and a colleague, Farnaz Fassihi, who wrote for the *Wall Street Journal*. We were both shaking. Aminzadeh, I knew, had been arrested in the same way two weeks earlier: government agents had sprayed pepper gas inside the car in which he was riding at the traffic light and dragged him out. But I hadn't realized how truly terrible such an experience could be until I witnessed it firsthand.

Just then, the metal door opened, and one of the students inside, Mehdi Habibi, a tall and lanky young man with dark skin, asked us if we would join them in the building. "We've called two members of Parliament, and they're on their way," he said breathlessly. "Will you stay with us until they come? You work for foreign media. . . . emm . . . Maybe they won't come back for us in front of you."

Still startled by what we'd seen, Farnaz and I stepped inside— partly in the interest of helping the students and partly to calm our own nerves. Inside, a couple of students sat on the floor hugging their knees. We left after two members of Parliament arrived. But none of these interventions did any good. Later, on their way home, all of the students were arrested.

A few nights after the arrest of the students outside the Office for Fostering Unity, Farnaz and I went to cover another protest. It stretched for over a mile, from the Tehran University student dormitory all the way east to Kurdistan Highway, sprawling into a tree-lined residential neighborhood. Moving slowly through the dimly lit Tehran streets, people chanted anti-regime slogans and demanded the release of political prisoners. Neighbors walked out of their homes to watch and take part in the mass demonstration. The crowd occupied the Kurdistan Highway, blocking the traffic.

I was with Farnaz near Kurdistan Highway when a colleague, a photographer who was closer to the dormitory, called me on my cell phone to say that he had just seen members of the Basij on motorcycles pour out of the mosque across from the dormitory. They were heading for the protestors closer to us.

The crowd on our side close to the highway continued chanting until, suddenly, the sea of people began screaming and diverging into smaller streams, disappearing into the narrow alleys on either side of the highway as the Basij approached on their bikes. They slammed their batons into people, yelling and swearing at them. Neighbors opened their doors to offer shelter to the protestors, and Farnaz and I ran with a dozen others inside the yard of a house. Its owner hurriedly shut the door behind us.

Cowering in the house's walled yard, we heard a collective cry of terror from beyond the brick walls, screams mixing with gunshots, the roar of motorbikes, and shattering glass. The Basij were smashing cars and windows, punishing people in the neighborhood for hosting the protest and harboring the demonstrators. I looked at our host, an older man, and saw him flinch at the sound of his intercom getting crushed outside.

We waited until the commotion died down and then ventured out again, this time moving westward through the side streets, heading toward the dormitory.

Arriving on the street where the dormitory was located, we saw a terrible confrontation play out. The asphalt surface of the road outside the dormitory gates glittered with shattered glass, illuminated by orange flames. On one side stood a skirmish line of young men and women, their faces wrapped in scarves. On the other side were a host of Basij, revving the engines of their bikes. We watched as two Basij on a bike tried to break through the protestors' line; the crowd swarmed the bike, pulled off its two riders, and set it on fire. A black cloud swirled over the scene, the smell of burned tires and gasoline filling the air as the two riders dashed back toward their fellows. Protestors booed at them, attracting more people, who came with us to watch.

Half an hour later, we heard the sound of rumbling from the mosque a few hundred feet north of the dormitory. Farnaz and I were on the main street when we saw a mob surging down the road from the direction of the mosque, screaming at the top of their lungs.

We ran into a narrow street with a large group of protestors. As before, residents on the side street opened their doors and let some of the crowd inside, but only so many people could take shelter at each home. Farnaz and I continued running until we reached a dark corner and began pounding on a closed door, praying that its resident would let us in. But no one opened the door.

As we stood helplessly at the door, several men came up behind us. Their wrinkled, untucked shirts hung over their pants. One of them brandished a sickle in front of our faces. "You whores, I'll slit your throats," he howled hoarsely. His eyes were red, his face sweaty.

Farnaz and I clung to each other, frantic with fear. While we were in a corner, pressed against a closed door, the man could do anything to us—and probably would, if he found out that we were reporters with American publications. "We are not protestors," Farnaz pleaded. "We were just going home," I added. Like helpless children, we begged the men to let us go: "Please, please, let us go. Forgive us. We did not do anything."

Two of the men began beating us with their batons—how hard I had no idea until the next day, when my hips and thighs turned purple and painful. At that moment, however, I was thankful: their beating had driven the man with the sickle away.

We ran off after our assailants ran after other people. We took refuge in an apartment building and watched from its third-floor window the horrible events of that night, as more men arrived on the streets below, some of them brought in riding in the backs of pickups. They were dressed in shabby clothes and holding sticks, batons, and daggers. Falling on any protestors who were unlucky enough to still be out on the streets, they beat some unconscious and stabbed others. We saw two Basij throw the limp body of one young man into the trunk of a car that then sped away.

Horrified, we stayed in our hideout until three AM, when the streets in the neighborhood finally cleared and we felt it was safe to leave. Even then, when our gracious host gave us a ride back to our homes, we saw on every corner clusters of men with ghastly expressions on their faces. The protestors had disappeared; the regime forces ruled the streets.

My body was still aching the next day when I opened the door for Nasrin, our housekeeper. She had been working for my aunt for several years, and now came to our apartment once a week as well.

When I told Nasrin about the beating I'd suffered the night before, her eyes lit up. She said that her son, Mehdi, had been there too. "He was on alert last night at the mosque across from the dormitory," she added, as though this were a happy coincidence.

"Was he with the Basij?" I asked.

"Yes, the entire month, he's been there on and off on alert."

Somehow, I had thought that the men I had seen brutalizing un-
armed protestors just hours earlier could not possibly have belonged to
the society I knew. I was doubly stunned because I could not imagine
how anyone in Nasrin's family could have ended up perpetrating such
violence on behalf of the regime. I knew Nasrin didn't support the regime; in fact, the regime had executed two of her brothers-in-law for
their leftist activism at the beginning of the revolution. And she had
always spoken highly of Mehdi, raving that he was the most mature out
of all her three children. Where in society did she and her son fit? Why
had he joined a militia group?

"Nasrin," I asked her innocuously. "Do you think Mehdi can call up
a couple of his friends from last night? I'd like to interview them."

CHAPTER TWENTY-ONE

THE "GOOD" CHILDREN OF THE REVOLUTION

I t took me two weeks to see Mehdi and three of his friends at his grandmother's home in Tehran. I spotted the four of them sitting cross-legged on a scarlet Persian carpet in the living room when I arrived with Kaveh Kazemi, a longtime photographer with the *New York Times*. The four youths, all Basij members and each of them just twenty years old, stood up as soon as they saw us. All four introduced themselves, reaching out to shake Kaveh's hand as they did so. But when they turned to me to say *Salam*—hello—they looked down at the flowers on the carpet in a sign of modesty.

Mehdi had suggested that we meet at his grandmother's home in a commercial neighborhood in southern Tehran. Nasrin and Mehdi lived in Malard, a blue-collar neighborhood over an hour's drive from Tehran, so presumably he figured his grandmother's place would be easier for me to get to.

I wore an ankle-length manteau to the meeting, and I had wrapped a black shawl around my head. Nasrin had stressed that I must cover all my hair when I met with the young men. "They are very religious," she told me after she called Mehdi from my home that day to plan the meeting. "They'll be offended if you show your hair."

After we greeted each other, all four men knelt in a line facing Ka-veh and me. I sat cross-legged across from them and examined their faces, trying to remember their names; I had been distracted by how they looked away when they introduced themselves. They all wore a bit of stubble on their faces; their eyes were nearly expressionless as they looked in the distance to avoid my gaze. But as we spoke, they opened up a bit, and their personalities and family histories began to shine through.

Mehdi, for starters, did not resemble his petite, gregarious mother; he had a thick chest and a large, fleshy face. But like his mother, he pulled his chin into his neck when he spoke. Mehdi had known the three other men since middle school, when they had all joined the Basij at the local mosque. His friend Ramin was the son of a female teacher; his father was out of work. Hassan, with slanted eyes, was one of five children. His father worked for the foreign ministry, and his mother was a homemaker. Saeed, sporting a pair of gold-rim glasses that pressed against his cheeks, had three siblings; his father, a civil servant, had passed away.

Wrapped in a floral chador, Nasrin emerged from the kitchen with tea for us. She was beaming with pride. She was proud that her son was in a position important enough that I would want to interview him.

Nasrin had a delicate face, and although she was forty-one, she looked younger. Born in a small, Turkish, Azari-speaking village, she was one of only a few members of her generation who, despite obliga-tory schooling, never received a formal education. She had learned to read the Koran at a mosque without learning the meaning of the Arabic words themselves. At the age of fifteen, she had married her cousin, a baker, and given birth to a girl. But the cousin abruptly divorced her and took the child away. Nasrin never revealed to me the reason behind the divorce or spoke of the pain of giving up her daughter; I got a sense that she saw her from time to time. She remarried, and after her two sons were born, she moved with her new family to Malard. A decade later, her second husband, a civil servant, retired early. To support the family, Nasrin began sewing linen for a store. It was around this time that my aunt hired her part-time as a maid.

Nasrin had nine siblings, and she often complained that her sisters had married better than she had. They lived in the capital, and their husbands, unlike hers, were hardworking. That didn't seem to be the only problem with Nasrin's husband; her daughter had grown into a young woman and was eager to move in with her, but Nasrin's husband was against it. Mehdi wasn't close to his father either; he was religious, while his father enjoyed liquor and hashish—two vices of which devout Muslims strongly disapprove.

Mehdi was serving the mandatory enlistment period for young men with the Basij but was hopeful that he'd be able to take advantage of university quotas for Basij members and study law. The other three men in Mehdi's Basij cohort were already at the university. Regular university students—those who had won their seats in a competitive entrance exam—viewed Basij students with contempt since they often performed poorly in academics, but reserving a certain number of spaces for Basij students in each class was one big way that the regime incentivized membership in the militia force.

Privileges like these were what made Nasrin thankful that Mehdi had joined the Basij—not the things he was required to do as part of the organization. After I had told her about the beating I had suffered at the hands of the Basij that night at the demonstration, she'd insisted that Mehdi would never get involved in any kind of violence. "He is a gentle boy," she said. "In our neighborhood, the kids either join the thugs or the Basij. Mehdi has always been religious, and at the mosque he has only learned to love Khamenei." Nasrin's younger son, I knew, had taken the opposite track; he was fourteen and a rebel, skipping school.

As we spoke to Mehdi and his friends, they, too, raved about the Basij. "Everything we have is from the Basij," said Saeed, as I jotted down notes on the conversation. "It has helped us mature; it has given us confidence, we feel we can do anything in life."

"Do you see all these young people only wanting a girlfriend or a boyfriend and to look fashionable?" added Ramin. "We are not like them. We have learned that those things weaken our will power."

"Basij is not just a military institution; it's also a cultural one," explained Mehdi. "It has helped us find our goals in life."

"What is your goal?" I asked him.

"To follow our *vali faqih*," replied Saeed, referring to Khamenei. "Without him, the Basij is nothing. Our job is to guide society toward the path that he has defined."

The young men said that they had weekly meetings at the mosque, where a commander and a preacher analyzed political events for them. "We must follow Khamenei's orders," said Saeed. "It's *haram* if we don't," he added, using the Arabic word for "sinful." His three comrades nodded their heads in unison.

"Many people call us freaks," Hassan said, surprising me. "I don't deny that there are freaks among the Basij, but we are part of this society—we haven't come from Mars. The Basij offers us good opportunities. Journalists have misrepresented us. If a couple of Basij members have done something wrong, that doesn't mean that we are all like them."

Hassan's tone wasn't accusatory, just defensive. What he was saying reminded me how polarized Iran's society was, not only economically, but also—and perhaps especially—culturally. Two different cultures lived side by side in our country; one was modern and relatively secular, the other traditional and intensely religious. The 1979 revolution had nurtured the hostility between these two different strains of Iranian culture by encouraging the religious people to police secular people, to dominate their lives by telling them what they must and must not do.

Mehdi picked up where Hassan had left off, talking about other people's sins, which he described as a threat to society. "Satellite television has a bad influence on the mind," he said. "I have noticed that my cousins have stopped praying and started showing their hair since they began watching satellite television."

Hassan jumped back in, interrupting Mehdi to explain to me, in a stern tone, "When they say satellite television is bad, it means that you cannot watch its programs. Period. It corrupts the mind and distances you from God. People must learn to follow directions, or they will get punished. Like Zahra Kazemi: she didn't listen, so she got what she deserved."

His comment startled me. Zahra Kazemi was an Iranian Canadian photographer (not related to Kaveh Kazemi, the photographer who had joined me for this interview) who had died in prison in July after being caught photographing people outside Evin prison as they looked for their loved ones who had been arrested during the protests. A week after her arrest, prison authorities transported her to the hospital in a coma. The doctor who examined her reported that she had suffered a severe blow to the head. She died nine days later. Reformist politicians launched an investigation into her death, but prison authorities buried her immediately to prevent an autopsy. The Canadian government summoned its ambassador home in protest and indicated that it held Judge Saeed Mortazavi, the notorious judge who'd been promoted to prosecutor general, responsible for Kazemi's death.

Naturally, the death of a journalist attracted the attention of the international press corps—myself included. Zahra and I were Iranians working for foreign media outlets, and perhaps for this reason her murder horrified me more than most atrocities I had seen in my line of work. Now, Hassan's offhand remark about Zahra made me question everything I thought I had figured out about him. Was this young man really a gentle, pious Muslim? How easily could his commanders mold him into a hardened killer?

One day before meeting Mehdi and his friends that August, I had rushed to see a senior official to find out more about the Basij. I'll call the official *Mohsen* to protect his identity.

Mohsen found the subject of the Basij so sensitive that before answering my questions, he picked up his cell phone and took out the battery and SIM card, placing the pieces on the table. I did the same to my phone. It was widely believed that the Revolutionary Guards had imported equipment that enabled them to use cell phones as listening devices. Turning off the phones wasn't enough to disable them, people thought; you had to take out the batteries too. Visitors to foreign embassies were not even allowed to bring their phones inside.

Even after we placed our dead phones on the table, Mohsen spoke in such a low whisper that I had to pull my chair closer to him. It was as if he feared that there was a listening device right under our table.

"After Khatami's election, the regime realized that it had no genuine support," he whispered, referring to the presidential election in

1997, when people had overwhelmingly elected the long-shot reformist candidate into one of the highest offices in the country. "The Revolutionary Guards embodied the revolution, but its members had voted for Khatami."

So, after the election, Mohsen explained, the Guards' senior commanders began investing in the Basij, which is the Guards' militia arm. It rewarded new members with jobs, bonuses, even property, depending on how involved the new members were. "The ones who beat people on the streets are rewarded better than the ones who participate only in pro-regime rallies," he said. "We did the same thing at the beginning of the revolution, but now they spend too much money on the Basij."

Mohsen leaned back in his seat and shook his head. He had been a senior Revolutionary Guard commander in the early days of the revolution, but over the years he had evolved into a reformist. In that time, he had seen the regime change as well—and had witnessed how changes in Iran's economy, particularly in relation to the country's oil industry, had served to both strengthen and undermine the regime.

"With more oil income coming in," he explained, "the regime can afford to splurge. But the high oil prices won't last. The regime is making the Basij too greedy. When oil prices collapse, the regime will lose these supporters, too."

The oil industry had fostered dictators since 1908, when crude oil was first discovered in Iran. Instead of relying on taxes, production, and a desire to increase internal revenues, the kings before the revolution and later the clerics after the revolution were intoxicated by the oil revenues. They no longer felt accountable to the Iranian people because they could now buy political support with the money they had earned from the oil trade. And they were earning a lot of money; on average, 60 percent of the government's income and 80 percent of its exports had come from oil and gas revenues in recent years. Oil prices had surged from $9 a barrel in 1997 to over $20 in 2003 and would continue to rise, surpassing $100 five years later—a windfall that would only make the regime less dependent on any sort of genuine support base.

Both before and after the revolution, this oil money helped the Iranian government to expand the public sector, the engine that had helped families move up in society. Iran had largely been a rural society early in the century, but beginning with the rule of Reza Shah and later, under his son and after the revolution, many Iranians received steady incomes from jobs at universities, government ministries, and other areas funded by the government that, in turn, nurtured a growing, urban middle class. The post-revolution regime invested in infrastructure—electricity and piped water—and expanded social services in health and education, which lay the foundation of the rise of the middle class in the 1980s. Between 1997 and 2009 the country enjoyed steady economic growth, fueled by rising oil prices. Per capita income climbed at an average rate of 3.5 percent during these years.

By 2009, according to surveys by the Statistical Center of Iran, the population of poor people had dropped to 7 percent (Khomeini had referred to nearly two-thirds of the population in 1979 as *mostazafin*, "the deprived"). Some 8 percent of the people were classified as rich, with an income of over $25 a day. The rest of society, 83 percent, were identified either as lower-middle-class, with an income of $3 to $9 a day, or middle-class (43 percent), earning over $9 a day—a demographic transformation that had serious political implications.

As I spoke with Mohsen, I speculated that he, like many other Iranians, had shed his revolutionary ideas as he moved up in society.

Mohsen asked me if I recalled the government's campaign to round up neighborhood criminals in poor neighborhoods. The regime had gone after neighborhood gangs several times, arresting them and then humiliating them on television. I did remember the campaign; in fact, I had visited one neighborhood and found out that its residents were truly relieved that the men were off their streets. They had bullied their neighbors, stolen from them, and raped women in the area.

Some of these thugs were hanged in public, but not all of them were punished, Mohsen told me. "They always execute some of the leaders," he whispered. "But they invite the rest to join the Basij. They take good care of them and their families. They put them up in camps, and in return they have to fight for the regime in the streets."

I was shocked by Mohsen's revelation, but it made sense that the men I'd seen stabbing people a week earlier were criminals. I looked up at the portraits of ayatollahs Khomeini and Khamenei hanging next to one another on the wall. They gazed down at you in every government building, both of them in black turbans, Ayatollah Khomeini wearing a permanent frown, Khamenei hiding behind his oversized glasses. What, I wondered, had the revolution come to?

Back in the living room with the Basij members, I bit my lip angrily at Hassan's comment about Zahra. Rather than respond to it, however, I decided to ask them what they had done during the recent protests. "Did you think the protestors needed to be punished too?" I asked, my voice a bit icier than I intended. "Where were you on the nights of the demonstrations?" I asked directly.

They looked at one another and shook their heads. "We go to the mountains every Friday," said Mehdi, "and urge women to cover their hair, or if they are with unmarried men, we explain that it's a sin for them to hang out together that way." His words reminded me of my own teenage years, when I had gone hiking and had encounters of my own with the Basij. I always resented them.

"But we don't get involved in street protests," Mehdi added, as though harassing hikers was all right, but harassing protestors would be beyond the pale.

Nasrin had clearly forgotten to tell the young men that I knew they had been at the mosque during the protests. I looked up to see if she was within earshot. It was a warm, sunny day, and she was sitting in the yard with her mother.

"So where were you on those nights?" I asked again.

"Home," said Ramin.

"We followed the news on the Internet," added Saeed.

"Which website?"

"Parskhabar," Hassan replied quickly. "Mr. Khamenei had ordered us not to intervene."

"I've never heard of Parskhabar," I said, turning to Kaveh. He shook his head in disbelief.

When I got home, I checked Parskhabar. It was a page with links to almost every Persian language blog, news website, newspaper, and television and radio program, regardless of their political affiliations. I was impressed that the Basij members were familiar with it while

Kaveh and I were not. They were clearly reading more than what their commanders were instructing them to.

I couldn't figure out why Mehdi and his friends were lying to me about their involvement in the protests, and even after my conversation with them ended, I could not tell whether they had actually been involved in the violence or even seemed capable of it. I wasn't able to write a story about the meeting, and Nasrin was quite disappointed. But one thing was clear to me: as obedient as they might have seemed, these four Basij were hungry for information, just like many other young Iranians. Their economic backgrounds had made them vulnerable to exploitation, which the regime surely knew by luring them into the Basij with promises of money and education. I couldn't help but wonder how long it would take, if their circumstances suddenly improved and they no longer needed the Basij, for them to morph into moderate young men.

CHAPTER TWENTY-TWO

THE "BAD" CHILDREN OF THE REVOLUTION

I met Mehdi Aminzadeh, the student leader, at a coffee shop in downtown Tehran two weeks after his release in 2003. He'd lost at least fifteen pounds since I'd last seen him. His lower lip trembled slightly when he spoke. But it was his eyes that looked the most changed. His pupils were dilated, and his eyes darted nervously around, just like those of other tortured activists I had met. "It was horrible," he said, shaking his head and stirring his cappuccino for a long time.

This had been his fourth arrest, and the jail term that followed had lasted for four months. The first time he had been imprisoned was when Mortazavi, the infamous hard-line judge, had sent him to Evin prison for a month during the presidential elections on the spurious pretense that Aminzadeh had insulted religious sanctities in a student publication. That imprisonment and the next ones had been a relative cakewalk: the food had been good, and the guards had been relatively lenient. This time, Aminzadeh had also been sent to Evin—but I could tell this latest experience had been different.

I'd seen Aminzadeh's friend, Ali Afshari, a few months after his televised confession at a press conference—a confession that was false, he told me, and that he claimed had been forced. Up to that point he had tolerated the psychological and physical pressure for nine months, he said. "It was wrong for me to make the confessions, but I couldn't take it anymore."

I knew Afshari and Aminzadeh weren't overstating their suffering. Another jailed activist, seventy years old, who had also spent over a decade in the shah's prison, which was notorious for torturing detainees, had smuggled a letter out of prison that summer saying how much worse this regime's prisons were than the shah's prisons. Death, he wrote, was preferable to the torment he was suffering at the hands of the Revolutionary Guards. He had two heart attacks before his release in February of that year.

Aminzadeh sipped his coffee, his head bowed, as he delved into his experiences over the past four months. I began taking notes.

Aminzadeh had known his captors were Revolutionary Guards the moment they had sprayed pepper gas in the back of his car as he had been sitting at a traffic light with his wife. Only the Guards surprised their victims that way. They pulled him out, handcuffed him, and shoved him in the back of a car that took him to Evin. On its compound, they had now built their own prison, called 305A.

Immediately a man who called himself Afzal began interrogating Aminzadeh. Always standing behind him (he warned that he would break Aminzadeh's neck if he attempted to look at his face), Afzal swore at Aminzadeh and threatened to arrest his sister, his wife, his father-in-law, and his friends. Aminzadeh sat on a chair blindfolded, listening to tapes of his telephone conversations. Afzal instructed him several times to remove his blindfold to look at photos of himself with other activists, including dozens of images of Aminzadeh outside his own home.

Aminzadeh suffered a range of psychological and physical torture while in Evin. Afzal threatened to lock him in the section that housed dangerous criminals, where convicts were known to rape young men like him. Sexual abuse, indeed, was the most devastating torture other activists had suffered. But Afzal was physically brutal too. Every ten minutes he punched and kicked Aminzadeh so hard that he fell off his chair and lay curled up on the floor.

"There was not a second that I did not fear the beating coming," Aminzadeh said, as he adjusted his glasses on his face. Afzal's oval-shaped ring, he said, left purple marks on his face for days after each beating. There was no trace of those marks on his face anymore, but I had also heard from other activists that they were often not released until after all signs of torture had disappeared from their bodies.

Afzal had wanted Aminzadeh to confess that the activists were plotting to overthrow the regime, and that one of their members had met and worked with the armed Iranian opposition group Mujahedin Khalgh Organization, which was based in Paris. Like many moderate Iranians, Aminzadeh despised the MKO; he also knew that the punishment for cooperating with them could be death. Afzal tried various forms of coercion to get Aminzadeh to comply; he told him that Khatami had resigned, reformist politicians had been arrested, and no one was campaigning on his behalf. "You'll rot here," he would tell him.

Aminzadeh kept reminding himself that Afzal was lying, but his torturer was his only link to the outside world. Even during his brief strolls in the yard, he was blindfolded and saw no one. He began to lose touch with reality.

Three weeks of grueling interrogation passed. Aminzadeh refused to confess to Afzal's fabricated story. Finally Afzal told him that a different interrogator ("a more brutal person," Aminzadeh remembered him saying) would replace him. And so it was that, before sunrise the next day, a guard woke Aminzadeh up and dragged him to the interrogation room. "I want you to think about the philosophy of standing," a new voice said. Then the new torturer slammed the door and left.

Confused, Aminzadeh stood there half asleep, blindfolded, and unable to think. As the man's remark bounced in his head, his eyes became heavy with sleep. Afzal had interrogated him for fourteen hours the previous day, and he was exhausted. Aminzadeh's head tilted sideways, and his knees began to shake. At that very moment, the door was flung open, and a torrent of ice water cut across his head like a dagger. Before he could take a deep breath, three or four men attacked him, punching and kicking him until he fell to the floor.

"Didn't I tell you just to stand and think?" the voice thundered. On the floor, Aminzadeh gasped for air as the blows landed on his stomach, head, and testicles. "Your fate will be decided here," the man shouted. "In this room of two by three meters. Do you know how big that is?

Huh? Huh? Not even five square meters." Then breathless, the man ordered him to stand.

Aminzadeh stood up but could not stop thinking about what the man had just said. The man must be a complete fool, Aminzadeh thought; every elementary school student knew that two times three is six! Aminzadeh told himself that he would defeat the idiot with his will power, that he would avoid falling asleep. But the room was silent and dark, and he was exhausted. He must have lost his balance half an hour later because they poured another bucket of cold water on him and attacked him again. Aminzadeh lost count of how many times they assaulted him like this; some of the time he was not sure if he had even dozed off when they swooped down on him. It was an endless cycle of torment, repeating itself every half hour. For three days and two nights, they deprived him of sleep in this way. Disoriented, cold, and wet, Aminzadeh kept track of time by counting the breaks he was given for lunch, dinner, and breakfast.

Close to sunrise at the end of the second night of his ordeal, the man dragged Aminzadeh out of the room, through the long corridors, and into the yard. Aminzadeh felt the sudden chill of a fall wind on his face as he staggered outside. The man pushed him against a tree trunk and placed the cold muzzle of a pistol against his head. "Under this sycamore tree I have killed many," the man said to him. "Your time has come too."

Aminzadeh told himself to remain calm, that this was just a mock execution, exactly what they had done to many others before him. But his body wasn't listening; it was shaking and sweating. "I was part of the team that carried out the chain murders," the man told him. "I am back to finish the job. But we can end this right now, right here, if you do what you've been asked to do."

Aminzadeh was shivering so hard that he couldn't say a word. The man cocked the gun and pressed the muzzle harder against his head. "'What if he is crazy enough to pull the trigger?' I asked myself," Aminzadeh said to me. "What if his finger just slips? What if they have really arrested everyone and are killing them?"

As we sat in the coffee shop, Aminzadeh paused and pulled a tissue from the box on the table. He folded it neatly and wiped the sweat off his forehead. It was a cool day, and I was wearing a heavy coat, but he was perspiring heavily.

"I was completely off balance," he said, continuing. He was out there for several hours, shivering and sweating weakly, before the man pulled the pistol away and announced: "I'll do something that will make you wish I'd killed you." With those words, he ordered a guard to take Aminzadeh to his cell.

Aminzadeh was so terrified that he refused to touch his food and water, even though he was ravenously hungry and thirsty. He knew their plan; they were just going to abandon him in the cell.

Three times a day, day after day, a guard knocked on his door to take him to the washroom and to slide in his meal tray through a small door that latched from the outside. No one said a word to him. No one came for him. Days passed. To sustain himself, Aminzadeh looked inward and came up with a project. He decided to pace his cell and imagine that he was walking to his hometown of Kerman. He needed to walk nine miles a day, fourteen hours a day. He counted: fourteen steps if he went around the cell and three steps if he went diagonally. Every 125 steps were 328 feet, and he needed to go over six hundred miles southeast of Evin. Aminzadeh tried to visualize every detail of the road: the newsstand at the corner, the kabob place near the city of Qom, the teahouse with sticky tablecloths, the beggar with an accordion singing Persian oldies.

I asked Aminzadeh if he had ever figured out who was in the cells around his, and for the first time in our conversation he smiled. "They sang," he said, "and sometimes we exchanged a few words." In his section of the prison were some other student leaders and a couple of older activists. "Hoda Saber sang beautifully," Aminzadeh said, and then began murmuring a Persian song for me. "Sing the bird of dawn, revive my scorching pain, break down this cage with your fire-drenched breath, demolish it and set me free," he sang. Another activist, he remembered, sang a pop love song: "I wish this wall would collapse, you and I would die together and hold hands in a different world."

This limited human contact obviously meant a great deal to Aminzadeh, but the isolation was still maddening. Day after day, Aminzadeh felt that the walls were closing in on him. He had no idea how long he was going to be trapped like this; Afshari had spent nine months in solitary, and several others, like Hoda, had been there for over a year.

Slowly, his mind began to turn against him. As Aminzadeh sat on the bright green carpet in his cell, under a lightbulb that never went off, Afzal's words plagued his mind. What if they *had* really arrested everybody?

After forty days, Afzal sent for him. As soon as Aminzadeh sat down on the chair in the interrogation room, he lost his composure. "You unscrupulous liar!" he shouted at Afzal. "You claim you are religious— hell no! You're not even human." He broke into uncontrollable sobs.

"I don't know how long I yelled and cried," Aminzadeh told me over our coffee. "When I calmed down, Afzal put his hand on my shoulder and told me to take off the blindfold. I'd never seen his face. I pulled down the blindfold and saw that his eyes were red. He had cried too."

Afzal was of medium height, with a black beard and a limp. The skin on one of his hands was red. Maybe he had really fought in the war, Aminzadeh thought.

Afzal told Aminzadeh that four of his friends had confessed to attempting to overthrow the regime in league with the Marxist group the MKO. Aminzadeh's resistance was useless; in fact, it was the only thing standing between him and freedom. If he wrote down everything, Afzal promised, he would secure his release.

To convince Aminzadeh of the futility of resisting, Afzal left him alone for two hours with other students' handwritten notes and recorded tapes. Afzal returned to the room with Reza, another student leader, who looked blankly at Aminzadeh and urged him to admit the story. "I could tell that he'd been tortured," Aminzadeh recalled to me.

Finally, Aminzadeh picked up the pen and jotted down the story that Afzal had pounded into his head so many times: the students and nationalist activists wanted to overthrow the regime with the help of the MKO. Still, it took several weeks for him to leave Evin.

I had heard many prison stories from other activists and had begun to have nightmares about their experiences, as if they'd happened to me. Some of these men and women had told me that their interrogators were obsessed with sex. To dehumanize them, they made them talk and write about their relationships and fantasies, play them out, and sometimes even make up sexual stories. Another young activist was locked in a tiny space like a coffin for hours on end. There were so many of these stories, yet I could only report a few of them. The rest of them simply festered in my mind, and in the minds of the people who told them to me.

I listened to their stories to find out what was shaping these activists. They were among the brightest of their generation of students. Aminzadeh had ranked two thousandth among over a hundred thousand hopefuls who had participated in the national entrance exam. He was getting his graduate degree in civil engineering from one of the top universities in Iran. He and his fellow activists weren't the kind of people who could be easily brainwashed or silenced. Yet one by one, they had been broken.

I said good-bye to Aminzadeh and decided to walk part of the way home. It was another polluted day in Tehran; a haze of grey smoke hung in the air, making me wish for a cleansing rain to clear the skies. I walked on Ferdowsi Avenue, where people had queued outside the British embassy to apply for visas. A little farther up, there was a longer line outside the German embassy. A woman with a mass of dyed blond hair peeking out from under her veil adjusted her reading glasses and paged through her documents. A mustached man sat on the curb with a typewriter, filling out visa application forms for people. Money changers hung whiteboards on their windows with the latest exchange rates. People bustled around, minding their own business.

Many students lived in this neighborhood because of its proximity to the city's universities. I couldn't help but wonder at the fact that they remained in the capital even as many of their classmates were being abducted and tortured on a regular basis.

To be sure, some of the activists did flee the country. They left for Europe or the United States and talked about their experiences on opposition satellite TV stations. Even local newspapers reported on them, and their stories floated around. Some people wrote books about their experiences. Many cab drivers told me different versions of stories I'd heard firsthand. It was no secret what the regime was still capable of doing to its opponents.

Aminzadeh, like many other activists, chose to stay in Iran and resume his activism. He gave talks and held events. But now he was more careful. He changed his tone and, as he put it, "weighed every single word" he uttered. After all, the regime was watching and had informants everywhere. And if there was one thing that terrified Aminzadeh, it was the thought of winding up back in Evin.

CHAPTER TWENTY-THREE

NASRIN

I was eight months pregnant and had just moved into a new apartment in March 2004 when Nasrin told me that she'd been kidnapped, beaten, and threatened by government agents who were looking for keys to our new apartment. She recounted the ordeal with such visual details that I believed her.

"I was on your street at eight AM," she said, sitting on the floor at my father's home, her shoulders visibly tense and her small eyes wide as she explained. "A big white car suddenly pulled up, and a man snatched me on the sidewalk and pushed me inside the car. A woman punched me in the stomach in the backseat and took my bag. I thought they were thieves, but after she emptied the bag on the seat, she asked for keys to your new apartment. When I told them that I didn't have them, the man said that they were Intelligence agents. He wore a beard and a big pair of sunglasses. He said you and Babak are opium smugglers. They asked me to introduce the woman as your new maid. She had large green eyes and delicate hands. I said that she'd never be able to do the kind of work I do. Then they asked that I let them into the house whenever you go out. I refused. When they dropped me off in Vanak Square, the man said that he'll find me and drop my corpse somewhere that no one would ever find it."

I could not breathe or move until my son began kicking inside me. Our home had come under surveillance again, by exactly the same men who had watched us in 1998, and I was already alarmed about being intimidated so brazenly. None of my colleagues who worked for foreign media had ever faced such harassment.

The men who watched us had returned several other times over the years. We'd written down their license plate numbers and the car models: two Peugeot 405 and a white Peykan. Two men sat in each vehicle and switched shifts precisely every eight hours. I was now also a Canadian citizen as well as an Iranian and had notified the Canadian embassy of the surveillance; one of the diplomats had suggested that we offer the men tea to start a conversation with them, but I never got around to it.

Babak had more luck than I did. One day he had walked out of our building to find the doors of the Peugeot flung open and the two men crawling under the steering wheel. He asked if they needed help, and they explained that they'd broken the wheel. When Babak looked, he noticed that they'd only unlocked the tilt. He taught them how to use the tilt to adjust the wheel, and the men thanked him profusely. From then on, Babak exchanged greetings with them whenever he left the house.

Although Nasrin looked terrified by the abduction she had described to me, she didn't quit. I was grateful for her steadfastness, but I ignored her request to keep her ordeal a secret and informed my foreign editor in New York, Susan Chira, who complained to Iran's ambassador at the mission in New York. The next day I received a call from the Foreign Ministry, saying that it was investigating Nasrin's kidnapping. I also informed Khoshvaght at Ershad and Mr. X at the Intelligence Ministry. I'd done nothing wrong and feared that if I kept quiet, the regime would try to intimidate me even further. The regime had arrested dozens of bloggers in a new wave of crackdowns, and it was clear it wanted to control the flow of information in and out of the country.

All three ministries asked for some time to make inquiries, and in the meantime, springtime came to Tehran. On March 21 the thirteen-day Nowruz holiday began, a time when people visit relatives and friends and finally picnic on Seezdah Bedar, April 2, to celebrate the awakening of nature. The trees bloomed; swallows and crows sat in the treetops again, and the sun sailed in a blue sky, the only time in the year that the grey smoke finally leaves the capital, along with most of its population. But despite all of the beauty around us, Nasrin's kidnapping never left my mind. The agents can open the lock on any door, I thought. If they were after me, they could simply break into my car and hide a bag of heroin to validate the story they had told Nasrin and give them an excuse to lock me up. Why kidnap and threaten Nasrin?

My son, Chayan, was born in May, and Nasrin made herself indispensable. She arrived at dawn so that I could rest after those early sleepless nights. She cradled my son lovingly and bathed him while singing in her native Azari language. We became dependent on her in no time.

A few weeks later, Mr. X summoned me to the same immigration office where I'd first met him. He congratulated me on the birth of my son and then said that he was saying good-bye. I was shocked. "Please forgive me if I ever offended you," he said, not acting like a security agent at all. He was about to leave the room to fetch the new agent who would be my contact at the Intelligence Ministry when I asked him about the cars that had been posted outside our building. "They are not with the Intelligence Ministry," he said. Then he warned me that Nasrin had lied. "Don't trust her," he urged me. "The Intelligence Ministry has never gone after her. She wants to blackmail you to get money."

I felt betrayed. I'd already emptied my savings account so that Nasrin could live closer to me. One morning at dawn she had told me that the two-hour trip was wearing her down, and that she would quit if I couldn't help her move to the city. Her husband had died of a stroke a year earlier, and I felt that I should help a fellow working woman who was devoted to my son. Two days after she asked to borrow money she announced that she had found an apartment and needed nearly twenty thousand dollars. With that money, she could buy an apartment in Tehran. She insisted that her sons wanted to move into a *modern* place. I found it interesting that Mehdi wasn't clinging to the simple life that the Basij endorsed. His conservatism was wearing off, I thought.

Nasrin wanted to leave the money with the landlord as a deposit—*rahn*—to avoid paying monthly rent. She owned two apartments in Malard and promised to return half of the money as soon as she rented out those units. As for the rest, I could deduct $100 a month from her $330 salary. I was fully aware that she was manipulating me, but still, in addition to all my savings, I borrowed money to buy her loyalty.

After telling me that Nasrin had been lying to me about her abduction, Mr. X brought in a young man, Mr. Ghoddoossi, who would be taking over as my liaison with the ministry. Mr. Ghoddoossi was short, and his jacket was so tight that I expected the buttons to pop at any minute. He bowed his head politely and said that he had been a fan of my articles since he was in high school. Baffled, I looked at him to see if he was making fun of me. I had been writing under my byline for only five years, and, if not older than I, he did not look that much younger than I. Or maybe, I thought, he was suggesting that unlike Mr. X, his English was good enough to read the *New York Times*. As I looked at him in silence, he added he had a graduate degree in communications. In the years that followed he would call me only once.

I should have been glad to have been left alone by the Intelligence Ministry's central office, but the truth is that without Mr. X, I was at a total loss. I had known him for nearly ten years and was aware that he dealt with all my colleagues. Given the murky history of the Intelligence Ministry and the awkward comments that Mr. Ghoddoossi had just made, I was suspicious of this new arrangement.

The next day, I rushed to see Khoshvaght to make sense of what had happened. The joy of becoming a mother had already given way to anxiety. I didn't know what or who to believe.

Khoshvaght was also surprised to hear that Mr. X had bid me farewell. But then he dropped another bomb: it was the prosecutor's office that had kidnapped Nasrin. The prosecutor was Judge Mortazavi, the man who had arrested activists and shut down newspapers. Mortazavi worked closely with the Revolutionary Guards and was accountable to no one.

The room began spinning around me. The prosecutor's office had a spy in my house and had managed to throw the Intelligence Ministry out of the picture. It suddenly dawned on me that the reformers' efforts had stalled, and their opponents were taking charge. All the horrifying stories I had heard from activists came flooding back. Now I was the one who needed to fear for my safety and freedom, I thought. I had also shackled myself to Nasrin by lending her money. If I sacked her, I might never get my money back. I also learned that it was only part of the problem.

"Don't fire her under any condition," Khoshvaght stressed. "As long as she is at your home, you're safe."

Babak and I began whispering in our own home, fearing that Nasrin might have helped install listening devices. We worried that if we dismissed her, we might get a nanny who came directly from the prosecutor's office. At least we knew Nasrin. In the end, we came up with an arrangement so as not to leave her alone in the house. My father volunteered to drop by every day to check on her. We didn't talk about her kidnapping, and Nasrin never mentioned it again.

Within a year of Nasrin telling us her story, it had become clear that she was an informant. We returned from a trip to Toronto and discovered that she had brought a strange woman to our apartment; my mother had dropped by early to pick up a key to our apartment and found the two women there with the contents of all the cabinets and closets scattered on the floors. When I confronted Nasrin about this, she said that she'd brought her own maid and that if I didn't like it, she would quit. I happily accepted her resignation, even though I still needed her help—but the next morning, she showed up for work as though we'd never had the conversation the day before.

Every day a woman called six or seven times on my landline to speak to Nasrin. She introduced herself as Nasrin's sister-in-law, but her authoritative tone differed from the voices of Nasrin's relatives, who spoke in a low and sheepish tone. I overheard Nasrin reporting my daily schedule to this lady.

On two separate occasions, when the kids weren't home and I had asked Nasrin to leave, I found her hiding in their bedroom while I had colleagues visiting. From then on, I escorted her out the door when her workday was over.

Nasrin's behavior, however, annoyed me more than her spying. I got the impression that her duties as an informant had given her a newfound confidence, and that suddenly she felt that she could rule our lives. Within an hour of her arrival every day, she littered the house by spilling food and garbage on the floors. As she walked around the apartment, she knocked picture frames off the walls. Bathroom faucets had turned black because she left detergent on them for too long. Our fifth-floor apartment flooded several times because she left her rag in the sink with the water running. Once I screamed and grabbed my three-month-old son away from her when I found her shaking him hysterically as a way of playing with him.

Many of my friends had dealt with dysfunctional domestic helpers. My mother constantly reminded us of her own horrible experiences. Ultimately, my last nanny had forced my mother to quit a good job. That nanny had gone so far as to make me afraid of birds, even of their photos, threatening that she would have them hurt me if I didn't listen to her. The bird phobia that she instilled in me stayed with me into adulthood, and to this day I keep my distance from the tiniest birds. As for Nasrin, I had sent her away several times on temporary leave to see if I could replace her with other candidates. One woman refused to change diapers; another would only come at noon and leave before dark. Another candidate, who changed diapers and worked long hours, confided after a few days that she worked as a prostitute in the evenings.

Deciding that the alternatives weren't any better, and that it was better to deal with a spy whom we knew than to risk having a new, more sinister spy assigned to us, we tried to manage Nasrin with constant supervision. I worked long hours and went on unexpected trips. During those times, Nasrin was devoted to Chayan. In the meantime, I did not mind her spying on me as long as she didn't try to dominate my life. We often had long conversations about her difficulties as a single mother raising a rebellious teenager, her youngest who wanted to quit high school. I respected her as a hardworking woman who wanted her children to do better in life than she had. My relationship with her had become like Iranians' relationship with the Islamic regime: I was stuck with her whether I liked it or not.

To me Nasrin personified the Iranians who were benefiting from the government's ability to splurge with the oil revenue of 2000. Money had intoxicated her in ways that she'd never experienced before, and the newfound wealth had increased her desire for power. She had joined the middle class, and her income would increase steadily along with that of the growing middle class during these years.

Oil prices had begun to rise in 2003, filling government coffers with a historic windfall—revenue that was directly and indirectly injected into Iranian society. Iran's middle class was growing, and the number of poor Iranians was dropping rapidly.

The biggest winners from these economic developments were Iranians who were linked to the regime. By fueling the economy, the oil money opened up new opportunities for people like Nasrin's family. Her son, Mehdi, got into a law school because of his affiliation with the Basij, and at the same time he was awarded an administrative job at a university.

I would learn several years later that, as an informant, Nasrin earned a salary three times greater than what I paid her. She never rented out her two apartments in Malard. Every time I asked her the reason (she had returned half of the money she owed me, but I was eager to get the ten thousand dollars I was still owed more quickly than through her monthly $100 payments), she explained that she feared tenants would damage her properties. She hired a maid and copied the improvements we made to our home in her apartments.

To me, Nasrin also represented the cultural transformation that was taking place during the first decade of the new millenium. Iranians' infatuation with modernity, their resentment toward restrictive laws, and their rising affluence had led to the decline of morality. Addiction soared. Official figures suggested that one out of every seven Iranians used some kind of drug, with crystal meth being the most popular substance by early 2000. Bootleggers would not deliver alcohol unless you ordered cases of liquor, so the availability of alcohol skyrocketed. The government's propaganda on chastity backlashed, and prostitution also became a problem.

Nasrin stopped wearing the chador after her husband passed away and inside our home wore such revealing clothes that an American friend who visited our apartment once thought she was hitting on him. Another time, when I was away and she was alone with Babak, she walked out of the shower with only a towel wrapped around her.

I felt sorry for her, knowing that she was confused and unaware of the impression she left on people. In some ways she seemed to want to defy the traditional restrictions on her behavior, just like the rest of us. All her life religion had dictated how she had to behave, but now she was reinventing herself. Nasrin no longer had a sense of what behaviors were inappropriate. In the old days, a man could engage in a polygamous relationship and wed his housemaid, but not in modern Iran. Babak could even have a temporary marriage with her according to Iranian laws, but contemporary Iranian society abhorred such behavior. Nasrin became the *sigheh* ("temporary wife") of her aunt's husband, a much older man. She complained to me that she was confused as to why her relatives, including the aunt, were angry.

When the June 2005 presidential race approached, Nasrin said that she was too disillusioned with politics to vote. No one in her family except for Mehdi was doing so, she claimed. As for Mehdi, I was surprised to hear that he was planning to defy orders from the Basij and vote for Rafsanjani. Rafsanjani had been the first president after Ayatollah Khomeini's death and had played an instrumental role in Khamenei's appointment as supreme leader. But relations between the two men had soured after Rafsanjani held the elections that led to Khatami's victory, and two of his children since then had openly backed the reform movement.

Rafsanjani was running against four other candidates, including the newly appointed mayor of Tehran, Mahmoud Ahmadinejad, who pledged to distribute the country's oil wealth among the poor. I would have expected Mehdi to have backed a candidate like the mayor, because the Basij commanders had accused Rafsanjani and his family of corruption, indicating that the regime favored one of the other candidates over him. But Mehdi had told Nasrin that Rafsanjani was a more seasoned politician.

Rafsanjani was benefiting from other popular perceptions as well. Reformists had lost key positions a year earlier, after the Guardian Council had barred many of them from running in parliamentary elections. Now they confronted another threat to their cause; Ahmadinejad, a short man with hollow cheeks, had denounced reform and said that he would resurrect revolutionary values if he were elected. Fearing that he would reverse the gains they'd made under Khatami, reformists threw their support behind Rafsanjani.

The elections were so close that they led to a runoff between Rafsanjani and Ahmadinejad. On Election Day, I went to different polling stations. At some of the polls in the poorer neighborhoods of south Tehran, people were bused in. Many of them refused to tell me whom they were voting for. Some of them said they wouldn't know until they reached the front of the line, when the person who'd brought them would write the candidate's name for them. Here it was clear that the Basij had mobilized people to vote for Ahmadinejad; later, after his victory, his rivals would accuse him of engineering the vote. At other stations, where people were not bused in, many had said proudly that they were voting for Rafsanjani to avoid getting a hard-line president.

The Basij played a key role in Ahmadinejad's election, but many people also voted for him because he wasn't a cleric or because he appeared as the champion of the poor. The next day, I was following the vote count—which put Ahmadinejad in the lead—when Nasrin announced that she and her entire family had voted for him, too. "My brother called in the morning and urged me to vote for him," she said. "He looked innocent on television, and we thought we were tired of having clerics as presidents." By "innocent," Nasrin meant not corrupt and perhaps a sign that Ahmadinejad was willing to share more of the oil wealth with the population. But I knew the reasons were more complicated than that: Nasrin's brother worked at the university where Ahmadinejad taught. The brother had hurriedly sold his house during the week leading to the runoff, hoping that the distribution of oil wealth would help him buy a bigger home. Nasrin and her family still belonged to a section of society that vied for long-lasting economic relief, and Ahmadinejad had cannily tapped into the vein of their economic uncertainty.

Nasrin added that Mehdi had voted for Rafsanjani, and I was so impressed by his decision that for a moment I forgot my disappointment at the fact that Ahmadinejad's victory seemed to be assured. I told Nasrin that I was going to her home the next day, even though she had avoided showing me the apartment I'd helped her rent. It was time to speak to Mehdi again.

Mehdi's chest had grown thicker in the two years since I'd seen him last. He looked more confident as he invited me to sit on an armchair by the fireplace. He sat across from me, resting one foot on another knee, picking at his toes. I let my headscarf slip back, the way I always wore it, and ignored Nasrin, who was standing behind the counter of the open-space kitchen and motioning at me to pull the headscarf over my forehead.

The vote counting had ended, and Ahmadinejad had been announced as the new president of Iran. He beat Rafsanjani with seventeen million votes, some 61 percent of the total. Rafsanjani's humiliating defeat after getting a little over ten million votes had prompted him to join other candidates in complaining that the Basij had tampered with the votes. But while I knew that Medhi and I were both disappointed with the election results, I was curious to find out if Mehdi had really changed course.

Mehdi told me that the Basij commanders had initially instructed him and his fellow militia members to vote for Mohammad Baqer Qalibaf, a former police chief. But then, a week before the first round of elections, they told them to vote for Ahmadinejad instead. Basij members were also required to persuade their families to vote the same way.

Mehdi had listened to Ahmadinejad's campaign speeches and watched his television debates, and he made his own decision. "He might be a good man," he told me. "But to run a country, you don't need a good man; you need a politician. I argued with many of my Basij friends that Ahmadinejad wouldn't make a good president.

"To persuade us to vote for him, our commanders told us that even Khamenei had favored Ahmadinejad and that his son was campaigning for him. This is wrong. Khamenei and his children should always stay neutral."

Mehdi's words were uncharacteristically progressive. Only two years earlier, he had believed that Khamenei was the nation's father, his word the country's law. Mehdi's parents hadn't dared to mention Khamenei's name in front of him, for fear of offending him. Now he was judging the man and had even voted against his wishes. I didn't know if this change in Mehdi had been triggered by living in the capital, attending law school, having a job at the university, or spending long hours surfing the Internet, but I could tell that despite his ties to the Basij, he had embraced the mentality of Iran's more educated citizens, those who favored moderation.

After I finished asking my questions, I closed my notebook and leaned back. "Mehdi," I said, "once you told me that Basij members were rewarded according to their contributions. What did you do to earn a staff job at the university and a spot at the law school?" As I posed the question, I glanced at Nasrin to see the expression on her face. Nasrin was resting her chin on one fist with her elbow on the countertop as she stared at her son.

"I did something that no one else could do for them," he said, without hesitation.

"What was that?"

"I cannot tell you."

Nasrin continued to look at her son, not making eye contact with me.

By the time my daughter, Tina, was born in December 2005, Nasrin had become a nightmare. I couldn't be sure whether the questions I had asked Mehdi had made her angry with me, or whether she was simply becoming even more intoxicated with power than she had been before the interview, but it was becoming clear that Nasrin was no longer my maid—she was something else entirely.

One day in March 2007, she screamed at me and threw her rag at me after I asked her to clean the kitchen, which she'd dirtied within an hour of her arrival. I had to tiptoe so that I wouldn't slip on the wet tile or step on the potato skins she had dropped on the floor while preparing lunch. "I am tired of taking orders from you," she barked. By noon that day, she had thrown a check on my desk for more than what she owed me. I was surprised that she had held the money even though she could pay her debt. I returned the check and asked her to give me one for the right amount. She never did.

Perhaps it was the spiritual emptiness of the years after the revolution, or maybe the easy money that filled her pocket, or simply a desire to be in charge, but Nasrin's behavior had become exasperating. And she wasn't alone. I tolerated her for a few more months because there was an army of people like her—people who felt their support for the regime entitled them to insult others and dominate their lives. They were everywhere, at a bank, on the street, in a government position, at the grocery store—and no one was immune from them. Nasrin quit on many more occasions; I fired her on many others. But she continued to show up for work.

In the summer of that year, two scholars were arrested on spying charges. They were both Iranian Americans, and so I reported their story in detail. Soon the state daily newspaper *Kayhan* ran a column and named me along with the two scholars. I was terrified; everyone in Iran feared *Kayhan*, because if it named you, it meant that you were on the regime's blacklist and your arrest could be imminent.

I had other reasons to be afraid. Another friend had been arrested a year earlier; he and his wife later found out that their servant was an informant and perhaps facilitated his arrest at the airport. I was traveling alone to Toronto a few days after the column in *Kayhan* appeared. I hadn't told Nasrin about my trip and was planning to send her home early on the day of my flight, but shortly after she arrived that day, she slammed the door and disappeared with the kids. She dropped them at my mother-in-law's home on our street and then left. She returned at noon and, sensing my anger, declared that I must not expect her to get permission to leave or drop the children at my in-laws' home.

I flew out of the country but was on the verge of a breakdown by the time I arrived at Paris's Charles de Gaulle Airport to catch my connecting flight to Toronto. I was hungry, but I was too tense to eat. I was exhausted, but I felt too jittery to sit. My bag weighed too much, but I was too nervous to put it down. As I stood there watching people pass by, a loud noise startled me. Behind me, two women had broken into laughter, a high-pitched carefree guffaw. As I listened to them, my cheeks became wet. How envious I was. Back home, none of my colleagues ever burst into laughter like that. Here, outside Iran, no one paid any attention to the two women or to my red eyes; you were entitled to your personal space. It was a freedom I had long since forgotten about, even in my home. The strain of coping with Nasrin on a daily basis had finally worn me down.

I returned home with a plan. Babak called Nasrin and told her not to come for a week. Babak called her the following week and asked her not to come for a month. We didn't let her show up at our doorstep anymore. She called my mother-in-law and pleaded over the phone to help her get her job back, but my mother-in-law ignored her. She went knocking on my father's door several times, saying that she missed my children, but he sent her away. As for the money, Babak instructed her to return it to his father, which she did in small installments over a year.

I put my kids in day care and did my best to forget about Nasrin. Soon she was all but out of my life.

I felt a spell had broken. And with Nasrin gone, I dared to hope that Iran itself might soon be freed from Ahmadinejad—a person who, like Nasrin, had earned his grip on power by deceit and who had turned the lives of most Iranians into a nightmare, just as Nasrin had done to mine.

Ahmadinejad had no political experience and little political acumen, as had become clear after he assumed the presidency. Under his leadership, the country had gone into a tailspin. As he looked for ways to spend the windfall petro-dollar, he turned to imports. It was cheaper to import anything, from Chilean apples to industrial goods from Europe or China, than to encourage Iranian farmers and industrialists to produce them. His policy of distributing Iran's oil wealth also slowed down the manufacturing sector. Many of those who were financially rewarded felt they didn't need to work. As the country's exports dropped and Iran became more dependent on imports, inflation skyrocketed and consequently hurt the poor who had voted for him. As far as I knew, Nasrin's brother was not able to replace his house.

Relations with the outside world worsened under Ahmadinejad as well. He sped up Iran's controversial nuclear program, which the West believed was aimed at making nuclear weapons. To punish him, the United Nations and Western countries imposed economic sanctions on Iran, worsening the country's economic plight. Ahmadinejad also made inflammatory remarks such as "The Holocaust is a myth," and "Israel must be wiped off the map." These comments, like Ahmadinejad's nuclear policies, were turning Iran back into a pariah state.

Ahmadinejad became a source of embarrassment for Iranians— but also many jokes. When a cholera outbreak killed several people that year, a joke went around that Ahmadinejad had spread the virus by washing his socks in the reservoir. When his government began segregating men and women at universities, another joke held that when Ahmadinejad parted his hair he ordered, "male lice to the left, female lice to the right." The jokes were circulated in the millions by text messaging—the latest form of technology to liberate Iranians from the yoke of the regime.

The humor was a welcome release for many Iranians, but it also veiled a deep anger. People were extremely upset that Ahmadinejad seemed to be undoing the great progress the country had made in recent years. Many were eagerly awaiting the next presidential elections in June 2009, when they hoped to repudiate Ahmadinejad and reinstall a reformer in his place.

A year and a half had passed since I fired Nasrin. Our life settled into a pleasant rhythm. I stopped worrying about who was visiting me or how Nasrin was playing with our kids. And while Ahmadinejad had made life harder for our family, Babak and I shared a sense that we were biding our time until he could be peacefully and democratically eased from power.

Then, in December 2008, when the cold winter weather had frozen puddles solid and made Tehran's polluted air even more suffocating, two Revolutionary Guards knocked on our neighbors' doors. They asked questions about us and implied that we were part of a drug and prostitution ring. They continued to phone one neighbor for four months after the visit.

Finally, in April 2009, one of the Revolutionary Guards called Babak. It was just eight weeks prior to the presidential election. The man asked to meet with Babak and me that afternoon.

This was the first time the Guards had directly contacted us. I informed Ershad about the phone call, and the new director instructed me that I must not open the door when the Revolutionary Guardsmen arrived. He said that he would ask the local police as well as Police *Amniyat*, the special Security Police, to come to our house. This was the first sign to me that the country's security apparatuses were competing over power. I reasoned that Ershad was worried about my fate because of what had happened to a colleague about the same time as when the Guards had first knocked on our neighbors' doors. In December, they had arrested an Iranian American freelancer, Roxana Saberi, who now faced spying charges.

Both the local police and the Special Security Police arrived early. We met them outside, and both groups urged us to avoid the Guards. "We will send them away," said the two stocky and intimidating men with the Special Security Police. We went home and from our living room window saw that the two Special Security Police officers lingered and the local police drove off. The Guardsmen arrived outside, and the Special Security Police seemed to check their identity cards—but then the officers mounted their motorbike and left, too, leaving the Guards behind.

The Guardsmen buzzed our doorbell, and when Babak went downstairs and answered, they asked for me. The two men were polite and friendly. They wore civilian clothes, and one of them carried a sling bag and had a hole in the knee of his dress pants. They showed me a printed webpage with mug shots of several people already arrested for running a prostitution ring and asked if I knew them. They must have seen the shock on my face because they apologized quickly and left. It seemed clear to me that the whole visit had been an excuse for them to find out what I looked like.

Ershad sent half a dozen people my way to figure out what the Guards' intentions had been, but no one explained to me what the two agents were actually up to.

I finally went to see Khoshvaght. He was no longer at Ershad—he was running a pro-reform news website instead—but he was still well connected. He had been honest with me when Nasrin was kidnapped, and I hoped he might offer some advice. This time, his first question was, "What did you do with your nanny?" When I said that I'd fired her, he warned that I should expect trouble. "The Guards have lost their eyes and ears in your house."

I immediately saw Khoshvaght's point. The Guards had lost their spy and had been forced to collect their own information on me. The

Intelligence Ministry must have refused to cooperate with them. It occurred to me then that the Guards were stepping far beyond their limits, trying to control duties that had been part of the Intelligence Ministry's job since the 1980s. This might have reassured me—the other ministries weren't targeting me, after all—but instead it made me very, very nervous.

CHAPTER TWENTY-FOUR

THE RISING TIDE

It soon became apparent just how desperate the Revolutionary Guards had grown. Not only were they willing to go against the other branches of government to target threats like me, but they were also willing to defy the will of the Iranian people to keep a grip on power.

The presidential elections took place that summer, as planned, but after the polls closed on June 12, 2009, a surprisingly early count put Ahmadinejad in the lead. His rival, Mir-Hussein Moussavi, held a press conference right before midnight and warned the Iranian and foreign media that the Guards, together with Ahmadinejad, were rigging the vote. Moussavi claimed that, according to his monitors at the polls, he'd actually won the election. But Ahmadinejad still held the reins of power, and the next day his own interior ministry announced that twenty-four million votes (out of a historic turnout of 85 percent of the Iranian electorate) had gone to Ahmadinejad, while only thirteen million had been cast for Moussavi.

These results flew in the face of most Iranians' expectations for the election. All signs leading up to the election had suggested that Ahmadinejad would lose. Moussavi, with a sliver beard, had served as the prime minister under Ayatollah Khomeini, something that might have made him anathema to many people, but his criticism of Ahmadinejad had drawn wide support. Reformist groups had thrown their support behind him, creating what became known as the Green Movement.

Predicting his victory, people had blocked the traffic in Tehran in cele-bratory convoys before the vote.

I had traveled with Moussavi to the city of Tabriz during the cam-paign. Tens of thousands of people had come to the airport, traffic snarling the road. The following day, police had to block off the streets near a stadium as thousands of his supporters marched there to hear him speak. "*Ya shasoon* Moussavi" ("Long live Moussavi"), they chanted in Azari.

This excitement had manifested itself in long lines of voters on Elec-tion Day, curling around polling stations. Many wore green wristbands, which had become the color of Moussavi's campaign. An overwhelm-ingly anti-incumbent mood, as well as the support of the reformists, had driven a huge population to stand behind Moussavi.

In truth, for many Iranians the choice between Moussavi and Ah-madinejad had been a choice between the lesser of two evils; as a mem-ber of the revolutionary government, even a reformed one, Moussavi was tainted in the eyes of many voters. But he was a more progressive alternative to Ahmadinejad and—just as importantly—a viable can-didate, and many Iranians had considered a vote for him to be a vote against Ahmadinejad.

That morning, I scanned the newspapers for some explanation of how Ahmadinejad could have won. The pro-regime daily *Kayhan* carried a front-page headline in a large font: "Minister of Intelligence Warns Against Demonstrations." (In truth, people had gathered in celebratory convoys before the election, but there had been no sign of protest.) Another strange announcement in *Kayhan* said that the gov-ernment was shutting down the universities for a week; universities were strongholds for activism, but they were quiet now because the stu-dents were taking final exams. The measure only signaled the regime's fear of demonstrations at universities.

Another newspaper, one that tended to take the reformist line, ap-peared with half of its front page completely blank. Local journalists had told me the night before, at Moussavi's press conference, that the judiciary had sent monitors into printing houses to check the contents of the papers and shut them down if they were publishing controversial stories. I assumed the monitors had disliked their cover story, and the editor had left the space blank as a sign of protest. Other newspapers refrained entirely from commenting on the results of the election.

I checked my cell phone and noticed that the text messaging service, which Moussavi had used to rally support, remained shut down. The service had abruptly become unavailable on Friday morning, when the polls opened. Moussavi's monitors at the polls had planned to text what they observed from around the country into a center in Tehran, so the timing of the shutdown seemed like more than just a coincidence.

What was happening? Was it possible that Ahmadinejad and the Guards had stolen the elections, just as Moussavi had warned the night before? Would the Green Movement, the millions who had rallied behind Moussavi, accept the results? Would all the reformist politicians remain silent? Moussavi, unlike Ahmadinejad, had roots in the revolution; he had served as the prime minister when Khamenei was president. Was it possible that Khamenei wanted to intimidate him now because Ayatollah Khomeini had never let him dismiss Moussavi? Hungry for information, I called a political analyst, a newspaper columnist I knew. "Ms. Fathi, forgive me, but I cannot talk," he said. "I promised my wife to avoid getting arrested this time."

I apologized and wished him luck. But his words made me realize how critical the situation must be if an analyst feared that a mere phone call from the *New York Times* could land him in jail. I felt as if I had gone to sleep in one country and woken up in a completely different one.

I dialed the number of a newspaper editor, Mahmoud Shamsolvaezin, who often analyzed complicated situations objectively, and who I hoped could explain what was going on. "They summoned all the editors last night," he explained. He didn't elaborate on who "they" were, but I knew he was referring to government forces. "They warned us not to speak to foreign reporters," he continued. "I am sorry."

I wasn't a foreigner, but suddenly I found myself being treated like one because I reported for a foreign outlet. Frustrated, I turned my attention to news websites, some of which had become reliable sources of information and published the kind of news that newspapers couldn't print. They were now reporting that government forces had arrested dozens of activists, journalists, and reformist politicians. The forces had stopped and beaten a former vice president, Abdollah Ramezanzadeh, while he was in his car with his son. Later there would be photographs online, showing the car stained with blood. Both the former vice president and his son were now in prison, although the charges against them were unclear.

I threw on my headscarf and slipped into my manteau to go out and get a sense of what was happening on the streets. I called Reza, the driver who'd taken me around the city for the past few days, and told him to meet me outside the convenience store on our street. The tiny store was packed with jars, cans, bottles, and boxes, so that the few customers who could fit inside at any given time could barely squeeze their way around the shop.

The store was often my first stop for some honest conversation with total strangers. People opened up quickly there because Karim, the smiling young man who ran the store, knew that I was a journalist and spoke his mind to me without hesitation. I'd learned that ordinary people liked speaking to journalists so long as they felt they could trust them not to reveal their identities. I usually threw a question at Karim and others jumped into the conversation.

On this day, I picked up a carton of milk and asked Karim, "Did your candidate get elected?" The fourteen-inch TV installed just below the ceiling was playing on mute, but it was tuned into the same channel I had been watching at home.

"I did not vote," Karim said, showing his white teeth. "What difference would it have made, anyway?"

"You were wise," a middle-aged man quickly interjected. "They're thieves. This was the second time I voted in thirty years, and it was certainly the last."

"I was just at the bank," commented a middle-aged woman, "and everyone there was appalled. So many of us have moved to Tehran from different cities and still have relatives there. We have a sense of how people vote even in small towns. Who can possibly believe that 63 percent of the people would vote for Ahmadinejad after what he has done?"

Both of these customers looked like people who lived in my upper-middle-class neighborhood, people who would vote pro-reform or refrain from voting all together. But they were not the activist type, and I was surprised to find them so angry.

I paid for the milk and spotted Reza outside the store. We drove downtown. The streets were unusually quiet. We went to Ahmadinejad's neighborhood, a lower-middle-class district in eastern Tehran where the president-elect had a large support base. When I asked people there if they were happy about his victory, most reacted with sheepish smiles. There were no signs of celebration.

In other parts of the city, people referred to the elections as a coup d'état staged by Ahmadinejad and the Revolutionary Guards. This was a new language, and so I took the comments as an indication of how angry these people were with the election results. I was about to find out just how widespread that anger was.

In the afternoon, as I was speaking to people on a street near the Interior Ministry, where the votes were counted, a group of about a hundred protestors appeared. "Death to the dictator," they chanted, a common reference to Khamenei since the protests in 1999. "Death to the Islamic Republic." They were shouting at the top of their lungs, their fists clenched.

Passersby joined them. A man with a briefcase got off a nearby bus and chanted with the protestors for a few minutes before leaving. Shopkeepers came out of their stores to watch. Drivers waved to signal their support. The outpouring appeared to be unorganized, spontaneous, and emotional.

A colleague called on my cell phone to say that she was at the scene of another rally. Small demonstrations, it seemed, were breaking out around the city. News websites would report dozens of other protests taking place around the country.

The demonstration I was witnessing had been going on for less than an hour, stretching and receding several times, when the Basij arrived. They drew their bikes in a circle around the protestors, drowning their chants with a chorus of roaring engines. Behind them followed a bus filled with Security Forces in olive-green uniforms. Wearing helmets and holding shields, they stepped off the bus. The Security Forces and the Basij had for years become the visible face of repression. But everyone knew that the Revolutionary Guards were involved in behind-the-scenes positions, leading the big crackdown.

An officer with three golden stars on the shoulders of his uniform spoke into a handheld speaker, asking people to disperse. "Please return to your homes. This gathering is illegal," he pleaded. "I beg you: go home." Members of the Security Forces are civil servants, not volunteers or necessarily regime supporters, and this man clearly wanted to avoid a clash.

But the crowd didn't waver. "Death to the dictator," they chanted.

The Security Forces pulled out their clubs, and the Basij members swirled heavy chains. Together, they attacked the protestors and began kicking, punching, and clubbing them. The Security Forces fired tear gas. People torched garbage bins or held flaming newspapers in front of their faces, in the hope that the smoke would alleviate the effect of the tear gas.

I ran to the car. Reza and I were sitting inside, coughing and rubbing our eyes, when a Basij member pounded on the hood. "Move!" he yelled. Reza lit a cigarette and put it between his teeth. As the man struck the hood again, Reza turned on the engine, and we began moving through the chaos.

I returned home and found Babak in front of the television with my mother, who had been coming to our home every day to look after our children after we fired Nasrin. They were watching the BBC Persian service, showing footage of the clashes in Tehran and other cities. People had shot videos on their cell phones and sent them to the network, showing government forces beating people violently and the country immersed in chaos.

In addition to the BBC Persian service, more than twenty opposition channels were broadcasting similar footage. People trusted these networks more than state-run television. The government had acknowledged that some 40 percent of the population watched satellite TV. But judging from anecdotal evidence, even this figure was an understatement; I'd seen the aluminum dishes popping up over mud houses in even the country's most remote and impoverished areas, and knew that at this very moment hundreds of thousands of my countrymen must be watching the same images that we were seeing on the screen in our Tehran apartment.

My mother and my husband cursed the government forces. "Look at that beast," Babak said as we watched one muscular Basij punch a young man in the face and then force the man's head back with one hand while dragging him by the arm along the pavement. Three green-clad troopers clubbed another young man.

"How many of them does it take to subdue one person?" moaned my mother.

A middle-aged woman threw herself between the young man and his assailants, and the forces began beating her too.

I left my mother and Babak in front of the TV and released myself from the embrace of my kids, who were playing nearby, to check the news websites. Many of them were operating from outside the country to avoid government harassment, but Moussavi and another pro-reform candidate, Mehdi Karroubi, still posted their statements and communications on their websites, *Kaleme* and *Sahamnews*. And ordinary Iranians continued posting their videos on the Internet, too, even though the government had slowed its speed to a crawl.

One of the websites suggested that the election results were completely fabricated, and that the number of votes for each candidate had been calculated based on how harshly he'd criticized Ahmadinejad. Karroubi, the most outspoken critic and a former Speaker of Parliament, finished with the lowest number of votes: a little over 300,000. The newspaper he published joked that he'd come in fifth even though there were only four candidates. He got fewer votes than the total number of ballots that had been declared void. Mohsen Rezaei, another candidate, fared slightly better, with a little over 600,000 votes. He was from the south, had served as the commander of the Revolutionary Guards during the war, and had repelled Iraqi forces from Iranian territories. His website claimed that his representatives at the polls had estimated between three and a half and seven million votes cast for him.

The thirteen million votes that had been announced for Moussavi seemed generous compared to the other two men's shares, yet most websites were already saying that the figure represented only a fraction of his actual votes.

Moussavi and Karroubi had met that day and issued a statement, vowing that together they would defend people's votes; to avoid offending Khamenei, however, the two candidates also pledged their loyalty to him. Other activists and reformist politicians issued statements condemning the election, too, but these tended to be similarly cautious.

But there was one statement, posted on all the websites and emailed to me by several people, that stood out from the others. The Green Movement was urging all Iranian ethnic and religious groups to stage silent rallies the next day:

> Ahmadinejad, the president appointed by the Supreme Leader, is planning to celebrate his fake victory tomorrow at five PM. But we, Iranians who are loyal to their vote and are opposed to this coup, are planning to march at the same time on Valiasr Avenue in Tehran, between Valiasr Square and Tajrish Square, to show our support for Mr. Karroubi and Moussavi, the two coalition leaders who are the true winners of the election. We will hold green and white cloths in a sign of unity. Kurds, Azaris, Baluchis, Turkmen, Bakhtiaris, Arabs, Persians, Sunnis, Shiites, Christians, Jews, Zoroastrians, Dervishes, Baha'is: this country belongs to you. The armed forces will certainly try to discourage us. Let us spread the word by phone, text messaging, on the Internet chat rooms, websites, blogs, by word of mouth and all other possible means of communication. We will meet tomorrow at five PM. Hand in hand, we will unite and give flowers to the Security Forces. Merchants of the bazaar, close your shops tomorrow and join us. If we allow this coup to prevail today, we will have to grieve for many years.

By calling out every single major Iranian ethnic group—even the Baha'is, followers of a faith that the regime had persecuted since 1979—the Green Movement was trying to bring all opposition forces together under the same umbrella. Its outreach didn't end at Iran's borders either. Besides calling for silent rallies in Iran, the statement also urged Iranians living abroad to stage protests in front of Iranian embassies around the world.

The next day, I went to Ahmadinejad's press conference with Roger Cohen, a columnist for the *New York Times*. Seated in a chandeliered hall, Ahmadinejad dismissed allegations of fraud and asked jokingly if reporters had asked all forty million voters whom they had voted for.

While we were at the press conference, tens of thousands of people marched on Valiasr Avenue. A huge crowd occupied a distance of several miles. No clashes occurred; images that people captured on their cell phones showed a sea of humans dotted with green, moving like a silent river.

Emboldened by the number of people they had galvanized, the opposition called for another massive rally the next day.

That night I received a letter by fax from Ershad. It banned resident journalists working for foreign media outlets from reporting on the streets and also suspended work permits for translators working with visiting reporters. Requests for visa extensions were denied, and all reporters were told to leave the country. The regime, I could tell, was circling its wagons.

Despite the ban, most of us reporters on the ground went to cover the march on Monday. Close to three PM, under a scorching sun, I headed out again with Roger Cohen, who no longer had a translator; I'd decided I could both interpret for him and fulfill my reporting duties for the *New York Times*.

At first Roger and I were hesitant. I hid my notebook in my bag, and we decided not to talk to one another so as to avoid drawing attention to ourselves by speaking English. If there were Basij or other Security Forces mingling with the protestors, English would surely make us a target.

But our concerns evaporated when we saw the swelling crowd. The smell of car exhaust—a common fragrance in Tehran—began to dissipate as the number of vehicles on the street grew sparser and the number of marchers increased. The sidewalks overflowed, and people spilled into the street. Many carried backpacks and bottles of cold water that sweated in the afternoon heat.

The silence was palpable once we reached Enghelab ("Revolution") Street. Normally teeming with roaring cars, screaming vendors, and swarms of motorcyclists, Enghelab was now filled with a single, silent body of people. A man with an amputated leg, perhaps a war veteran, limped past on a pair of crutches. A young woman pushed the wheelchair of an elderly woman through the throng. Some of the protestors had taped their lips shut to show they had no intention of chanting slogans. Every few minutes we could hear a "shush" coming from the crowd. I looked down and noticed that most people were wearing running shoes. They were prepared for a confrontation.

Groups of police in black riot gear sat on the pavement, their batons and shields scattered around them. It was an embarrassing scene; the demonstrators must have surged onto the streets in such unexpected numbers that the riot police could neither confront them nor flee. In an act of compassion, demonstrators offered their water bottles to these men, whose heavy, dark gear had left them particularly parched.

Roger and I interviewed people to find out why they'd dared to come out despite the fact that state television and radio had been warning people against staging any rallies.

"They have insulted our intelligence," whispered a young woman, wearing a shimmering lipstick. "We are not violent, and we are not the enemy. But the regime must realize that we are not ignorant."

"What's your name?" I asked her.

"Iran," she said. "We all have the same name and the same voice today."

After an hour, the crowd stopped marching, the people around us no longer able to move forward toward Azadi Square—the largest square in the capital, capable of holding hundreds of thousands of people. We climbed the stairs of a pedestrian overpass to get a clearer view. The steel bridge creaked as hundreds of people crammed onto it, trying to get a better vantage point so they could use their cell phones to capture the scene below.

When we reached the top, I held my breath. People filled Enghelab as far as the eye could see. From every single alley, groups of people were pouring onto Enghelab like small rivers. But despite the assembled masses, the entire scene was eerily still. The marchers' deafening silence echoed in the distance between Enghelab to Azadi, "Revolution" to "Freedom," appropriately enough. "Where is my vote?" flashed on hundreds of handwritten sheets of paper. In the middle of the silent crowd was a long green banner, nearly a mile long. The abundant cloth fluttered in the air as people held it over their heads.

More than three million people attended the rally that day. More significant than the turnout, however, was the behavior of the crowd; people had expressed their dissent in the most civilized fashion. Had the crowed veered off a few blocks south of Enghelab Street, they would have reached Khamenei's compound. They never did.

The demonstrators remained silent, restrained, and peaceful until later that afternoon, when a few men ran toward a Basij headquarters. Fearing that they would climb the wall, an armed watchman opened fire on the crowd, killing seven people.

Angered by the violence, people packed downtown Tehran for three more days of silent rallies. Iranians demanded new elections. News of the protests dominated the international media. Everyone was eager to find out if this massive outpouring of opposition would force the regime to hold new elections and accept Ahmadinejad's defeat. People had risen up in massive numbers to protest against the regime, and for the first time they had two leaders on their side. Karroubi and Moussavi had been part of the establishment. Both men had been Ayatollah Khomeini's allies. And now they, too, were demanding that his successor, Khamenei, bend to the will of the Iranian people.

CHAPTER TWENTY-FIVE

END OF AN ERA

On Friday, June 19, a week after the election, Khamenei took the podium at Tehran University to lead the Friday prayers. All eyes were fixed on him. For an entire week, massive rallies had rocked the country. People openly referred to the elections as a coup d'état. Khamenei had the final word on state matters and could call for new elections. His predecessor, Ayatollah Khomeini, had famously said, "The regime derives its legitimacy from the people's vote." Yet a few days earlier, Khamenei had congratulated Ahmadinejad on an electoral victory that most Iranians apparently considered a farce.

It seemed strange that Khamenei would have cheated Moussavi out of office if he had been legitimately voted into it. After all, he had been allowed to run in the first place; the watchdog Guardian Council had screened and approved Moussavi, when it could have simply barred him from running, as it had hundreds of other would-be candidates. It was possible that the Council had not considered him a threat to Ahmadinejad; Moussavi wasn't a liberal, and his campaign had gained no momentum until the reformers, with no other viable candidates, had thrown their support behind him and used their networks to mobilize voters on his behalf.

Khamenei stood at the podium that Friday, one hand resting on a rifle. I still remembered my morality teachers explaining that the rifle, which the Friday prayer leader had with him, was meant to strike fear into the hearts of the enemy and show that the leader was prepared to fight for Islam. In the front row was Ahmadinejad, kneeling.

In a firm voice, Khamenei denounced the protests. "Flexing muscles on the streets after the election isn't right," he said. "It means challenging the elections and our democracy." Without naming Moussavi and Karroubi, he warned, "If the political elite ignore the law—whether they respect it or not—they will be responsible for the ensuing bloodshed and chaos."

With those words, Khamenei reminded the Iranian people that he still viewed compromise as a sign of weakness. He had also come out clearly on the side of Ahmadinejad and against the reformists and their candidate; rather than accepting the demonstrations as a legitimate expression of the political will of the Iranian people, he called the protests *lashgar keshi Khyabani*, "street trooping." Khamenei lost any claim to impartiality that day, putting himself at the forefront of the battle over the contested election.

Karroubi challenged Khamenei that same day by sending a letter to the Guardian Council and demanding that the Council must nullify the results of the election. By ignoring the people's demands, the letter said, the regime would only intensify their rage. No one had ever gone against Khamenei as publicly as Karroubi did that day, but he and Moussavi would pay a heavy price for their opposition.

The protestors, meanwhile, refused to give in. They called for another rally on Enghelab Street the next day.

Roger and I headed to Enghelab Street at three PM on June 20. This time, we were in a car, but as we neared Enghelab Street, we found ourselves carried through Tehran on another human tide.

No one doubted that Khamenei's forces would use violence; he'd used the word "bloodshed" in his speech the day before, after all. Yet people were streaming down the streets in running shoes all the same, still wearing bright green shirts and wristbands.

To prevent people from forming the massive rallies of the previous week, the government had brought out a huge number of pro-regime forces, armed with clubs, chains, and guns. These men stood at every corner leading to Enghelab. Some of them wore olive-green fatigues, while others wore menacing black, Robocop-style outfits, and yet others were in civilian clothes.

On a narrow street about twenty feet away from Enghelab, we passed a group of Basij forces attacking people. The men screamed religious Shiite slogans such as "Ya Hussein," referring to the grandson of Prophet Muhammad, as though he would have endorsed their crusade against the protestors. People fled before the onslaught but returned within minutes in greater numbers. Our car got caught in the middle of this second confrontation.

A group of regime gunmen stood in front of our car. Over a hundred people began running in the opposite direction, rocking our vehicle from side to side.

One pro-regime gunman, in his early twenties, lifted his shotgun right in front of our car and took aim at the protestors, then slowly lowered the barrel until it was pointing straight at me where I sat in the backseat. Our eyes met through the windshield. I screamed and tensed my body, as though I could make myself disappear. His finger rested on the trigger. But he didn't fire. Instead, he grinned maliciously.

Roger and I realized it would be better to be on foot than trapped in a car, so we got out and sent the driver home. Pro-regime forces were everywhere, so we agreed again to minimize our conversation to avoid attracting attention to ourselves. As journalists, we weren't even allowed to be there, since Ershad had banned resident journalists from reporting on the streets for foreign media, and foreign reporters had been forced to leave after their visas expired. Roger had luckily received a longer-term visa than anyone else.

Marching with a group of about fifty protestors, we reached Enghelab Street. The crowd was smaller than the previous week but more tightly knit. They gathered in a huddle and looked around hesitantly. A woman's voice broke the silence: "Don't be scared, don't be scared, we're all together," she shouted rhythmically in Persian. Everybody began chanting the words along with her.

Within minutes, a rumbling of rushing feet drowned their voices. People behind us were under attack. We began running, perhaps more than a hundred of us in one direction. At the next intersection the crowd turned right, but Roger and I froze in our tracks in front of a shuttered store.

On the opposite side of the intersection, a large crowd of protestors had formed a line. Women stood in the front row, their bags slung over their shoulders and their scarves wrapped around their faces to hide their identity. Some leaned forward, knees bent, as though they were ready for a footrace.

Just then the Basij appeared. Some of them were on foot, swinging their batons in the air; others were on brand-new red motorcycles.

A roar erupted from the dense rows of the protestors: *"Hamleh!"* they shouted—"Attack!" From their sling bags the women pulled out rocks and hurled them at the Basij. The men behind them began advancing too. The Basij who were on foot staggered and turned back; the ones on bikes wobbled and turned around. The protestors outnumbered them, and within minutes not a single Basij was in sight.

Victory. Hundreds raised their arms in the air and screamed with joy. The store shutter went up, and a few men emerged into the center of the street. Among them was a young man in olive-green fatigues—a defector. In a dance-like move, he tossed his hat in the air. *"Namarda,"* he shouted, meaning "men of no honor." *"Gomshid"*—"Get lost."

As we were standing at the intersection, organized rows of Security Forces with helmets and shields appeared on the street across from us. The protestors quickly pulled together. Again, it was the women who took the lead. "Get up, collect some rocks," a slim woman shouted at a male spectator sitting on the curb. He looked up, stunned. "Quickly!" she snapped. Protestors ran into the side streets, seeking construction sites and any other places they could find rocks and pieces of brick.

"Hamleh!" came the call, and once again the protestors began pelting the advancing men. But this time, the troopers held their shields over their heads and marched on unharmed. From behind them, gunmen shot tear gas at the protestors.

This time the line broke, and the protestors began running. Roger and I were following them when a canister, with white smoke billowing out, landed in front of us. I pulled my scarf over my nose and mouth as I jumped over it. But I quickly felt a sharp sting in my lungs and lost my balance as my eyes got teary. I slowed down, pulled out my water bottle, and poured some water onto my scarf.

Bad idea. As soon as I put the wet cloth on my nose and mouth, my chest burned. My head began spinning, and I staggered forward with my eyes shut. I'd been tear-gassed before, but never this badly. I heard the sound of footsteps running by. I'd lost Roger.

At that moment, a hand grabbed my arm and pulled me along, directing me to a quieter street, where a man instructed me to lean against a wall. "Open your eyes," he said a few minutes later. "Let me blow cigarette smoke into your eyes."

I had to separate my wet eyelids with my fingers. My savior, a young man, blew smoke into my face, but my eyes and nose were still wet and my head was spinning. I located a small fire and took a step toward it, hoping that more smoke might help. We were in a dead-end alley, and people were scurrying around. An old man shuffled out of a house with a pile of newspapers for people to burn. Residents opened their doors and ushered people inside.

People were still chanting in the distance, "Oppressor, get lost," referring to the forces. The sound of gunshots ripped through the air. "They are coming," somebody shouted.

A door opened nearby, and the same man who had pulled me into the alley drew me inside. It was cool, and I slumped to the floor as the door shut. Somewhere nearby a man was moaning in pain.

"Keep quiet," a woman whispered. "They will come in if they hear you."

I felt better after a few minutes and was able to open my eyes. A dozen of us were inside the hallway of a small apartment building. I spotted Roger sitting against a wall, taking a drag on a cigarette. He was not a smoker but seemed to have become one. His eyes were red.

Two men were carrying a long-haired fellow down the stairs. He had no visible injuries, but one of the men explained that he'd been hit by a stun baton and was in pain. He was cursing: "May they burn in hell. My father fought for this regime in the war. This is how they repay their Guards."

I turned and thanked the man who had rescued me. His shoes were worn out and pointy, the kind that many lower-middle-class Iranians wore. His eyes were red. He was young, in his early twenties. He smiled.

A nervous woman appeared in a traditional, floral, head-to-toe chador. "They have moved up the street. Please leave now," she pleaded. "We'll get into trouble if they find you here."

I recognized her voice. It was the woman who had urged us to stay quiet. The injured man could stay behind, she said. We decided to leave in pairs every five minutes to avoid drawing attention to the house.

When Roger and I appeared on the street, we saw government forces nabbing people and shoving them into black vans. One soldier in black riot gear pulled a young man up from the back of his collar, as though he was lifting a kitten, and shot pepper spray into his face. The man screamed and raised both hands to his face.

"Give me your phone, or I'll spray again!" the trooper commanded.

The young man dropped the phone on the pavement, and the soldier stamped his boot on it. I assumed that he must have seen the young man taking a video on his phone. He shoved the man into the van.

Roger and I looked down and walked away. The air smelled of tear gas and smoke. Black soot littered the ground. Grey smoke still whirled out of metal garbage bins that people had dragged into the middle of the street. The neighborhood was deserted of the men and women who'd been roaring victoriously only half an hour earlier.

A few blocks to the west, we reached a large intersection called Nosrat. It was another battlefield, with women leading the attacks against the Basij, advancing and retreating, their voices ringing in the air. We stood and watched for a while. Hundreds of people were standing on the curb, and many others occupied an overpass, taking video with their cell phones.

One such video shot in the streets of Tehran that day captured a tragic scene. A few blocks north of Nosrat, on Kargar Street, a twenty-seven-year-old woman named Neda Aghasoltan was in the backseat of a car with her silver-haired singing instructor, Hamid Panahi. They were caught in the traffic behind a protest scene. It was hot, so Aghasoltan unknotted her headscarf under her chin and tied it behind her head, revealing a long pale neck—an unacceptable act in Islamic Iran.

Aghasoltan had come out to protest in solidarity with other Iranians, but she hadn't voted and wasn't interested in politics—even though politics had shrouded her entire life and had turned her into something of a rebel despite herself. She loved dancing and singing, but before she was born, the regime had banned women from taking part in such things, so all her adult life, like many women of her generation,

Aghasoltan had defied the rules. A divorcee, she set herself up as a tour leader and took like-minded Iranians to neighboring Turkey—a popular destination for its beaches, discos, and bars. At home, she ignored the ban on singing and took lessons privately.

The air in Aghasoltan's car was suffocating. The traffic wasn't moving, and people were getting out of their vehicles. Aghasoltan and Panahi stepped out, too, and retreated into a side street for some fresh air.

Suddenly Panahi heard a gunshot. He turned and saw Aghasoltan fall to the ground. She landed on her back as he rushed over to her, reaching her side at the same time as a young man who said he was a doctor. A bullet had pierced Aghasoltan's chest. The doctor bent over and pressed his palm on her wound to stop the bleeding. Another man approached with his cell phone, recording the scene.

"*Sookhtam*," she said—"It burns." Aghasoltan's eyes looked straight into the camera. She opened her mouth again, as though to breathe. Instead, blood gushed out of her mouth and eyes.

I learned about her death when I returned home that day; the video had already gone viral. Television networks around the world were broadcasting it repeatedly, as were Persian-language satellite networks. I had heard gunshots, and many people were killed that day, including a young man at the Nosrat intersection. But inside and outside Iran, people reacted with sadness and sympathy to her killing. Karroubi called her a *shahid*, meaning "martyr," a term that was normally reserved for men. As the video of her death spread, Aghasoltan became the face of the Iranian uprising.

My mother was sobbing when she called me that evening. "Did you hear what they did to an innocent girl?" she asked. She had been talking to her friends, and they were angry, too. In those young eyes, my mother said, they had seen their own children, many of whom were protesting in the streets just as Aghasoltan had been.

"First they stole the election, and now they are silencing people's children with bullets," my mother said. "This regime is doomed."

Late on the night of June 19, a TV show called *Parazit* on Voice of America Persian, which soon drew the largest audience in the country, put Iran's newly emerged citizen journalism on the right track. The show's host, Kambiz Hosseini, offered viewers "a few tips" on how to use their cell phones to shoot video.

"Stretch your arm out with the phone," Hosseini explained as he stood in front of the National Museum of American History in Washington, DC, with a phone in his hand. He told viewers to hold the other hand under the elbow of the stretched arm to prevent it from shaking. "Avoid close-up shots and zooming," he added. "And don't speak while shooting, so that we can hear the background noise. Give a brief description of the date, location, and what you are seeing."

Two days later, on a Sunday, the Green Movement posted a message online calling for a protest in Valiasr Square in central Tehran. Dozens had been killed the day before, but the violence had only fanned people's anger.

Only two hours before the opposition's rally was expected to begin, the authorities announced on state television that pro-Ahmadinejad forces would stage a demonstration in Valiasr Square, too. It meant that they were planning another confrontation. Valiasr Square was a small roundabout, with dozens of manteaux stores and restaurants. The government forces could easily contain any Green Movement protestors there, beat them, and arrest them.

I linked up with Roger, and together we headed toward Valiasr Square. Bus drivers had parked their vehicles half a mile away, and people were walking the rest of the distance to the square. We got out of our taxi and joined them. Most of the men were bearded and grinning and carried huge banners; the women walked separately in black head-to-toe chadors. It was blisteringly hot, and many of the people in the crowd held small silver juice packages and sipped from them leisurely through straws. These demonstrators looked and acted drastically different from the protestors we had seen at the previous rallies. A group of them told us that they'd come from the industrial city of Karaj, a forty-five-minute drive west of Tehran.

As we approached Valiasr Square, there was no visible sign of the opposition. The street leading to the square was quiet except for ordinary passersby, who threw unfriendly looks at the waves of men and women headed toward the demonstration. A few young people, their political affiliation unclear, sat listlessly in front of the shops in the square.

Then I heard a whisper. "The rally has moved to Vanak Square," said a young woman, as normally as if she were telling me what a beautiful day it was. She passed by without looking back at me, and when I turned around, I saw that she was carrying a bag of diapers. A few minutes later a man who was carrying a bag containing a watermelon said into my ear, "Go to Vanak."

Vanak Square was six miles north of Valiasr Square on Valiasr Avenue, a much larger space and a good distance away from the pro-regime protestors.

At this point, the authorities had arrested over a hundred leading activists and former politicians who'd sided with Karroubi and Moussavi. The Revolutionary Guards had used sophisticated equipment to track down activists in hiding using their cell phone signals. Several thousand demonstrators had been arrested and dozens were killed. The Green Movement never had a clear leadership but had now also lost many of its prominent figures.

None of that, I could see, had intimidated the opposition. Disguised as shoppers, they were using word of mouth to mobilize their supporters.

About an hour later, we were interviewing a Basij commander at Valiasr Square when one of his men rushed over. "Demonstrators have gathered in Vanak Square," he said.

The Basij members gunned the engines of their motorbikes. A few of them raised the front wheels of their bikes, wheelie-style, before speeding off. We hopped into a taxi and headed north to Vanak Square.

There was no sign of the usual traffic until we got close to the square, where the traffic stopped moving. We got out and walked the rest of the way. Many other people were walking in the same direction, casting gentle looks at one another as though they were sympathizing over the violence they had all suffered the previous week.

Once we got to Vanak, we found the square and Valiasr Avenue—which stretches south to north of Vanak—occupied by tens of thousands of people. Security Forces stood by idly, not knowing what to do with the massive crowd. People flashed their fingers in triumphant V signs to each other.

As we walked among the crowd, I noticed some of the protestors' faces fall when they looked at Roger. Thrilled by what we'd seen, he was giving them the thumbs-up sign. I elbowed him; this is the foulest sign in Persian culture.

All along the square I noticed hundreds of people standing on the curb holding their cell phones in the exact posture that the VOA program had taught the night before: they stretched the arm that held the phone and held their elbows with the other hand. This was their weapon. It was impossible to stop the flow of information; it was travelling faster and farther than ever.

When I called my editor later that day to tell her that I was filing a story about the protest, she mentioned that the state-run IRNA news agency and one of the international wires had reported only two thousand people had shown up at the opposition's rally. I assumed that the reporter with the international wire agency had not defied the ban and instead had based their reporting on the IRNA story. But as we were talking on the phone, people's videos were finding their way onto YouTube, showing that the rally was actually much, much larger than the regime was admitting.

The authorities were at a loss and groped for a scapegoat. The next day, they expelled the BBC resident journalist Jon Leyne from the country, accusing him of plotting Aghasoltan's death; he had paid thugs to kill her, prime time news announced. But everyone knew that Leyne was innocent. The regime wanted to punish the BBC, and Leyne was the closest that the regime could get to the network. The BBC Persian television continued to broadcast scenes of the protests and stir the public's anger, making the government feel even more threatened.

Leyne left the country, but the videos continued flowing on YouTube and other websites. Technology was evolving faster than repression could, and it was clear that the government was increasingly at a loss for how to respond.

CHAPTER TWENTY-SIX

EXILE

During the last week of June 2009, Tehran became a police state dominated by pro-regime forces. Some of the armed men who roamed the streets of the capital were so young that they had no facial hair yet. Others sported provincial, cone-shaped beards. Many had helmets but no batons; others had batons but no helmets.

The opposition had deserted the city's streets. Even drivers who normally blocked the traffic disappeared. The violence seemed to have sapped everyone's energy.

During that week, I drove out of my garage and noticed that a car and two motorcycles were tailing me. After I circled around the block and returned home, I realized that my house was under surveillance by some sixteen men.

I stopped going out, worried that, although the forces might not have a warrant to arrest me at my home, they might nab me on the street. I filed stories based on what appeared on websites and Persian wires. None of my sources spoke to me. They were in jail or in hiding. I began spending more time with my children. I felt completely alone. All the international correspondents I knew had left the capital, and my colleague, Maziar Bahari, the *Newsweek* correspondent, had been arrested a day after he visited me at my home.

I was also haunted by the memory of a call I had received the week after Aghasoltan's death. The Basij commander I had interviewed during one of the demonstrations, and whom I later visited at his office, had phoned to urge me to stop going outside. "They have given your photo to snipers with orders to shoot you," he said. I'd been so overwhelmed by the events that I ignored his warning. But the more I ruminated on his call, the more I was reminded of Aghasoltan's last words to her music teacher: "*Sookhtam*"—"It burns."

I had tickets for Babak, our children, and me to fly to Toronto a few nights later, on July 1—a vacation we had planned months earlier. The *Times* foreign editor had asked me to cancel the trip and stay in Iran. But now, with the surveillance starting all over again, we were eager to leave. We had heard about what Bahari's arrest had been like. Government forces had come knocking at dawn and barged in after his mother opened the door. They pulled him out of his bed and dragged him away. The scene had replayed in many other households, traumatizing young children. Babak and I were determined to avoid it if we could.

Unlike the previous surveillance teams, which had watched us twenty-four hours a day, the men assigned to our house this time left every night at midnight. On the evening before our flight, we packed a few pieces of clothing and drove to the airport after midnight with Babak's parents and my father. I thought we would be back in a few weeks, everyone would be released, and life would return to normal again—crazy, perhaps, but a manageable kind of crazy.

During the two-hour car ride to the airport I held Tina and Chayan's tiny hands, wondering if this would be the last time I held them for a while. Many people had been arrested at the airport. My fears seemed confirmed when officials at passport control held us for no reason. While we waited, I gazed at my two children with guilt. Sitting excitedly in their twin stroller, Chayan clasped a pair of pink sunglasses he was planning to wear in Toronto. Tina was still asking if I had packed her red glittery shoes, the ones I'd taken away from her before leaving the house. At that moment, it struck me that I should prepare them for the worst. I leaned down and looked them in the eyes. "I don't want you to worry if I end up going to Canada alone," I said, thinking it would be better for them to think that their mother was in Canada than in prison.

I don't remember how long the officials at passport control held us, but it felt like the longest wait of my life. I looked around nervously and promised myself that I would keep my composure if they came for me. It turned out they were scanning the pages of our Canadian passports— part of a new regulation. Finally, an officer handed the passports back and wished us a nice flight. I relaxed my muscles and waved at my father, who was standing behind a glassed wall, to signal our safe departure.

As our Austrian Airlines flight took off, many other Iranians were fleeing, too—part of a mass exodus I would only become aware of later. I was lucky to be leaving on a plane and with a Canadian passport; many local reporters, including ones who had travelled with me during the past months covering the campaign, escaped on foot, with nothing but a backpack. They followed human smugglers through rugged mountains into neighboring Turkey or Iraq. It would take months, even years, for them to settle down in new, faraway homes.

In Toronto we kept postponing our return. Gradually several people I knew were released from prison back in Iran. They phoned and urged me not to return. I had become the longest-serving reporter for an American publication in all of Iran, and my name had come up time and time again during their interrogations. The regime was claiming that foreign media had instigated the protests, and people like Bahari and I had become actors in that fictional narrative. When Bahari was released, he told me that he had learned about my departure from his interrogator. "She escaped before we could arrest her," the man told Bahari, seeming disappointed.

Babak and I settled into a life in exile and put our kids in kindergarten. They began speaking English within a week, remembering the language I had spoken to them since birth. When we told them we were not returning to Iran, my son's eyes filled with tears. "Will I see Grandpa again?" Chayan called my father his best friend in the world. Then he wrote my father's name on dozens of papers and pasted them around the house, as though he was worried he might forget him. Tina repeated every day, "I will remember Grandpa's face, and when he comes to visit, I will recognize him in the airport." My dad was eighty-one. Secretly, I wondered whether I would see my parents again, too.

Babak, who was paying a steep price for being my pillar of support, fell into a depression. He couldn't hold back his tears and would lie in bed for long stretches of time, becoming reluctant to even leave the house alone. Years later, he would tell me that he thought of committing suicide during this period but never found the courage.

At night, I dreamed again and again that I was back in our apartment in Tehran, scrambling to find something precious to take with me. But before I could find anything, the government forces began banging on the door. I would wake up sweating and breathless, and ask myself why I would even consider going back. But I knew the answer: I had left part of me behind without saying good-bye.

I continued to cover Iran for the *New York Times* as massive rallies rocked the country. To intimidate the opposition, government forces raped detainees and tortured them to death. Conditions back home seemed to be getting worse by the day.

Surprisingly, people inside Iran began speaking to me. They felt more secure knowing that my phone wasn't tapped in Toronto, and many of them weren't overtly political and so assumed that the government wasn't listening in on their phone lines. Protestors put me in touch with others, such as doctors and nurses at hospitals who were treating the injured. Once they found a safe way to communicate, often on Skype, people wanted to tell the world what they and their fellow Iranians were going through.

The 2009 crisis turned out to be a crisis within the regime too. In February 2010, Grand Ayatollah Abdolkarim Moussavi Ardebili, a senior cleric close to Ayatollah Khomeini who had helped revise the constitution after his death, travelled from Qom to Tehran to appeal to Khamenei. He was more senior than Khamenei, and along with other senior clerics, he had backed Khamenei's appointment as supreme leader. Back then the clerics had thought the modest Khamenei would serve a symbolic position and let them lead the country. But fearing that he would never command their respect, Khamenei alienated Ardebili and other senior clerics after they had elevated him to the supreme post. He dismissed Ardebili, who served as head of the judiciary, and replaced him with a more junior cleric. Ardebili pretended that he was resigning and retreated to Qom, but now the chickens were coming home to roost.

Ardebili's trip to Tehran showed just how critical conditions within the country had become. Dissent had reached new heights among the youth in Qom; children and grandchildren of clerics had been arrested for protesting. During their meeting, Ardebili urged Khamenei to find a compromise with the protestors. "Your failure is the failure of the revolution, Islam, and the Shiites," he told Khamenei, and then asked him to order the release of all detainees and to distance himself from Ahmadinejad.

Khamenei declined both requests.

The truth is that when he served as president and Ardebili was head of the judiciary, Ayatollah Khomeini had simply killed his opponents. What Khamenei was doing was lenient by comparison. Human rights groups had registered the deaths of more than a hundred people, but this was still far less than the thousands Khamenei's predecessor had murdered. Still, Iranians were referring to the recent violence as *Sarkoub-e-Khooneen*, meaning "the bloody crackdown." Pictures of the victims circulated widely, and people knew their stories as though they were family members. Killing was proving harder to get away with in the Internet age, even if the numbers involved were smaller.

But while Khamenei was under pressure to ease up on the opposition, his brutal tactics seemed to be working. By March 2010, the protests had diminished. People felt that they were achieving no progress. Initially they had tried to force the regime to respect their votes; they knew there was no alternative to the Islamic Republic—at least, not one within sight—but they still wanted to have a say in how that republic was run. Moussavi and Karroubi were both regime men who would not have posed a fundamental threat to the regime. But when the regime confronted the protestors brutally, their anger had snowballed. The opposition had gambled that the regime wouldn't slay millions of Iranian citizens and would back down instead. But the country's leaders seemed to feel that the protests were threatening the regime's very existence, or at least their own hold on power, and resorted to extreme violence to intimidate the protestors.

When it was reported that Mohsen Rouhol-Amini, the twenty-five-year-old son of a senior Revolutionary Guard commander, had died in prison, many in the Green Movement began to feel that they had misjudged the regime. It seemed to have no mercy, even toward the child of one of its own people. Rouhol-Amini's jaw had been smashed, and his bones had been broken. For two weeks after his arrest, his father had appealed to every senior official for his release, including Khamenei. But Rouhol-Amini remained incarcerated until his injuries became infected and he died of meningitis.

The violence reminded many people of the bloodshed after the 1979 revolution, and reawakened in many Iranians a sense of caution that had deep historical roots. During the time of the revolution, as the brutality had escalated, people forgot about democracy and longed for calm and security, slowly coming to accept the new regime as a guarantor of safety and stability. Then came the war, which only traumatized the Iranian people further. When the war finally ended, Iranians remained politically passive for nearly a decade, until the reform movement flourished in 1997.

Yet even while reformists were steering the country in a new direction, they encountered new hurdles that forced them to slow down and work more gradually to transform their country. The fall of Saddam Hussein in 2004, which brought Iraq to the brink of a civil war, reminded Iranians that chaos is only one institutional breakdown away. Reformers became more determined to seek gradual grassroots change, of the kind that Khatami had introduced, instead of radical breaks with the existing order.

In 2009, people had tried to bring about change at the polls—a simple democratic right that the constitution granted them. When this right seemed to be denied to them, they fought to reassert it. But following six months of confrontation, and after realizing that the regime wouldn't budge, the opposition withdrew from the streets. Many people told me that they didn't see the point in dying on the streets or in prison to effect change; any regime that feared its own children, as the Islamic Republic did, was bound to collapse or change. All the people had to do was wait.

But the regime's fear of the protests didn't disappear. Two years after the Green Movement receded, in 2011, when Tunisians and Egyptians toppled their leaders after a few weeks of protests, the Iranian regime frantically snatched Karroubi from his home and detained him in an unknown location. Moussavi and his wife, Zahra Rahnavard, were put under house arrest. The regime feared that the two leaders might lead similar revolutions in Iran. Moussavi and Karroubi, who had bravely kept their pledges of loyalty, vanished from the public eye. These developments sent shock waves through Iran's leadership.

The Arab Spring, as it would come to be known, only deepened the Iranian regime's resistance to change or compromise. High-profile reformers and activists remained incarcerated. Those who had fled, like me, stayed in exile. Many others, like the activist Aminzadeh, left the country too.

On the surface, it seemed that the regime had prevailed.

EPILOGUE

Many observers had pronounced the death of the Green Movement as early as 2010, when the protestors had disappeared from the streets of Tehran and other cities across Iran. But if it were dead, I wondered, why did the regime go as far as banning even the mere use of the term "the Green Movement"? Green, which had been the traditional color of Islam, evoked such terror that the regime outlawed the color too.

I'd witnessed the formation of this modern movement throughout the years, like a steadily rising tide. Young people, vying for social and cultural liberties as well as economic prosperity, had loaned it momentum; it contained Iranians from various backgrounds, as well as from both genders. Indeed, women were at its core, trying to assert themselves against a chauvinistic culture and an oppressive regime. On June 15, from the overpass on Enghelab Street, I'd seen the magnitude of this tide as it rolled silently toward the locus of tyranny in our country, promising to wash it all away.

The tide may seem to have receded since then, but in truth, it is timeless. At one juncture of history it was called the Constitutional Revolution of 1906, another time the Islamic Revolution of 1979, and finally the Green Movement of 2009. All along, it ebbs and flows depending on whether Iranians have remained silent in the face of despotism, whether monarchial or religious in nature, or whether they have cried out against it.

In 2009, as at several other points in our recent history, Iranians spoke with one voice. This time our cries were particularly forceful because religion, which after the revolution had held such great promise for Iran, had become a tool of oppression. Iranians today cherish religion, as they always have, but their leaders have also made many of them deeply skeptical of political Islam.

The events of 2009 marked not the death of the movement but rather a new chapter in the history of Iranians' struggle for democracy. Ironically, this episode has much in common with the Revolution of 1979, for both were stoked by civil movements aimed at procuring freedom, respect, and prosperity for all of Iran's citizens. This impulse may seem to have gone dormant, but its longings have passed from one generation to another, and they have not gone away.

Khamenei was wrong if he thought that he, alone, could control the affairs of the country simply by stealing the vote for his candidate and crushing dissent. Relations between him and Ahmadinejad grew bitter even before the protests had ended. When Ahmadinejad tried to replace the sensitive positions of interior, foreign, and intelligence minister (all three of whom Khamenei had handpicked), Khamenei stepped in and reinstated the intelligence minister, while appointing new men to the other two posts. In this, he was following in the path of Ayatollah Khomeini, who had blocked Khamenei himself from sacking Moussavi as prime minister in the 1980s.

Khamenei seemed to have bet on the wrong horse with Ahmadinejad—not only because the former professor didn't have much of a flair for governing, but also because he was continuing to wreak havoc on Iran's economy. The country's failing economy was further squeezed by mismanagement, corruption, and international sanctions imposed to punish Iran for pursuing its controversial nuclear program. The value of Iran's currency, the rial, plunged: the exchange rate rose from 9,000 in 2009 to 32,000 rials for one US dollar a year later. Oil revenue shrunk to half after the West tightened its noose on Iran's oil exports, limiting the amount of crude that Iran could ship around the world. Inflation shot above 40 percent in 2013, the last year Ahmadinejad was in office.

A new presidential election was slated for June 2013, but people expected only another sham. Rafsanjani, whose two children had been jailed for supporting the Green Movement, nominated himself to unite the country. But the watchdog Guardian Council barred him from running. A member of Parliament wrote scornfully in a letter to Khamenei that if Ayatollah Khomeini were alive, he would be rejected by the Council too. Khamenei clearly felt threatened by Rafsanjani, but in disqualifying him, Khamenei was rejecting his own legitimacy; Rafsanjani, after all, had paved the way for Khamenei's rise to power.

The Council cleared eight candidates, among them Hassan Rohani, a relatively moderate cleric close to Rafsanjani. People widely believed that the regime would falsify the votes, as it had in 2009, in favor of a forty-eight-year-old candidate, Saeed Jalili—a favorite of Khamenei. The Basij and the Revolutionary Guards had thrown their support behind Jalili. He had fought as a volunteer during the war, but it was not until 2001 that he quickly climbed the ladders of power and became a senior director of policy planning at Khamenei's office. Khamenei promoted him to membership in the Supreme National Security Council a year later and then appointed him as Iran's nuclear negotiator in 2007.

During the campaign, Rohani spoke in support of the Green Movement. He said that Moussavi and Karroubi must be released, he promised to seek rapprochement with the West to save Iran's ailing economy, and he pledged to distance the country from Ahmadinejad's policies. Voters backed him, if only to send signals to a regime that hears and understands such coded messages even if it never responds to them. People had little confidence that their vote would count—but this time, it would turn out that they were mistaken.

When millions of Iranians took to the streets in celebration of Rohani's victory, one of the many slogans people chanted was: "Thank you, dictator." The eighteen million votes cast for Rohani were a testament that the movement was alive and that it had reason to hope for the future. Khamenei, by then seventy-four years old, had finally given in and counted people's votes. Many assumed that he had only done so because Rohani was not a threat; Rohani had not tried to share power with him as Rafsanjani and Moussavi had in the past. But the regime was also on edge; it had lost legitimacy inside and outside the country. Khamenei needed Rohani to restore part of Iran's lost legitimacy at home as well as its international standing.

Khamenei went even further. Right after Rohani took office, he gave his blessing to the president to end Iran's nuclear crisis with the

West and mend ties with the United States—Iran's arch-enemy in the 1979 revolution and a country that Ayatollah Khomeini had labeled the Great Satan. Secret talks between Washington and Tehran had resumed in February 2013, but in a speech to members of the Revolutionary Guards on September 17, 2013, Khamenei openly called for "historic leniency," urging the force not to oppose Rohani's efforts. A week after that speech, President *Hassan* Rohani spoke on the phone with President Barack *Hussein* Obama—the first time the two countries' heads of state had spoken to each other since 1979. Iranians joked that the spell had been broken after thirty-four years only because the two presidents happened to be the namesakes of Prophet Muhammad's two grandsons, the brothers Hassan and Hussein. But in reality, Rohani needed to try to reestablish relations with the United States in order to take a first step toward reintegrating Iran in the international community and righting the country's economy. Either way, one of the major pillars of the revolution had finally collapsed.

Repression at home did not diminish following Rohani's election, and the memory of the protests in 2009 continued to haunt the regime. Iranians who had fled the country during that time were warned not to return. The regime asked Karroubi and Moussavi to admit publicly that they had mistakenly claimed the 2009 elections were stolen, but both men refused and so remained incarcerated along with many others.

The 2009 protests had made the regime paranoid. Khamenei, who doesn't give interviews but who is famously candid during his public speeches, revealed his fear of those protests in one of his speeches after Rohani's election. Without naming Karroubi or Moussavi directly, he explained to his countrymen that the ringleaders of the Green Movement had risked the stability that all Iranians cherished so much and that they were continuing to do so. "One must not forget the main issue," he told the nation.

> Why did they resort to street trooping in 2009? Why don't they answer? We have asked them many times privately so that they can respond. Why don't they apologize? Privately they have admitted that no rigging took place. If there had been no rigging, why did they put the country at such risk? If God hadn't helped

us, they could have set off a war in society. You can see today what is happening in several countries in the region where people are fighting against one another. They took the country to the edge, and it was only God that helped us. This is the main issue.

It is impossible to make predictions—to say if the Islamic Republic will collapse or if it will survive in its current form. Certainly its current form isn't the one it took in the immediate wake of the revolution. Although Khamenei has been committed to safeguarding the revolution, he has also created a new theocracy—one that relies on the greed of the Revolutionary Guards and the Basij instead of the loyalty of its founding fathers. Khamenei has banished nearly all the clerics who held power when Ayatollah Khomeini was alive. Despite falling oil prices and economic sanctions, Khamenei had enough petro-dollar to satisfy his military base of support: the Guards and the Basij.

The oil revenue has been the biggest deterrent to democracy in Iran, even though the windfall has transformed the fabric of Iranian society. The Iranian middle class, more than two-thirds of the population, relies on the revenue instead of contributing to economic growth, and thus has been less likely to fulfill a historic mission to create institutional reform. It has been incapable of placing demands on Iranian leadership for political reform because of its small role in producing wealth, as in other developing countries.

The regime is still an autocracy, to be sure, but democracy has been spreading at the grassroots level, even among members of the Basij and the children of Iran's rulers. The desire for moderation goes beyond a special class. As I am writing these lines, Khamenei's followers are shifting alliances and building new coalitions. Civil society, despite the repression it has long endured, has turned into a dynamic force. Khamenei still has the final word in Iranian politics, but the country's political culture is not monolithic. Like Ayatollah Khomeini, who claimed he had to drink the cup of poison in order to end the war with Iraq, Khamenei has been forced to compromise. The fact that he signed off on Rohani's historic effort to improve ties with the United States signals that the regime is moving in a different direction, and that further compromises are possible.

The revolution is evolving, and Iran's story is still playing itself out—as is my own. I do not know when I will get to go home again, and with every year that passes my children grow further and further away from the country of their birth. So, too, do Babak and I. But if the opportunity presents itself, I would like to return to Iran. I would like to see, one more time, the sun shining off the Alborz mountains and glimmering on the surface of a Tehran swimming pool. In my heart of hearts, I long to swim in those waters again.

ACKNOWLEDGMENTS

A host of people opened their hearts and minds to me over the two decades that I worked as a journalist in Iran. In this book you hear the voices of a broad swath of Iranian society—from ordinary people to activists and officials—who welcomed me into their homes and offices with tea and sweets. Many of them, unfortunately, have been tried, jailed, and tortured; some are still serving sentences. I have decided not to thank any of them by name, but they know who they are. As we say in Persian, "*Yek donya tashakor*"—"A world of thanks." Those conversations and interviews enabled me to write this book.

In Tehran, Ershad, the bureau that deals with foreign media at the Ministry of Culture and Islamic Guidance, arranged my press credentials for ten years, beginning in 1999. Hossein Khoshvaght and his team—Alireza Shiravi, Efatol Sadat Iqbali-Namin, Masoumeh Mahmoudi, and Gelareh Pardakhti—and later his successor, Mohsen Moghadaszadeh, were always helpful and courteous.

Several foreign editors at the *New York Times* gave me assignments and space in its pages. Andrew Rosenthal, Roger Cohen, and Susan Chira trusted my instincts and encouraged my ideas.

Bob Giles, the Nieman Foundation curator, gave me one of the best opportunities of my life when he accepted me as a Nieman Fellow at Harvard. I am grateful to him and his wife, Nancy Giles, who helped me and my family find a home in Cambridge, Massachusetts. Several Nieman Fellows generously helped during the different stages of this book. Joshua Prager patiently read the proposal and helped construct it, Fernando Berguido read the early chapters, and Antigone Barton offered editorial advice on the entire manuscript. Rose Moss and Martha Bebinger were my most loyal and brutal critics—exactly what I needed. Melissa Lutke was always there to have coffee and fill me with good cheer.

Alex Jones hosted me next as a Shorenstein Fellow at Harvard Kennedy School, where I wrote many of the chapters of this book. Jeff Seglin, Edith Holway, Luciana Herman, Richard Parker, and Thomas Patterson made me feel at home at the Shorenstein Center. My assistant there, Patrick Johnson, made certain we met the deadlines we set. Nicholas Burns and Cathryn Cluver gave me an affiliation with Harvard's Belfer Center for Science and International Affairs, where I almost finished writing the manuscript.

I am grateful to friends who helped with different parts of the book: Fatemeh Haghighatjoo and Mohammad Tahavori shared their insights with me; Shahala Haeri and Mehrangiz Kar shed light on women's issues; Mehdi Khalaji answered my endless questions on Islam; and Djavad Salehi-Isfahani generously shared his economic analysis and in the course of our discussions helped me hone my ideas. Greg and Michel Harris, gracious friends, read the manuscript and commented over savory dinners. Hassan Sarbakhshian enriched this book with his photos. Farnaz Fassihi, a constant friend, offered me encouragement not only with the book, but in life.

I am grateful to other people for reading the manuscript and lending me counsel along the way. In Cambridge, Massachusetts, Lois Fiore, Beena Sarwar, Dina Kraft, Alysia Abbott, and Andrea Meyer were thorough readers. In Washington, DC, Mathew Roberts and Kim Alexandra offered their comments with a wonderful sense of humor.

I was lucky to have Elaine Sciolino as my mentor when I started my career in 1992. She gave me my first reporter's notebook, then my first tape recorder, and later brought my first laptop from the United States to Iran, always urging me to take good notes. Without those notes, this book couldn't exist.

I would like to thank Greg Myre for introducing me to Alice Martell. Alice gave me crucial advice and steered me through the world of publishing. Alex Littlefield, my editor, put his faith in me and with his great skill and literary sense transformed the manuscript. Sandra Beris and Beth Wright improved the rough spots.

I owe boundless thanks to my family, who understood from the beginning what an important project this was for me. My talented sister, Golnaz Fathi, never failed to nourish my hunger for art and thus gave me positive energy. My husband, Babak Pasha, was my constant pillar of support who reminded me to remain conscious and sensible every time I was consumed by despair. Tina and Chayan kept me going with their endless love. Iradj and Shahin Pasha, my in-laws, were always there for me and my family at crucial times. Most important, I am forever indebted to my parents, Jaffar Fathi and Azar Saei, who never held me back; instead, they gave me wings to fly.

NOTES

PREFACE

xi **more than 70 percent:** "Iran: Urban Population," Index Mundi, 2011, http://www
.indexmundi.com/facts/iran/urban-population.

xi **By 2009, 43 percent:** Djavad Salehi-Isfahani and Amir Kermani, "The Middle
Class in Iran," paper presented at the Iran Economy Conference, University of
Chicago, Oct. 15–17, 2010, http://iraneconomy.csames.illinois.edu/program.

xi **Yet the regime also rewarded:** Followers of the Baha'i faith have been banned
from attending university in Iran since the revolution.

xi **Since the mid-1990s:** Djavad Salehi-Isfahani, "The Revolution and the Rural
Poor," *Radical History Review* 105 (Fall 2009): 139.

xii **"that is a far cry":** "Pedar, Modar, Ma Baz Ham Motahamim" ("Father, Mother,
We Are to Be Blamed"), http://www.kaleme.com/1389/03/24/klm-22713, June 14,
2010 (author's translation).

xii **Another revolutionary who fled:** Mojtaba Vahedi, "Farewell to My Mentor, Mr.
Karoubi," Sahamnews.com, July 20, 2013.

CHAPTER ONE: THE REVOLUTION

14 **It was clearly not an accident:** Anwar Abdulrahman, "From the 1978 Cinema Rex
Atrocity in Iran to a 2013 Riffa Mosque Bombing in Bahrain," *Gulf Daily News*, July
19, 2013, http://www.gulf-daily-news.com/NewsDetails.aspx?storyid=357499, and
also in Persian, "Ahmad Khomeini Ordered the Arson in Qom Cinema," *Keyhan*,
Dec. 14, 1979 (23 Azar, 1358). Hossein Lahouti, a senior cleric close to Khomeini,
said in an interview that Khomeini's son, Ahmad Khomeini, was behind the burning of another cinema in the city of Qom. The intention was to blame it on the shah
to provoke anti-regime sentiments. "Ahmad Khomeini was eager to overthrow the
regime and show that the clerics were part of a dynamic movement, so he issued the
order to blow up the cinema," Lahouti said. Lahouti died mysteriously in prison
shortly after this interview.

16 **state network TV camera captured:** In Persian, http://www.youtube.com/watch
?v=b2jtA5guMQ8, and in English, "Feb. 1, 1979: Ayatollah Khomeini Returns,"
ABC News, Jan. 26, 2011, http://abcnews.go.com/Archives/video/feb-1979
-ayatollah-khomeini-returns-12769714.

16 **"We are going to elevate":** Khomeini's speech at Behesht Zahra cemetery, You-Tube video, 9:57, posted by BaMoshiri, July 21, 2011, http://www.youtube.com/watch?v=cFMnG4NguBc (author's translation).

17 **when a full-bearded man sitting:** The man was Mahmoud Mortezaee-far, later nicknamed the Minister of Slogans for his role later at the Friday prayers, leading the slogans people were to chant (http://javgiriattt.blogsky.com/1392/02/21/post-1122).

CHAPTER TWO: NESSA

24 **But Khomeini claimed that the shah:** Ruhollah Khomeini, speech given on Jan. 8, 1979, in *Sahifeh Nour*, vol. 3 (Tehran: Moasesh Nashr va Tanzim Asar Imam Khomeini, 1999), 75. All Khomeini's interviews and speeches were published in Persian in *Sahifeh Nour*.

CHAPTER THREE: THE TIME OF HORROR

30 **the worst bloodshed:** "Iran's Srebrenica: How Ayatollah Khomeini Sanctioned the Deaths of 20,000 'Enemies of the State,'" *Independent* (London), Feb. 7, 2013. A tribunal in the Hague documented and published its final report in February 2013, concluding that the regime killed between fifteen thousand to twenty thousand dissidents in the 1980s.

30 **At the trial, which lasted:** Iranian journalist Alireza Nourizadeh, with the daily *Etelaat*, who was one of the reporters present during the trial and execution, reported it in detail. "Thirty Years After the Revolution: They Speak About February 1979," Feb. 10, 2009, http://www.radiofarda.com/content/f1_Memories_revolution/1490722.html.

31 **"And I believe":** Sadeq Khalkhali, *Ayatollah Khalkhali's Memoir* (Tehran: Sayeh, 2001), 12 (author's translation).

32 **"And prepare against them":** Sura 19, Maryam, Aye 1.

CHAPTER FOUR: "WORLD POWERS DID IT!"

38 **he sold the Iranian tobacco industry:** Stephen Kinzer, *All the Shah's Men: An American Coup and the Roots of Middle East Terror* (Hoboken, NJ: Wiley & Sons, 2003), 32.

38 **required to seek permits:** Mansour Moaddel, "Shi'i Political Discourse and Class Mobilization in the Tobacco Movement of 1890–1892," *Sociological Forum* 7, no. 3 (Sept. 1992): 459.

39 **He called for the establishment of a parliament:** In Persian: http://fa.wikipedia.org/wiki/اسماعیل_ممتاز.

40 **the British paid 20,000 rials:** Kinzer, *All the Shah's Men*, 42.

41 **the British ordered Reza Shah:** Ryszard Kapuscinski, *Shah of Shahs*, trans. William R. Brand and Katarzyna Mroczkowska-Brand (New York: Penguin Books, 2006), 25.

43 **the CIA agent Kermit Roosevelt:** Kinzer, *All the Shah's Men*.

43 **He allocated a budget of $11,000:** Ibid., 163.

CHAPTER FIVE: THE CLEANSING

48 **only 2 percent of Iranians:** Kaveh Ehsani, "The Urban Provincial Periphery in Iran: Revolution and War in Ramhormoz," in *Contemporary Iran: Economy, Society, Politics,* ed. Ali Gheissari (New York: Oxford University Press, 2009), 43.

49 **the strike by the workers in the oil sector:** The shah acknowledged in his last speech before leaving Iran that the strike at the oil industry had paralyzed the country; YouTube video, 0:27, posted by irantito, Oct. 17, 2008, http://www.youtube.com/watch?v=Xl5SGno5Kcs.

49 **Millions of Iranians had moved:** According to the country's first census, in 1956 70 percent of the population of 19 million lived in rural areas. The proportion dropped to 61 percent in 1966 and 53 percent in 1976.

50 **the public sector would swell:** Ehsani, "The Urban Provincial Periphery," 45. According to one estimate, within three years after the revolution, one in every six Iranians above the age of fifteen belonged to one or more revolutionary agencies.

50 **more than 60 percent of villages:** Ehsani, "The Urban Provincial Periphery," 21. By 2004, electricity and clean water would reach all villages, and some 20 percent would have natural gas pipelines.

52 **"the training of our youth":** Shaul Bakhash, *The Reign of the Ayatollahs: Iran and the Islamic Revolution* (New York: Basic Books, 1984), 122.

53 **women who showed their hair as "nude":** Ali Motahari, *Mass'aleh-ye Hijab* [*The Problem of the Hijab*] (Tehran: Sadra Publication-Qum, 1969), 12 (author's translation).

53 **"one that can never be fulfilled":** Ibid., 68.

53 **avoid provoking their sexual desires:** Ibid., 80.

CHAPTER SEVEN: OUR BODIES, OUR BATTLEFIELDS

61 **Under the Islamic Penal Code:** Article 638 of the Islamic Penal Code states, "Anyone who explicitly violates any religious taboo in public besides being punished for the act should also be imprisoned from ten days to two months, or should be flogged (74 lashes). Note: women who appear in public without a proper *hijab* should be imprisoned from ten days to two months or pay a fine of 50,000 to 500,000 rial."

CHAPTER EIGHT: MASOUD

77 **Television ownership would increase:** Djavad Salehi-Isfahani, "Oil Wealth and Economic Growth in Iran," in *Contemporary Iran: Economy, Society, Politics*, ed. Ali Gheissari (New York: Oxford University Press, 2009), 19.

CHAPTER NINE: THE WAR ENDS

83 **by 2013, one out of every four:** "Az Har Chahar Ezdevaj Yeki beh Talagh Mianjamad" ("One Out of Every Four Marriages Leads to Divorce"), Oct. 13, 2012, http://www.tabnak.ir/fa/news/278441/ازدواج-یکی-به-طلاق-می-انجامد٪E2٪80٪8C٪از-هر-چهار .

84 **It was genocide:** "CIA Files Prove America Helped Saddam as He Gassed Iran," *Foreign Policy*, Aug. 26, 2013, http://www.foreignpolicy.com/articles/2013/08/25/secret_cia_files_prove_america_helped_saddam_as_he_gassed_iran.

85 **The United States claimed:** In 1990, the captain of the vessel, William C. Rogers, was awarded the Legion of Merit award for his service from 1984 to 1989, which included the time he ordered the shooting of the Iranian plane. The citation made no mention of downing the aircraft, which further angered Iranians.

85 **The Iran-Iraq War was the longest conflict:** Kaveh Ehsani, "The Urban Provincial Periphery in Iran: Revolution and War in Ramhormoz," in *Contemporary Iran: Economy, Society, Politics*, ed. Ali Gheissari (New York: Oxford University Press, 2009), 49.

CHAPTER TEN: AFTER KHOMEINI

90 **People pounced on the shroud:** See photos of the funeral in Alex Selwyn-Holmes, "Khomeini's Frenzied Funeral," *Iconic Photos*, June 1, 2009, http://iconicphotos .wordpress.com/2009/06/01/khomeinis-frenzied-funeral.

90 **When the footage returned:** "Ayatollah Khomeini Funeral," YouTube video, 3:01, posted by hijazna, Sept. 12, 2009, http://www.youtube.com/watch?v =2k7mpnPJWDo.

91 **the release of seven American hostages:** The United States imposed sanctions on Iran after Islamist students attacked the US embassy in Tehran and took fifty-two diplomats hostage for 444 days.

91 **"You and Khamenei must stay close":** *Sazandeghi va Bazsazi* [*Building and Reconstruction*] (Tehran: Daftar Nashr Maaref Enghelab, 1391 [2012]), 15.

92 **State-run television showed the clerics:** Fars News Agency footage of Council of Experts meeting, YouTube video, 5:49, posted by faridostadi, Oct. 9, 2010, http:// www.youtube.com/watch?v=sT4KKcPNDaM.

93 **he had befriended a communist activist:** Houshang Asadi, *Letters to My Torturer: Love, Revolution, and Imprisonment in Iran* (Oxford: Oneworld, 2010).

CHAPTER ELEVEN: MEETING A HAWK

97 **"My brothers":** Author's notes.

99 **"His words ripped through me":** Ali Akbar Mohtashamipour, *Memoirs of Seyed Ali Akbar Mohtashamipour* (Tehran: Hozeh Honari, 1997), 28.

102 **he fell to his death:** "Information on a 14 April 1996 incident in Teheran . . . ," European Country of Origin Information Network, Sept. 12, 1997, http://www.ecoi .net/local_link/181324/283920_en.html.

CHAPTER TWELVE: THE INTELLIGENCE MINISTRY

104 **Khomeini had opposed its formation:** "Hajarian Says How Ministry of Intelligence Was Established," Participation Front publication, Sept. 6, 2005.

110 **I will call him Mr. X:** Another colleague, Azadeh Moaveni, referred to the same agent as Mr. X in *The Lipstick Jihad* (New York: PublicAffairs, 2005).

111 **"Some 13 years after the revolution":** Judith Miller, "Movies of Iran Struggle for Acceptance," *New York Times*, July 19, 1992.

CHAPTER FOURTEEN: THE WALLS COME CRASHING DOWN

126 **he authorized Iran's connection:** Cyrus Farivar, *The Internet of Elsewhere: The Emergent Effects of a Wired World* (New Brunswick, NJ: Rutgers University Press, 2011), 163.

126 **Commercial Internet service still cost:** Carroll Bogert, "Chat Rooms and Chadors (Internet Users in Iran)," *Newsweek*, Aug. 21, 1995, 36.

128 **Khamenei had funded the Computer Research Center:** "The Ayatollah's 'Computer Research Center of Islamic Sciences,'" *Society for Internet Research*, report no. 4, June 2, 2005, http://www.sofir.org/sarchives/004208.php.

128 **one of the country's first Internet centers:** The center was called the Center for Islamic Jurisprudence in Qom.

129 **the largest number in the Middle East:** Farivar, *The Internet of Elsewhere*, 164.

CHAPTER FIFTEEN: NESSA MOURNS

132 **Shortly after the war ended:** Djavad Salehi-Isfahani, "Oil Wealth and Economic Growth in Iran," in *Contemporary Iran: Economy, Society, Politics*, ed. Ali Gheissari (New York: Oxford University Press, 2009), 7.

133 **a booklet called *Ranj-nameh*:** See http://rangnameh.blogsky.com.

134 **sidelining him after his father's death:** Akbar Hashemi Rafsanjani, *Sazandeghi va Bazsazi [Building and Reconstruction]* (Tehran: Daftar Nashr Maaref Enghelab, 1391 [2012]), 266, 341, 406, 513, 535.

134 **Rafsanjani had moved quickly to reverse:** Ibid., 271, 275, 278, 280.

135 **To rebuild the country:** Salehi-Isfahani, "Oil Wealth and Economic Growth," 7.

135 **an unofficial inflation rate of 40 percent:** "World News Brief: Iran Policy Patrol After Day of Rioting," *New York Times*, April 6, 1995, http://www.nytimes.com /1995/04/06/world/world-news-brief-iran-police-patrol-after-day-of-rioting.html.

136 **Some ten people were killed:** "Fear of Torture / Legal Concern," Amnesty International, April 7, 1995, http://www.amnesty.org/en/library/asset/MDE13/005/1995 /pt/0caf8c58–55f7–4af7–8f90–9af7e6225fd1/mde13005199sen.pdf.

CHAPTER SIXTEEN: A FORCE FOR CHANGE

141 **Iran's population had swelled to sixty million:** Population figures and literacy statistics according to the Iran national census.

141 **"Justice cannot be religious":** Abdolkarim Soroush, "Modara va Modiriyat-eh Momenan" ("Tolerance and Management of the Faithful") *Kiyan*, no. 21 (1994): 2, (author's translation).

142 **"The faithful have given the right":** Abdolkarim Soroush writing in *Kiyan*, no. 11 (1993): 12 (author's translation). Sharia is Islamic law.

143 **the law gave the custody of their children:** Articles 1180 and 1188 of the constitution state that the father is the child's guardian and, after his death, the right is transferred to the paternal grandfather.

143 **the holy text endorses:** An-Nisaa 34 states: "Men are the managers of the affairs of women for that God has preferred in bounty one of them over another, and for that they have expended of their property. Righteous women are therefore obedient, guarding the secret for God's guarding. And those you fear may be rebellious admonish them, and banish them to their couches and beat them. Then if they then obey you look not for any way against them; God is All-high, All-great" (*The Koran Interpreted*, trans. Arthur J. Arberry [New York: Macmillan, 1955], 105–106).

143 **Women needed their husbands' permission:** Paragraph 3, article 18, of the Passport Law.

144 **Once, it quoted the conservative Speaker:** *Zanan*, no. 47 (Sept. 1998): 56–57 (author's translation).

145 **"The Three Musketeers" was the name:** Alexandre Dumas's *The Three Musketeers*, translated into Persian, is a popular novel in Iran.

145 **"Stand outside for ten minutes":** In Persian, Mehrangiz Kar, *Iman Beh Khoon Aloodeh [The Bloodied Faith: A Memoir]* (Berlin: Gardoon, 2012), 46 (author's translation).

145 **"How dare you speak to a strange man":** Ibid., 105.

146 **Families became smaller:** Fertility figures according to surveys in 1997 by Statistical Center of Iran.

146 **in the old days women hadn't contributed:** According to the national census from the Statistical Center of Iran, literacy among women over the age of fifteen increased from 24 percent to 66 percent, but their labor participation fluctuated between 8 and 12 percent from 1976 to 1996. However, when the numbers are broken down, they show that women's employment in rural work dropped from 26 to 23 percent, while employment in the social and financial sector, which requires higher education, increased from 25 to 43 percent during this period. Similarly, women's employment in the manufacturing sector would drop from over 50 percent in 1976 to less than 30 percent in 2006, another indicator that women acquired positions that needed better education.

148 **Literacy rates among young rural women:** Figures according to the national census of 1996.

CHAPTER SEVENTEEN: REFORM

153 **Iranians could vote starting at age fifteen:** The voting age was raised to eighteen in 2007 in an effort to limit the number of younger voters, who tended to vote for reformist politicians.

154 **there was no tyranny in an Islamic republic:** *Etelaat Daily*, April 1, 1979, 8.

154 **former officials would acknowledge:** In Persian: Mohammad Maleki, "Election Lessons from the Past," Nov. 26, 2011, http://www.roozonline.com/persian/opinion/opinion-article/archive/2011/november/26/article/-31c3a941bf.html. Maleki was the dean of Tehran University and involved in the election process; he revealed in a public letter that Khomeini's supporters rigged the vote in favor of an Islamic republic.

155 **resigned in protest:** Khatami's resignation letter can be found at http://fa.wiki source.org/wiki/نامه_استعفای_محمد_خاتمی_از_وزارت_ارشاد.

155 **"It is not right to confine religion":** *Zanan*, no. 34 (April 1997): 3 (author's translation).

156 **"The West has a large and unique":** Ibid., 4.

158 **"Nateq-Nouri would put an end":** Author's notes.

CHAPTER EIGHTEEN: THE REGIME STRIKES BACK

163 **The new interior minister:** Abdullah Nouri had served as Ayatollah Khomeini's religious envoy to the Revolutionary Guards and later as interior minister under Rafsanjani.

164 **he viewed compromise as a sign of weakness:** Analysts rely on Khamenei's speeches to analyze his policies. He has repeatedly made references to compromise as a sign of weakness in his public addresses. For example, on talks with the United States, he brushed them off as a gesture of compromise: "negotiation in political terms means a deal," he said in May 1990. "It means compromise; it means that you need to give something to get something else in return. What do you want to give away from the Islamic Revolution? The United States wants your loyalty to the Revolution. It wants your pride. Are you willing to give it away?" (*Archive of Speeches in 1369* [1990–1991], http://farsi.khamenei.ir/newspart-index?tid=1045#2204; author's translation).

166 **Investigative journalists would soon claim:** "Unveiling the Truth about the Murder of Ahmad Khomeini by a Conservative Activist," YouTube video, 4:07, posted by TelevisionWashington.com, Jan. 29, 2010, http://www.youtube.com/watch?v=6iy4io9xGA0. In a speech on Feb. 15, 1999, Emadedin Baghi, an investigative journalist, confirmed allegations of Ahmad Khomeini's murder based on the information that Ali Yunessi, a pro-reform intelligence minister, had given to Ahmad's family.

166 **Reporters wrote articles and books:** The daily *Sobh Emrouz* published dozens of articles by Akbar Ganji, an investigative journalist who pointed the finger at Intelligence Minister Ali Fallahian under President Rafsanjani. A German court had also issued an arrest warrant for Fallahian for his role in the killing of dissident Kurdish leaders in Berlin. Ganji wrote two books on the chain murders: *The Dungeon of Ghosts* and *The Red Eminence, the Grey Eminence*.

168 **Another man was blinded:** "Kooyeh Daneshgha, yek parvandeh, chand dadgah" ("Student Dormitory, One Case, Several Courts"), BBC Persian.com, July 7, 2007, http://www.bbc.co.uk/persian/iran/story/2004/07/040707_a_jb_18tir_court.shtml.

168 **The Office had branches:** This is an unofficial estimation given and confirmed by student leaders.

169 **a few hundred students in Tehran:** "A Two-Hour Interview with Saeed Hajarian," *Fars* news agency, 2007, http://farsnews.com/newstext.php?nn=8508060195.

170 **"At one corner stood the Guards":** Ibid. (author's translation). Saeed Hajarian was the same individual who persuaded Khomeini in 1984 to found the Intelligence Ministry.

170 **a deputy interior minister slept:** Ibid. The deputy interior minister was Mostafa Tajzadeh.

170 **"the price he had to pay":** "What Led to the Events at the Dormitory?" http://www.farhangnews.ir/category/کلیدواژه-جانبی/خاتمی (author's translation).

170 **Seven people had been killed:** author's notes.

171 **Reza Khatami, the president's brother:** Reza Khatami is the president's younger brother and a physician who served as a member of Parliament from 2001 to 2005. He is married to Zahra Eshraghi, Khomeini's granddaughter.

172 **"He wasn't prepared":** Author's notes.

172 **"I never promised":** Author's notes on Khatami's speech, given on Student Day at Sharif University in Tehran, Dec. 6, 1998.

174 **seminary schools to train female clerics:** The regime founded Kanoon Center, a religious seminary for women after the revolution. The center was later expanded and renamed Jame-atol-Zahra (the Zahra Society), and thousands of women attended it over the years.

174 **a few other reformers had angered feminists:** *Zanan*, no. 58 (Nov. 1999): 38. Abbas Abdi, a leading reformist journalist, said women's issues were not urgent: "Resolving women's issues before establishing democracy is meaningless."

CHAPTER NINETEEN: THE REFORMERS SPEAK OUT

180 **Windows software had enabled Persian speakers:** Behdad Esfahbod, *Persian Computing with Unicode*, 25th Internationalization and Unicode Conference, Washington, DC, March/April 2004, http://behdad.org/download/Publications/persiancomputing/a007.pdf.

180 **Persian as the most common language for blogging:** Mehdi Semati, "The Pro-democracy Movement in Iran," in *Negotiating Democracy: Media Transformation in Emerging Democracies*, ed. Isaac A. Blankson and Patrick D. Murphy (Albany: State University of New York Press, 2007), 155.

181 **"I have always been under":** Author's notes.

182 **Mohsen Kadivar, who had served eighteen months:** Kadivar was released on July 17, 2000. He left the country in 2009 and is currently a visiting professor of Islamic studies at Duke University.

183 **"a minor jurisprudential hypothesis":** Mahmoud Sadri, "Attack from Within: Dissident Political Theology in Contemporary Iran," *Iranian*, Feb. 13, 2002, http://web.archive.org/web/20030226124152/; http://kadivar.com/Htm/English/Reviews/reform.htm#22.

183 **"Religion has performed badly":** All quotations from Hashem Aghajari's speech that day are from the author's notes.

CHAPTER TWENTY: NO FEAR OF AUTHORITY

185 **"I apologize to the supreme leader":** Author's notes.

186 **the students had used their networks:** Five student leaders ran in the 2000 parliamentary elections, and all were elected: Fatemeh Haghighatjoo, Meisam Saeedi, Ali Tajernia, Reza Yousefian, and Akbar Mousavi Khoini.

186 **"Society needs freedom":** Author's notes.

186 **a member of the Basij had attempted:** The assailant, Saeed Asgar, was later arrested and sentenced to fifteen years in prison. But he was released shortly after his arrest and never served the sentence.

188 **Afshari and eighteen other activists:** The detainees belonged to the religious-nationalist group called the Freedom Movement. The eighteen men were held under harsh conditions for a year. Their leader, Ezatollah Sahabi, made confessions on national television before they were tried behind closed doors in Jan. 2002.

189 **the court sentenced four of them to jail:** Fatemeh Haghighatjoo received twenty-two months in prison, Hossein Loghmanian thirteen months, Issa Mousavianejad one year, and Mohammad Dadfar seven months.

190 **the US interest section at the Swiss embassy:** The United States has had no diplomatic presence in Iran since Islamist students attacked its embassy in 1979.

190 **"Islam condemns the massacre":** "Iran Softens Tone Against the United States," *New York Times*, Sept. 19, 2001.

191 **Iran had an ambitious missile program:** "Iran Searching for Nuclear Bomb Materials: Cables," Reuters, Jan. 16, 2011, http://www.reuters.com/article/2011/01/16/us-iran-wikileaks-idUSTRE70F19Y20110116.

192 **In October 2001, Zia Attabay:** His television channel was called National Iranian Television, known as NITV.

192 **Talks of returning the former Afghan king:** Mohammad Zaher Shah of Afghanistan was ousted in 1973.

192 **Newspapers reported that the security forces:** "Opposition TV Stations Stir Unrest in Fundamentalist Iran," *New York Times*, Oct. 25, 2001.

192 **most detainees were young:** Ibid.

193 **"I should have died":** Author's notes. Aghajari's lawyer, Saleh Nikbakht, read the letter in a press conference in Tehran on Nov. 13, 2002.

193 **"The regime must understand":** Author's notes.

195 **after two members of Parliament arrived:** Elaheh Koulaee and Fatemeh Haghighatjoo.

CHAPTER TWENTY-ONE: THE "GOOD" CHILDREN OF THE REVOLUTION

201 **"Everything we have is":** All the dialogue in this chapter comes from the author's notes.

203 **The Canadian government summoned:** "Iran Jails Notorious Prosecutor Who Sent Canadian to Her Death," *Globe and Mail* (Toronto), Feb. 4, 2013.

203 **It was widely believed that the Revolutionary Guards:** "Iran's Web Spying Aided by Western Technology," *Wall Street Journal*, June 22, 2009, http://online.wsj.com/news/articles/SB124562668777335653. In 2009, Iranians also boycotted Nokia phones after news leaked out that Nokia Siemens Network, a Nokia subsidiary that specialized in communications services and networks, had provided the Iranian government with monitoring equipment that helped trace activists through their cell phones and listen to their conversations.

204 **60 percent of the government's income:** "Iran: Analysis," US Energy Information Administration, March 23, 2013, http://www.eia.gov/countries/cab.cfm?fips=ir.

205 **By 2009, according to surveys:** Djavad Salehi-Isfahani and Amir Kermani, "The Middle Class in Iran," paper presented at the Iran Economy Conference, University of Chicago, Oct. 15–17, 2010, http://iraneconomy.csames.illinois.edu/program. The figures used in Salehi-Isfahani and Kermani's paper came from the surveys of the Statistical Center of Iran.

CHAPTER TWENTY-TWO: THE "BAD" CHILDREN OF THE REVOLUTION

210 **smuggled a letter out of prison:** The author of the letter was Ezatollah Sahabi, who was in his mid seventies. See Elaine Sciolino, "A Lifelong Dissident Defies Iran's Rulers on Torture; Former Political Prisoners Battle a Judicial System Run by Islamic Clerics," *New York Times*, Feb. 22, 2003, http://find.galegroup.com/gic/infomark.do?&source=gale&idigest=e00c570417b0eb514f1a6e98f0db297d&prodId=GIC&userGroupName=king46652&tabID=T004&docId=A98005785&type=retrieve&contentSet=IAC-Documents&version=1.0.

213 **"Hoda sang beautifully":** Hoda Saber was a religious-nationalist activist who was jailed several times. He passed away of a heart attack in prison in 2012 while he was on a hunger strike in protest.

215 **Some people wrote books:** Farhad Behbehani and Habibolah Davar, *Two Prison Memoirs* (Tehran: Omid-e Farda Publishing, 2003).

CHAPTER TWENTY-THREE: NASRIN

218 **Iran's ambassador at the mission:** This was Javad Zarif, who became Iran's foreign minister in 2012.

219 **money with the landlord as a deposit:** *Rahn* is a common method of renting in Iran. Landlords take the interest rate from the deposit or invest the money in business. They return the entire amount when the tenant leaves.

220 **their opponents were taking charge:** The watchdog Guardian Council had barred reformist politicians from running in parliamentary elections earlier that year.

222 **benefiting from the government's ability to splurge:** "Iran's Per Capita Income at $13,000, Says Economy Minister," *Tehran Times*, May 9, 2012, http://www.tehrantimes.com/economy-and-business/97657-irans-per-capita-income-at-13000-says

-economy-minister. Per capita income steadily grew in Iran from $4,000 in 2003 to $8,000 in 2008 (Tino, "The Iranian Economy," *Super-Economy*, Nov. 12, 2010, http://super-economy.blogspot.com/2010/11/iranian-economy.html) and ultimately to $13,000 in 2012.

223 **Oil prices had begun to rise in 2003:** "Iran Oil, Gas Revenues Top $80 bln in 2007–8," Agence France-Presse, Sept. 8, 2008. Iran's oil revenue reached $81.7 billion in 2007, a steady increase from $62 billion a year earlier, according to a report by Iran's central bank.

223 **one out of every seven Iranians:** Iran has ten million addicts, according to Minister of Health Marzieh Dastjerdi in June 2012 (http://sahamnews.org/1391/04/217451).

224 **four other candidates:** Rafsanjani was running against a former Speaker of the Parliament, Mehdi Karroubi; former Revolutionary Guard Commander, Mohsen Rezai; former police chief Mohammad Baqer Qalibaf; and the mayor of Tehran, Mahmoud Ahmadinejad.

226 **"To persuade us to vote for him":** Author's notes.

228 **two scholars were arrested:** Kian Tajbakhsh and Haleh Esfandiari. Esfandiari was the director of the Middle East Program at the Woodrow Wilson International Center.

228 **Another friend had been arrested:** Ramin Jahanbegloo was an Iranian Canadian philosopher and a good friend who was arrested in the summer of 2006.

229 **the country had gone into a tailspin:** "Bankeh Markazi Nerkheh Tavaromeh 76 Sal Ra Elam Kard" ("The Central Bank Announced the Inflation Rate of the Past Seventy-Six Years"), July 24, 2013, http://www.mehrnews.com/detail/News/2103266.

229 **the country's exports dropped:** This is famously referred to as the "Dutch disease" in economics, caused by an increase in revenues from natural resources that make a nation's currency stronger compared to that of other nations, resulting in its exports becoming more expensive for other countries to buy.

229 **inflation skyrocketed and consequently hurt the poor:** Djavad Salehi-Isfahani, "Iran: Poverty and Inequality Since the Revolution," Brookings, Jan. 29, 2009, http://www.brookings.edu/research/opinions/2009/01/29-iran-salehi-isfahani:

> Significantly, during the first two years of the Ahmadinejad Administration (2005–06) inequality worsened in both rural and urban areas, possibly because higher inflation hurt those below the median income level more than those above it. This is not so much an indication that Ahmadinejad was insincere in promising redistribution but how difficult it is to redistribute income without fundamental changes in the country's distribution of earning power (wealth and human capital) and political power, which determines access to government transfers from oil rent.

CHAPTER TWENTY-FOUR: THE RISING TIDE

235 **the text messaging service:** The text messaging service was not available for forty days after the election, which also cost the government millions of dollars in income.

235 **"Ms. Fathi, forgive me":** Author's notes.

235 **"They summoned all the editors":** Ibid.

235 **The forces had stopped and beaten:** "Asareh Khoon Dar Masheen Hengameh Dastgiri" ("Signs of Blood in the Car During the Arrest"), July 27, 2009, http://ramazanzadeh.wordpress.com/tag/ماشین--خون--رمضان-زاده--دستگیری/.

238 **watching the BBC Persian service:** Stephen Williams, "The Power of TV News: An Insider's Perspective on the Launch of BBC Persian TV in Year of Iranian Uprising," Joan Shorenstein Center on the Press, Politics and Public Policy, February 2010, http://shorensteincenter.org/wp-content/uploads/2012/03/d54_williams.pdf. He writes, "Internet pictures, e-mails, text messages and alike were coming into BBC Persian TV in London at the rate of between six and eight a minute at the height of the upheaval" (4).

238 **The government had acknowledged:** "Darabi: 40 Darsad Mardom Mahvareh Negah Mikonand" ("Darabi: 40 Percent of People Watch Satellite TV"), Nov. 14, 2009, http://www.gunaz.tv/?id=2&vmode=1&sID=30511&lang=2. The number rose to 60 percent in 2011 and 71 percent in 2013; "Chand Darsadeh Mardomeh Iran Mahvareh Tamasha Mikonand?" ("What Percentage of Iranians Watch Satellite TV?"), 2013, http://www.fardanews.com/fa/print/145631, and "Vazir Ershad: 71 Darsad mardom Mahvareh Mibinand" ("Ershad Minister: 71 Percent of People Watch Satellite TV"), Dec. 18, 2013, http://www.roozonline.com/persian/news/newsitem/archive/2013/december/18/article/71-1.html.

239 **the government had slowed its speed:** People had learned to circumvent Internet restrictions years earlier, when the regime blocked access to independent news websites. Via the Bluetooth feature on their cell phones, people shared the software at public places—even at demonstrations. Some of the software enabled users to upload and download videos while using slower Internet speeds. Others helped users view blocked websites. Civil servants and students used the fast Internet connection at their workplaces and at universities to send videos.

239 **the two candidates also pledged:** Moussavi's statement number 2, Sunday, June 14, 2009: "We pursue our demands within the constitution of the Islamic Republic, which we believe in, and consider the rule of the supreme leader (*vali faqih*) as one of the principles of the establishment" (author's translation).

240 **Ahmadinejad, the president appointed:** Author's translation.

242 **"Iran," she said:** Author's notes.

243 **a long green banner, nearly a mile long:** The banner traveled around the world and finally came to New York, where later in 2009 Iranians in exile marched with it on the Brooklyn Bridge.

243 **More than three million people:** Tehran's municipality announced in the daily Hamshahri that three million people had occupied Enghelab Street that day. But the number did not include those who packed the side streets and the highway north of Azadi Square, which was also filled with cars.

CHAPTER TWENTY-FIVE: END OF AN ERA

250 **a tragic scene:** Mr. Panahi recounted the story to the author on the day of the funeral, June 22, 2009.

251 **Late on the night of:** The video can be accessed here: https://www.facebook.com/photo.php?v=120982467941&set=vb.76683931440&type=3&theater.

CHAPTER TWENTY-SIX: EXILE

258 **government forces raped detainees:** Human rights groups named at least five men who were tortured to death in Kahrizak detention center: Mohsen Rouhlol-Amini, Mohammad Kamrani, Amir Javadifar, Ramin Ghahramani, and Ahmad Nejati Kargar.

258 **He dismissed Ardebili:** Akbar Hashemi Rafsanjani, *Sazandeghi va Bazsazi* [*Building and Reconstruction*] (Tehran: Daftar Nashr Maaref Enghelab, 1391 [2012]), 278.

258 **Ardebili pretended that he was resigning:** Ibid.

259 **Khomeini had simply killed his opponents:** "Deedar Moussavi Ardebili va Khamenei" ("Moussavi Ardebili's Meeting with Khamenei"), Feb. 8, 2010, http://www.pyknet.net/1388/02bahman/21/page/32Ardabili.htm.

260 **he died of meningitis:** "Ravayati is Nahveyeh Marg-eh Rouhol-Amini" ("An Account of How Rouhol-Amini Died"), July 25, 2009, http://news.gooya.com/politics/archives/2009/07/091280.php.

EPILOGUE

264 **The country's failing economy:** Iran's economy ranked among the most corrupt countries on the corruption index ("Corruption Perceptions Index 2012," Transparency International, http://www.transparency.org/cpi2012/results).

264 **limiting the amount of crude:** Timothy Gardner, "Iran's Oil Revenues Drop 58 Percent Since 2011 as Sanctions Bite: U.S.," Reuters, Aug. 30, 2013, http://www.reuters.com/article/2013/08/30/us-usa-iran-sanctions-idUSBRE97T0S220130830.

264 **Inflation shot above 40 percent:** "Khabarhayeh Dagheh Seif az Tavarom va Hadafmandi" ("Seif's News on Inflation and Subsidy Reform"), Oct. 14, 2013, http://www.iraneconomist.com/fa/news/41889/خبرهای-داغ-سیف-از-تورم-و-هدفمندی.

264 **A member of Parliament wrote scornfully:** Ali Motahari made the comment in a letter to Khamenei (http://www.asriran.com/fa/news/275175).

266 **Secret talks between Washington and Tehran:** Laura Rozen, "Three Days in March: New Details on U.S. Iran Direct Talks," *Al-Monitor*, Jan. 8, 2004, http://backchannel.al-monitor.com/index.php/2014/01/7484/three-days-in-march-new-details-on-the-u-s-iran-backchannel.

266 **Khamenei openly called for "historic leniency":** YouTube video, 1:21, Sept. 17, 2013, https://www.youtube.com/watch?v=XBz_wmLvvXg (author's translation).

266 **"One must not forget":** Khamenei's speech, July 28, 2013, http://farsi.khamenei.ir/speech-content?id=23346 (author's translation).

INDEX